LOVE STORIES OF OLD CALIFORNIA

SENORITA MARIA IGNACIA BONIFACIO.

LOVE STORIES

OF

OLD CALIFORNIA

BY

Cora Miranda Baggerly Older

WITH A FOREWORD BY
Gertrude Atherton

APPLEWOOD BOOKS
Bedford, Massachusetts

Love Stories of Old California was originally published in 1940.

ISBN 1-55709-400-4

Thank you for purchasing an Applewood Book. Applewood reprints America's lively classics—books from the past that are still of interest to modern readers. For a free copy of our current catalog, please write to Applewood Books, 18 North Road, Bedford, MA 01730.

10 9 8 7 6 5 4 3 2 1

Library of Congress Cataloging-in-Publication Data:
Older, Fremont, Mrs., 1875-1968.
    Love Stories of old California / by Cora Miranda Baggerly Older; with a foreword by Gertrude Atherton.
        p.   cm.
    Originally published: New York: Coward McCann, 1940.
    ISBN 1-55709-400-4
    1. California—History.   2. California—Biography.   3. Love stories, American —California.   I. Title.
F861.6.042   1995
979.4–dc20   94-43777
                                                                    CIP

TO EVELYN WELLS

Godmother of *Love Stories of Old California*

FOREWORD

WE have no more thorough scholar of Old California, and no more valuable contributor to Californiana, than Mrs. Fremont Older. In these twenty-four stories ranging from 1775 to 1881 one gathers the impression that no love story worthy of record during those 106 years has escaped her discerning eye. A few have been used before in the form of short story or novel, and some were newspaper sensations, notably the tragic incident of David Terry and Sarah Althea Hill, but the majority will be new even to California readers. And her uncommon gift for patient research, selection, and completeness would make her work salient if she had merely presented the result of her labors in the form of "historical sketches"—useful material for writers of fiction.

But she has left little for any one else to work on. Each episode in the progressive and curiously varied romantic side of California history has been treated with the more cunning methods of fiction. Bare outlines have been filled in and dramatized with the aid of a general knowledge of the period and its atmosphere, notably the sixteen stories of Spanish California, but with no less facility in those closer to our own day. In short, Mrs. Older has presented pictures of our past that will be welcomed by those who read for entertainment not instruction. They will get both.

GERTRUDE ATHERTON

CONTENTS

INTRODUCTION   xi

I. LOVE RIDES INTO CALIFORNIA   1775   3

II. THE FIRST LADY'S DIVORCE   1783   19

III. AMATIL AND OLANA   1799   37

IV. REZANOV AND CALIFORNIA'S FIRST NUN   1806   48

V. GUADALUPE'S PIRATE   1818   64

VI. SAN DIEGO'S RUNAWAYS   1829   78

VII. YOSCOLO AND PERFECTA   1829   92

VIII. LARKIN'S ROMANCE OF THE SEA   1831   102

IX. HUGO REID'S INDIAN WIFE   1832   111

X. SANTA BARBARA'S INTERNATIONAL WEDDING   1836   119

XI. LOS ANGELES' INFERNAL COUPLE   1836   128

XII. CALIFORNIA'S WORST GOVERNOR   1836   141

XIII. CALIFORNIA'S FIRST PRINCESS   1840   151

XIV. REED OF '46   1846   169

XV. TAMSEN DONNER OF THE BISON TRAIL   1846   184

XVI. DOÑA RAMONA CONQUERS THE CONQUEROR 1846   194

XVII. THE SHERMAN ROSE   1850   207

XVIII. JUANITA OF DOWNIEVILLE   1851   217

XIX. LOLA MONTEZ AND PATRICK HULL   1853   229

XX. JOAQUIN, THE TERRIBLE   1853   242

XXI. MOTHER OF MYSTERY   1853   254

XXII. VASQUEZ AND ROSARIO   1873   266

XXIII. SHARON'S ROSE AND TERRY   1881   280

XXIV. STEVENSON AND FANNY OSBOURNE   1880   295

ILLUSTRATIONS

Senorita Maria Ignacia Bonifacio   *Frontispiece*

FACING PAGE

Indians on San Francisco Bay   10

The San Francisco Presidio   11

San Diego from the Old Fort   84

Mission San José Indians   85

Thomas Oliver Larkin and Mrs. Larkin   106

The Founding of Los Angeles   107

Ana de la Guerra de Robinson   124

Senorita Delfina de la Guerra   125

Chief Solano   160

A California Picnic Party   161

Mr. and Mrs. Reed, Martha Jane Reed, and Her Doll   174

The Donner Monument   175

The Sherman Rose Home: In the Original and
    Reconstructed   212

Sherman's Headquarters, Monterey   213

Doctor and Mrs. Aiken   224

Robert Louis Stevenson and Fanny Osbourne   225

Two Studies of Lola Montez   232

The House Where Lola and Patrick Hull Lived   233

Lola and Patrick Hull at Grass Valley   238

Joaquin, the Terrible   239

Tiburcio Vasquez and His Birthplace   272

Lynch Law in California   273

INTRODUCTION

ATLANTIS, a mythical lost continent in the Atlantic Ocean, had long cast its spell over dreamers. Plato was first to mention the legend describing how Egyptian priests had revealed to Solon this vast land situated just beyond the Pillars of Hercules—the Strait of Gibraltar. These priests said Atlantis had been a powerful kingdom nine thousand years before the birth of Solon. Its armies overran lands bordering the Mediterranean. Athens alone withstood them. Finally the sea overswept Atlantis, and from that time men sought this lost paradise.

Perhaps even Columbus on setting sail for the Far East of Marco Polo was under the enchantment of the legend. Instead of Atlantis, Cypango or Cathay, he found the Bahama island with troglodytes and maneaters, self-called *caribs*.

Columbus had estimated that India was not more than six thousand miles distant, for the map of the then known world indicated no America. It was not until 1503 that Martin Waldseemüller, in his *Cosmographiae Introductio,* mapped the land of the western hemisphere. Europe and Asia, declared he, had been named for women; it was but fair that the new land should bear the name of the intrepid Amerigo Vespucci who had touched the new-found continent's coastline.

Pope Alexander VI bestowed Columbus's discovery, the entire western hemisphere, upon King Charles the Fifth of Spain on condition that he Christianize the inhabitants. *Conquistador* Cortés came to claim the new possession. Upon arriving in the Aztec kingdom, he wrote his sovereign in 1519 that he would make him ruler of the whole world.

Soon Cortés heard of fabulous islands to the northwest—one of gold, one of silver, and another of pearl, coral, amber. This brought back to his memory the romance of Ordoñez de Montalvo, *Las Sergas*

de Esplandian, published in Madrid in 1510. In it he read of black
Amazons ruling California, the island to the right of the Indies, "very
near the terrestrial paradise." Their horses were harnessed with gold,
their dishes made of gold, but no man was allowed on the island.
Even the *conquistador* was beglamoured by the Northern Mystery.
Believing, he went to seek it. Then he discovered Lower California,
made the settlement Santa Cruz for the king, and one of his followers
for the first time applied the word *California* to its tawny hot soil.
Like many another dreamer Cortés died in exile. Neither he nor
Charles the Fifth realized that California, rich as Montalvo's romance-
land, had been found.

New California slumbered under its crystal peaks. Forests thousands of years old were untouched and none came to wrest the gold
and silver from the mountains. All this pleasant land abloom with
beauty was the playground of a few thousand red men and the wild
creatures. Once every twelve months the Philippine galleon freighted
with musky silken cargo drifted down the California coast, and Cape
Mendocino and Santa Lucia Peak were glimpsed by the eyes of
civilized man.

Viceroy Antonio de Mendoza of Mexico carried on Cortés' work
when in 1542 he sent Portuguese Juan Rodriguez Cabrillo northward
to explore with two vessels, the *San Salvador* and *La Vitoria.* Cabrillo
was the first white man to enter San Diego Bay and touch the California shore line. Later he was the guest of the superior Santa Barbara
Indians who grouped by thousands about the Channel. Cabrillo
adventured along the California coast, but his dust now mingles with
the dust of the island of San Miguel off Santa Barbara, where, dying
in 1543, he urged his followers to carry on his work.

Elizabeth's gentleman privateer, Francis Drake, also wished to
bestow a continent upon his sovereign, and in 1579 he boldly flaunted
the flag of England over northern California. Brandishing a sword
on the high white cliffs he named the land New Albion. Then he
turned his ship homeward to receive knighthood—Sir Francis Drake.
Shortly after the new century dawned Sebastian Vizcaíno came

seeking the fabled islands of gold, silver and pearls. He discovered the sites of San Diego and Monterey but sailed on, leaving riches behind greater than he had dreamed. For a century and a half silence settled over California, then rumors came to Mexico that English privateers had rounded Cape Horn and had menacingly entered the Pacific— Swan, Dampier, Rogers—all seeking galleons and gold.

Like an inexorable glacier Russia moved steadily toward the strait separating Siberia from present-day Alaska. In 1728 Vitus Behring drove his small bark through the strait. Later North America was sighted, and then came descent upon the Aleutian Islands. By 1760 trade in otter skins had begun. Before Spain awoke the Russian Bear had rumbled down the coast.

What could save California? The Missions—Spain's sword of the spirit! In the Philippines, Paraguay and Mexico, Missions had been used with success to protect conquest and subdue natives. Alta California must have Missions.

Since 1697 the Jesuits had entered Lower California and founded seventeen Missions, but they were expelled by Carlos the Third and their property given to the Franciscans. When the Dominicans took over the Franciscan Missions in Lower California, followers of Saint Francis were assigned to Alta California to be led by *Padre* Miguel José Serra, better known as *Padre* Junípero Serra.

Courtly Viceroy Francisco de Croix, bluff *Visitador*-General José de Galvez and seraphic *Padre* Junípero Serra—these three shared in the founding of Alta California. The plan was to establish Missions at San Diego and Monterey, with one midway between to be called San Buenaventura.

Two hundred and twenty-five men in four divisions, two by sea and two by land, were to go to New California. Day and night Galvez and Serra worked to fit out the land expeditions, and the ships *San Carlos* and *San Antonio* that were to sail for San Diego. Costly vestments, silver vessels and supplies were made ready. When from the hilltop in Lower California Galvez saw the eleven sails of the brigantine *San Carlos* disappear northward, he knew Alta California was assured. "The Lord conduct it prosperously! The undertaking is all His."

Soon followed the first land expedition, headed by Don Fernando Rivera y Moncada, and the second, by Governor Gaspar de Portolá, forty-seven-year-old Catalonian noble. With him was Serra, head of the Missions-to-be, fifty-six years old, lame, carried part of the way on a litter. Portolá tried to send him back to Lower California, but the sandal-shod friar had his leg treated by a muleteer, and over the trail he came chanting the praises of Our Lord and the saints, delighting in the delicious grapes and the beautiful roses. Serra was a beholder of visions, a believer in miracles. At San Diego he found his lameness had lessened. He had courage for arduous toil and wisdom for the most baffling situations.

At San Diego Serra learned that scurvy had reduced the pioneers by thirty-one. No seaman remained. Monterey must be occupied by land. Portolá set out immediately with young Lieutenant Pedro Fages, a future governor of California. With them went the strongest men to find Monterey Bay.

Serra was left to found Mission San Diego de Alcalá and it almost cost him his life at the hands of the Indians. But he never doubted the future of New California, and this first Mission made July 16, 1769, California's natal day.

In the uncharted north Portolá and Fages did not recognize Monterey Bay, although they planted a cross on one shore of Carmel Bay. Near today's Santa Cruz they discovered the mighty redwood trees, and farther on they were the first white men to behold San Francisco Bay. Living on mule meat they reached San Diego with no loss of life, but at the new settlement they found that fifty pioneers had died in the winter. For a few days it seemed that New California must fail. Portolá, saying, "My men shall not starve," wished to return to Lower California.

Serra replied, "If necessary, we *padres* will remain at San Diego and starve."

Rivera was dispatched to drive cattle up from Velicatá to San Diego.

The *San Antonio* which had been sent to Mexico for supplies did not
return. Serra made a novena, but before the nine days of prayer was
completed a sail flashed white on the horizon—the *San Antonio!*
Mission San Diego was saved—New California entered history.

Although Portolá and Rivera declared that the Bay of Monterey,
supposedly discovered by Vizcaíno in 1602, was either an illusion then
or had since been filled with sand, Serra himself went northward on
the *San Antonio* to find the Bay.

Once more Portolá and Fages marched overland, but again they
were bewildered until they saw the *San Antonio* sail into the O-shaped
body of blue water described by Vizcaíno. Rejoicing, the land and sea
expeditions rushed into embrace, and on June 3, 1770, California's
second Mission, San Carlos Borromeo [today's Carmel], was established. Salvos sounded; messengers dashed down the valleys, across
deserts and over mountains to the Viceroy. In Mexico City cathedral
bells pealed forth the tidings; Spain had a new frontier. This Mission
San Carlos Borromeo was to be Serra's California home, and here
he was to be entombed.

Thirty-five leagues from Carmel near the Sierra of Santa Lucia
Serra established Mission San Antonio de Padua on July 14, 1771.
Mission activity was impeded by the new governor of *Las Californias,*
Felipe de Barri, at Loreto: but harmony was restored when he was
succeeded by Don Felipe de Neve.

In the same year that Serra founded Mission San Antonio, Mission
San Gabriel Arcángel [today's San Gabriel near Los Angeles] was
established, September 8, 1771. The following year Serra founded
another Mission in mid-California—San Luis Obispo de Tolosa, fifty
leagues southeast of Monterey, near the ocean.

In spite of five Mission establishments with Presidios at San Diego
and Monterey, fears that England or Russia might claim Upper California were not allayed. The inviting hills surrounding the bay of San
Francisco seemed to await inhabitants. English and Russian they
should not be—the Viceroy was determined; Spain's glory must march
onward.

Another imposing Mission and Presidio should be established on the great northern bay. Spain would give a royal sum for the foundation. The expedition was to be commanded by Captain Juan Bautista Anza, son of the great captain and Indian fighter of that name, and himself aglow with the ardor of the *conquistadores* for extending the Spanish kingdom.

Now for the first time women colonists entered California. With women came romance.

LOVE STORIES OF OLD CALIFORNIA

I

LOVE RIDES INTO CALIFORNIA

1775

LOVE rode into California with Doña María Feliciana Arballo de Gutiérrez. She was just twenty years old and, in her linen jacket, baize skirt, bright new hair ribbons, fine Brussels stockings and Spanish shoes—all from the coffers of King Carlos III of Spain—she felt herself again a bride. In the Plaza of the Royal Presidio de Horcasitas, on that September day in 1775, she sat her horse like a *vaquerista*. Don Juan Bautista de Anza's expedition was about to set out on its sixteen-hundred-mile journey to Spain's northern frontier, there to found San Francisco; and María, a widow, was the only woman of the company traveling alone.

Before her in the saddle sat her four-year-old daughter Estaquia, and clinging behind was Tomasa, aged six. In tribute to the valiant woman, blue- and gray-clad soldiers swept their hats to the ground. But to fierce Corporal Pablo, of the heavy, black-lidded, shoebutton eyes—a leather-jacket soldier with a coat a yard and a quarter long— she was *the* woman; he raised his hat to María as if he were saluting the Virgin.

The first trumpet sounded in the crowded Plaza. Shaggy-bearded Don Juan Bautista, frontiersman and soldier, flung a striped blue *serape* over his shoulder and tore himself from his sobbing wife, Doña Ana. Again and again the weeping Arballo family embraced María and her children.

"Ah, why do you go?" sobbed her mother.

"I go to the new life in the Indian country!"

"*Carita*, we'll never see you again!"

"My saint will bring me back, *Mamacita*."

3

The last shrill bugle sounded its summons. Again and again, her eyes shining with the thrill of her great adventure, María turned her prancing horse to wave to her dear ones. Already she rode as if she were a woman of California. She had two mares, a saddle, a fine bridle, and a mule to carry her luggage. With royal generosity the King had supplied the children and even the men with new hair ribbons. These two hundred and forty colonists, descendants of the soldiers of Cortés, felt like heroes on that afternoon of September 29, 1775, as they set out with Anza on the march toward the Bay of San Francisco. The people of the Presidio applauded; dogs barked; and María's children shouted with the others:

"Viva Dios y el Rey! Viva Anza! Viva California!"

Anza, grandson and son of Indian fighters, rode ahead, with the keen gray-habited Franciscan chaplain, Pedro Font, at his side. To Anza the expedition was for the glory of the King, but to the Franciscan it was for the glory of God and he began to chant the *Alabado,* a hymn of praise.

What with all the colonists, and their mules, horses and cattle, the procession was a mile long. One hundred and sixty women and children were being sent to California—some of the soldiers' horses bore as many as three shouting youngsters. The mules carried huge supplies for the long journey, as well as eleven tents for sheltering the various families and their stores.

On the first night out, after the soldiers had fashioned their barracks from brush and blankets, the camp looked like a town. But many women were weeping. To cheer them María sang folk songs of Spain and Mexico; Corporal Pablo's deep voice boomed out the *Alma de mi corazón,* and Father Font fingered the strings of his psaltery.

They had a delicious supper—barbecued beef, *tortillas,* chocolate. Unrestrained by her family, María felt free and gay. She and her children had been put into a tent with the Santiago Picos and their seven offspring. The youngsters were shouting at play—going to California was fun!

María sprang up and became one with the children. She banded her hair with beads green, red and yellow, bought for barter with the Indians, and to Santiago Pico she said mischievously,

"Please, *Señor,* teach me to roll *cigarrillos!*"

The Picos laughed at the young widow, dizzied from her first smoke; but Father Font, whose tent was also the church of the expedition, was not amused, and he gazed sternly at María as he passed through the camp:

"*Señora,* do nothing to scandalize the heathen!" he said. "We go to San Francisco Bay to found a Mission for the glory of our father Saint Francis. Let us behave as Christians!"

Reluctantly María extinguished her *cigarrillo.* "*Sí, sí,* Your Reverence!"

Before a portable altar of which the center was a painting of the Virgin of Guadalupe, the principal patron of the expedition, Father Font prepared to celebrate Mass. Striking on Anza's tankard, he summoned the colonists. All the women attended and Anza made a dutiful appearance, but Father Font noted that many soldiers were absent. Corporal Pablo prayed among the men, but his eyes frequently turned toward María as she knelt with the Pico family.

As the days went on, all discovered that travel with Anza was not easy. The hard-riding Captain ate on horseback—nothing but bread; he himself had no need of food until four o'clock of the afternoon. It was slow going—four leagues, five, finally six in one day! Apaches began to steal their cattle. It became dangerous for Father Font to say Mass, but he continued to preach, "Fear not, little flock!" The missionary became ill of chills, fever and a sore mouth; he clashed with Anza, who looked on him as a fussy pedant.

When the colonists left Tubac in southern Arizona—the last Spanish settlement—on October 23rd, the heroic part of the journey began. They were following the *Camino del Diablo* and it was the devil's own road! This was Anza's country—here he had been born. Save Anza and twenty soldiers who had been here the year before, no white man had ever traveled this trail. That intrepid scouting trip had resulted in Anza's promotion by Viceroy Bucareli and in his command of this present colonizing venture. So hope rode with the leader as he set out through a sterile dead land with his people, bound for heathen California with no more than four half-starved Missions for protection.

But the way was hard. Sometimes, for coolness in the torrid desert, the colonists traveled all night and lay by during the day. Soon a woman died in childbirth and Anza shuddered—he recalled that his lovely wife Doña Ana had had a premonition of misfortune. Father Garcés—a quaint figure in his brown robe, broad-brimmed hat and flowing cape—accompanied the four soldiers who carried the dead woman's body to Mission San Xavier, near today's Tucson, for burial. And pioneer mothers suckled the half-orphaned infant.

Phantom ships at sea appeared in the wide waste of sand dunes rising ever before them. Starved coyotes yapped at night when the travelers camped among date palms and the giant-handed columnar cacti. In this weird land made weirder by the Indian chants sounding through the darkness, María often wondered why she had ever left sunny Sinaloa. But even in the desert Corporal Pablo rode through buzzing rattlesnakes to pluck gaudy flowers for her, and the morning bugle always fortified her courage. Valiant Father Font sang the hymn of praise and she tried to sing with him, but in the dust and wind she could scarcely breathe or see. Silently the colonists moved through the dust cloud raised by their horses and herds; and Anza goaded them forward twenty-seven miles a day.

But fording the half-dry Gila River three times was pure joy; María and her children laughed through the adventure. And always at her side to give her all aid was Corporal Pablo.

Another diversion that broke the monotony was Chief Palma's visit; he came with a turquoise ring in his nose, along with a horde of Yumas painted black, red and white. With the Chief was his daughter and they brought gifts to Anza—calabashes, beans, watermelons and maize.

Anza flattered the Chief by giving him a gold-trimmed blue suit in the name of the Viceroy, and his guest was delighted by the breeches and the cap with its dragoon's cockade. Then the coin of the expedition was generously distributed, tobacco and glass beads.

"I have told my people not to steal from you," said the deep-voiced Palma. "If they do I will kill them."

Father Font protested: "God doesn't like killing."

Palma compromised: "I will flog them!"

But when Chief Palma embraced María, saying, "I will take this *señora* for my wife! I'm a Spaniard!" Pablo's eyes blazed.

"Only one wife for a Spaniard—" Anza replied.

"—and a Christian," added Father Font.

"Ave María!" Palma shouted. "I have six!" He crossed himself, to the amusement of all save Father Font, who urged him to speak with reverence. And Palma's daughter, painted with red and white spots, said in broken Spanish: "I wish to be white and beautiful like the Virgin."

Palma embraced Anza, Father Font, the soldiers, the men and women; he exhibited the scalps of Apaches he and his men had killed the day before and said:

"I wish to be Christian, go to Heaven with good people—not live underground with animals!"

That night the Yumas danced before Anza's tent for hours, playing on drums with *coritas* or baskets. The next day they were back in gala dress, their bodies freshly painted with stripes. They helped the travelers ford the shallow Colorado River, one-third of a mile wide. María and her children shouted like Yumas when, in mid-river, the soldiers emptied their muskets to amuse the Indians. She envied Chief Palma's daughter who swam the Colorado many times, carrying over baskets in return for a few beads. The Yumas bore Father Garcés on their shoulders, two at his head, one at his feet. A naked soldier supported Father Font; another guided his horse across the river. The missionary himself escaped immersion but he said, "I can't understand why my vestments and the holy oils should have been wet," and glanced sharply at María—he thought he heard her giggle.

After four hours and without mishap, the last colonist crossed the Colorado; but not until Anza promised to return and establish a Mission in that country would Palma leave. "I will build a pueblo for you," he promised. "You and the Fathers must come and help kill Apaches." Then with a great hullabaloo the Indians departed.

That night after the campfire supper, María arranged her hair crown-wise on her head, and into it she thrust feathers and ornaments. She painted her face red and white, hung pendants from her ears and in a Yuma deerskin dress danced like Palma's daughter.

Father Font protested: "*Señora,* do not dress like a heathen! Wash your face!"

"This is desert *fiesta,* Your Reverence," smiled María.

Thereupon Father Font brought forth soap and scrubbed her face clean. "Now," he said, "you look like a Christian!"

"*Gracias,* Father!" applauded Corporal Pablo.

In the glaring sunlight, through chamiso and salty bushes, the travelers went on at an average of eighteen miles a day. Some of their animals died from exhaustion and lack of pasture. Occasionally Anza gave the soldiers *aguardiente,* and then from the barrack tents would come sounds of raucous revelry. At such times Father Font would expostulate with the *Comandante:*

"I could not sleep, *Señor.* Some of your men were drunk last night."

"There are worse things than drunkenness, Father—failure to reach San Francisco Bay!"

In Latin Father Font would retort: "Lord deliver us from soldiers!"

Now to the northwest the bleak hills stepped up to lofty San Sebastian and the Sierra of California. "Beyond," Anza told them, "lies the rarest part of California, more beautiful than Spain. But first we must cross the desert and reach the wells of Santa Rosa."

At three o'clock the next morning Anza was out of his tent and feeding his horses. The colonists were placed in three divisions—

every one had to carry corn, grass and water. Cold winds swept down from the mountains, and María and her children donned extra clothing. They went in the first company with Anza and Font, who led with twelve soldiers, several families, and the pack train. By six o'clock the company began to struggle through sand dunes, and soon even the horses were a sorry sight—some gave out. The colonists suffered increasingly from aching backs and scratched hands; their eyes and throats smarted from the alkali dust and their clothing was pierced by cactus needles. But in eleven hours they made forty-two miles! Before nightfall, shivering with cold, they were at Santa Rosa's wells. But the water would not flow!

Anza threw off his cloak and wielded a shovel to deepen a well. From six o'clock that night until ten the next morning he worked with the men. Father Font invoked the patron saint of the expedition. "Water will come," he promised. "The most holy Virgin of Guadalupe will bring it. Tomorrow is her feast day."

On the feast day water began to flow, and the people were jubilant. The wells were so deep that the horses had to be watered from *coritas*—baskets. But María's gay spirits began to sink at last and as she was passing Anza's tent she called to him:

"*Señor Comandante,* why should we go farther into this terrible California? Our own Sinaloa and Sonora are beautiful."

"Wait, *Señora,*" urged Anza, "until you see California over the mountains. Russia is threatening us in the north, and Spain needs women like you. I shall report to the Viceroy your heroism in making this journey with your little girls—California's first and only lone woman colonist!"

In such wise Anza subdued all murmuring. And after packs and saddles were adjusted to galled animal backs, the travelers again began to crawl northward over shapeless hills of loose rock. At last they reached San Sebastian and camped in Coyote Canyon, today called Harper's Well. Here, in a narrow valley with precipitous sides, were grass, mesquite for animals, and a spring of water.

For a time only two of the three companies were in camp, and

Anza sent out a relief party to bring in the struggling third company. Meantime, soldiers were busy driving in half-dead cattle—those not lost in the journey. Some were too exhausted to eat but drank water till they died in the cruel cold. Many horses and mules belonging to the third company had dropped in the sand, but eventually all the colonists came safely through. At last the desert was conquered!

Now came snow and rain. Only Anza's large tent had a fire. Rejoicing that they had all crossed the desert in safety, Anza gave each one a pint of *aguardiente,* in an effort to warm them. Excited talk and loud laughter followed. María put on a new serge skirt, adjusted coquettish ribbons, then danced and sang in one of the tents until the crowd shouted, "Well done, *carita!*" An excited soldier kissed her, but Corporal Pablo caught her wrists and dragged her away.

"Who are you," she demanded, "to chastise me!"

Pablo shook her violently. "Vile widow of Satan! your lips are soiled!"

Hearing the uproar, Anza and Father Font entered the tent to expostulate: "Corporal! you would not treat a mule so!"

"*Señor Comandante,* a woman must be ruled by force!" thundered Pablo. "I'm going to marry her!"

"Never!" cried María.

Father Font interrupted: "*Señor Comandante,* the Corporal is right. The *Señora* should be punished! Her song was indecent!"

"Not to me, Father," said Anza. "The *Señora* shall not be chastised! She is brave!"

So saying, Anza left the tent, taking Pablo with him, and all night the *fandango* went on, María dancing with leather-jacketed soldiers to the delight and applause of the crowd.

The next morning they discovered that their cattle and horses had stampeded. The colonists gathered about the fire to keep from freezing—it was too cold for Father Font to say Mass. When they met in the large tent he reproached María:

"You're ruining this expedition! No wonder you don't come to confession." Then, to the rest, "The Virgin of Guadalupe delivered

INDIANS ON SAN FRANCISCO BAY IN 1776 [From a drawing by Louis Choris, 1816].

VIEW OF THE SAN FRANCISCO PRESIDIO [From a drawing by Louis Choris, 1816].

us, but instead of thanking God for sparing our lives you hold a *fiesta* in honor of the devil! Your gratitude is nothing but this—that you *fandango* all night, drunk and evil-minded! What must the Indians think of our religion!"

With their horses lost or dead, many of the colonists were obliged to cross the mountains on foot. And now they found themselves in a hostile country whose natives they could not hope to convert. Here, subsisting on roots and grass seeds, small naked men and women lived in rock grottos on arid mountain sides seemingly made of sweepings of the world. The women would not let themselves be seen, and the men disappeared over the boulders like fauns. A chief attempted to prevent the colonists from passing, but soldiers emptied their muskets and the Anza expedition went forward.

On a snowy Christmas Eve the eighth child since leaving Tubac was born and Father Font listened to the mother's confession. The colonists dined on already dying cattle which they had killed, on beans and chili, and wept, remembering Sonora and Sinaloa. When Anza brought forth holiday *aguardiente,* again Father Font protested:

"Sir, it does not seem right to me to celebrate the birth of Jesus with drunkenness."

"Father," Anza replied, *"aguardiente* is His Majesty's gift to his soldiers. I deliver it."

"But you know they are sure to get drunk, *Señor."*

Anza at once satisfied his conscience and stimulated California colonization by warning his followers: "Be careful you don't get drunk! If I find you drunk outside your tents, I will punish you!" Then he closed his ears to the noisy, night-long singing and dancing. The colonists forgot that it was raining, that horses were exhausted and cattle dying, and surrendered themselves to mirth.

In his next sermon Father Font burst forth: "Throughout this whole journey you have not come to confession, although I have urged you. On the eve of Christ's birth there is eating here, drinking, dancing, lewdness and drunkenness. His sacred day is profaned. You

sigh for your fatherland, but not for your true fatherland—Heaven!"
But the austere Franciscan closed on an indulgent note: "May you
all have a happy holiday!"

After Christmas the colonists passed over the Sierra summit through
blinding sleet. They left behind the hediondilla—vile-smelling shrub
of evil augury. Pine trees appeared. During an earthquake the travelers descended into a green leafy valley with fragrant rose bushes
where poppy lamps burned bright.

Pablo tried to make peace with María. "Forgive me, I love you,"
he said, placing scarlet toyon berries in her hair. "Forgive me! Let us
be married at Mission San Gabriel."

María shook her head: "I shall go back to Sonora."

The Corporal wooed her with glittering rock: "Look, María! There
is gold in California!" But all his words were vain.

Now the colonists camped in a wild vineyard on the banks of the
Santa Ana River, and gazed their fill on Mount Rubidoux. Soon
María and her children were gathering wild lavender, rosemary and
sunflowers. Larks sang in the valley. "Paradise!" breathed María.
And on a sycamore tree Father Font carved:

"IHS. In the year 1776 came the San Francisco expedition."

From San Gabriel rode Don Fernando Rivera y Moncada with
Father Antonio Paterna to welcome the travelers. The Mission guard
shot volley on volley; the Fathers Antonio Cruzado and Miguel
Sanchez rang bells, and Te Deums were chanted.

When María was welcomed by her countrymen at San Gabriel, she
felt herself back at San Miguel de Horcasitas. Perhaps it was a soldier
of the guard, Juan Francisco Lopez, with round merry face, eyes like
black diamonds and jovial manner, who made her feel that all through
its five years of existence San Gabriel had been awaiting her. Juan
had come through with Portolá and Serra in 1769—he knew the trail
—and he said in admiring marvel:

"Señora, you traveled all that thousand miles from Sonora—without a husband?"

"I was with Doña María," Corporal Pablo interrupted fiercely.

"And took all the care of your two little girls?" Juan Francisco went on.

Pablo tried to explain further, but María said, "I was both mother and father!" and Juan Francisco's eyes moistened.

Rivera had tragic news for Anza: "*Amigo,* Mother Mission San Diego is wiped out. Father Jayme and two servants are dead. Founding San Francisco can wait. We must put down the San Diego Indians at once."

To María's relief, when Anza left for San Diego, Pablo was ordered along. Father Font went with them and María was rid for a time not only of the Corporal's jealous interference but of the missionary's too keen observation. She and her children were in the Picos' tent, among the other colonists encamped in the Mission Plaza. Near by the soldiers erected their barracks of brush and blankets. Never far from María was Juan Francisco Lopez. He brought Indian toys for the children; with Anza's cook traded his tobacco for chocolate to delight them. When María thanked him, he said:

"But it's nothing! Alone we men hate each other. Women make the world fit to live in. I don't blame Spaniards for marrying Indian girls! You and your children have made San Gabriel a heaven."

Strolling with Juan Francisco about the irregular Plaza, María soon felt at home in San Gabriel. The church was within a rectangular shed. A granary housed the Fathers. Eight soldiers held the guard house. Five hundred Indians, neophytes from the mountains, lived in huts across the *acequia*—an irrigation ditch. With all its crudeness Mission San Gabriel seemed beautiful to her.

"What wonderful things the Fathers have done!" she said to her guide. "I like even the Indians!"

"They're not much like our Apaches," Juan objected.

"But they're far superior to mountain Indians," she replied, looking at the barefoot neophytes, some wearing smocks but more of them clothed in deer and rabbit skins. "The Fathers have been fairly good dressmakers!"

"They do the best they can, but they are better at plowing. The Indian girls need a woman to look after them—"

They came on Father Paterna, his gray habit pulled up to his sun-burned knees, driving oxen and showing Indian boys how to use horses and plows from Mexico. He had even taught them how to make plows. With his many responsibilities he often felt as if he were a beast of burden.

For his days were packed to the full. After the sunrise hymn of praise and Mass, the Fathers and the Indian neophytes breakfasted on a corn porridge, over which they made the sign of the Cross and sang the *Bendito*. At noon they gathered from the gardens and fields for *pozole* or stew, and after a long *siesta* they returned to work. At sunset came supper and prayers recited either in their native idiom or in Castilian. The evenings brought games in the Plaza, and songs to the music of elderwood flutes. Such were the Fathers' daily labors.

María had been at San Gabriel only a few days before Juan Francisco quietly put her in charge of the Indian girls.

"We shall still have rain," he told her. "You and your children will be more comfortable in the nuns' good log house where there is a nice lambs'-wool bed for you."

The children Estaquia and Tomas delighted in the nuns' spacious quarters, and María, mother of only two children—some of the women had nine—had almost the freedom of an unmarried woman. During the day she taught the Indian girls how to cook, to sew, to weave. They whispered prayers after her. She showed them how to make the sign of the Cross reverently and how to follow Mass. In teaching them how to keep the house clean, she made it a laughing game—to sweep the earthen floors with tarwood brushes in unison. And she taught them how to scrub themselves with the San Gabriel soap. "*Maestra*," the girls called her.

She had visitors. Juan Francisco often appeared with a native basket or a piece of pottery to adorn the nunnery. Father Paterna called. "Forgive me, Doña María, but I am ragged almost to indecency!

I implored the College of San Fernando to send me a new habit, but— Have you a patch for this one?"

"Reverend Father, pardon me, but let me patch your habit!"

The missionary blushed violently: *"Señora, gracias, gracias!* It is the only one I have!" He took the patch from her hand and departed for the privacy of his cell.

"Poor Father!" sighed María.

"Caramba, Señora!" said Juan Francisco. "I hope the *Comandante* doesn't hurry back from San Diego—San Gabriel needs you!"

"But I enlisted for the new Mission on San Francisco Bay!"

"Madre de Dios, María! Don't take your little girls to that wild country! Even San Diego has just been wiped out!"

"I'd like to see that wonderful Father Serra at Carmel, and that northern country."

"But María, what shall we do without you! San Gabriel is the most civilized part of California—the Viceroy has promised us mail from Sonora every three months."

For a fortnight Mission San Gabriel lavished hospitality on its two hundred guests; then its supplies began to diminish; meals were less bountiful and the San Francisco colonists murmured. Why were they not paid? Why did not Anza return? Some of the most discontented seized horses and set out at night over the trail across the mountains, bound for their homeland, Sonora. At once swift messengers were rushed to Anza and he returned from his problems at San Diego to face new ones.

At San Diego, Rivera had been excommunicated for denying an Indian rebel sanctuary; and Rivera, in turn, opposed the San Francisco foundation. San Gabriel could no longer feed the colonists— north or south they must go! Although Anza was a seasoned campaigner, his digestion failed him. He refused to eat from an old greasy door with no tablecloth! What if he should die!—what would become of his expedition then? Action! that was Anza's way of life! Quickly he gave his people the order: "Forward to San Francisco Bay!"

Without his usual smile Juan Francisco Lopez brought María word of Anza's command. "Don't go, María," he pleaded.

"But I must! My husband was one of Don Juan Bautista's soldiers! We were to have come together on this expedition. But he was killed —I'm his substitute."

Juan Francisco placed his hand on María's: "The Indian nuns need their *maestra*, María. Spain will grant us valleys and mountains near San Gabriel. Stay here with me! Don't take the babies into that wilderness! Here we'll raise a race of giants—Californians!"

Estaquia and Tomasa made their appeal on Juan Francisco's side: "Please, *Mamacita*, no more snow! No more mountains or desert!"

Should she stay? Her hand was on his blue-coated shoulder. Suddenly Corporal Pablo, his eyes blurred with rage, sprang into the room. His knife flashed and Juan Francisco's knife met it! Screaming in terror, María flung herself into the fray, only to realize that Anza and Father Font were there also, holding the foes.

"*Señora*," Father Font said, "ever since we left San Miguel de Horcasitas you have caused turmoil!"

"I helped that woman over the Colorado!" Pablo shouted in fury. "I wish I had drowned her!"

"I am sorry, Your Reverence," said María, "and I shall cause no more turmoil for you. I'm going to marry *Señor* Juan Francisco and live here at San Gabriel."

On the instant Father Font became as benign as Saint Francis. "*Señora,* you are too young to be without a husband! May you be happy!"

"San Gabriel is fortunate in gaining San Francisco's bravest colonist," said Anza as he went out, taking with him the raging Pablo.

On the morning when bugles sounded for the colonists' departure northward, María felt a sharp pang—for months she had obeyed its summons! Again and again she embraced her friends, and again and again doubt assailed her. Was she failing Anza? Was it right for her to stay behind? When she turned back to glowing, protecting Juan Francisco, she knew all was right.

Soon the San Gabriel bells pealed out to celebrate the marriage of María Feliciana Arballo de Gutiérrez to Juan Francisco Lopez. For their *maestra*, the Indian nuns decorated the altar of the little log church with spring flowers and brought out the filmiest altar linen. With an exalted light in his eyes, gaunt Father Garcés came from the Indian village to bestow his blessing upon María and Juan. Then, trusting to his guardian spirit, protected only by a banner bearing a picture of the Virgin, he set out alone across Tejon Pass for the Colorado River. There, later, he and Rivera were to be killed in a massacre fostered by the suddenly hostile Chief Palma.

After founding San Francisco, Anza returned to San Gabriel, and he and Father Font assured themselves of a welcome by the simple expedient of bringing from Carmel to the Mission two cats and numerous kittens—the joy of the Indians! All too soon Anza's spurs were jingling down the valley and over the mountains toward the great desert. Later, New Mexico was to have him for its Governor, but California never saw him again.

María remained at San Gabriel where, thirteen years later, her daughter Estaquia married José Maria Pico. One of their sons became Governor Pio Pico. Through the Picos María and Juan became the grandparents of Doña Trinidad Ortega de la Guerra whose loveliness is still a living legend in Los Angeles. La Primavera—springtime— she was called, and Spring Street is named in her honor. Another of their granddaughters was lovely Doña Ramona Carrillo of San Diego who was married to Lieutenant Romualdo Pacheco, later killed in a duel near San Gabriel. Their infant son Romualdo became the only Spanish Governor after American occupation. Another granddaughter of this happy pair was Doña Josefa Carrillo who in the 1830's defied Governor Echiandía by eloping with the American sea captain, Henry Delano Fitch, from San Diego. Still another granddaughter was Doña Francisca Carrillo who became the wife of General Mariano Guadalupe Vallejo and gave to California several of the State's most beautiful women.

Other descendants of Doña María Feliciana are the picturesque polo-playing Tevis brothers, and the actors Leo Carrillo and William Gaxton. Probably no woman has so greatly endowed California's beauty and art as this singing, dancing, laughing María Feliciana Arballo de Gutiérrez who deserted the Anza expedition at San Gabriel to become the wife of Juan Francisco Lopez. Her adobe dwelling has been appropriately restored at 330 South Santa Anita Street, San Gabriel.

II

THE FIRST LADY'S DIVORCE

1783

KING CARLOS III of Spain had become alarmed upon discovering, in 1767, that the Russians had crossed Bering Strait and were encroaching on Spanish territory on the Pacific Coast. Immediately he ordered the founding of the California Missions.

In 1769 the first expedition was sent northward to establish a Mission at San Diego. Visitador-General José de Galvez, in charge of the venture, summoned Don Pedro Fages, a young lieutenant from Catalonia who had been fighting Indians in Sonora, Mexico. Recognizing Fages' stormy energy, Galvez sent him on the California expedition as military chief of its sea branch. A Mission and a Presidio were to be founded at San Diego, and two Missions farther north. This young lieutenant Fages was to become California's fourth governor, and he and his wife, Doña Eulalia, were to disturb its history.

After more than three months at sea Fages arrived at San Diego before Governor Gaspar de Portolá and Padre Junipero Serra came overland. All but seven of Fages' men had died of or been disabled by scurvy. With those seven he joined Portolá and a company hurrying northward to found a Mission on the Bay of Monterey, which had been described in 1602 by Viscaíno.

On their first trip Portolá and Fages did not find this bay, but they and their company were the first white men to behold redwood trees and to discover San Francisco Bay. Starvation drove them back to San Diego, but they were not defeated. On their second march northward they found Monterey Bay and there established Mission San Carlos de Borromeo [Carmel].

Until 1774 Fages remained at Monterey as Comandante of the

California establishments. He cared little about founding Missions or saving souls, but he explored California. He had the first private orchard—six hundred trees planted at his own expense. Proudly he wrote of his garden, his shrubs, sheep and goats. He stormed over trifles and quarrelled with Serra because the padre insisted on having soldiers to guard the Missions. This resulted in Fages' removal from Monterey in 1774, but he wrote an excellent pamphlet describing California.

On his return to Mexico he again fought Indians. Then at Serra's request he was brought back to Monterey in 1782 as California's governor. He might have gone on indefinitely had it not been for his longing to see his wife, and her consequent coming to California.

FOR eight years His Excellency Don Pedro Fages, California's fourth governor, had not seen his wife, lovely Doña Eulalia Celis of Barcelona, or his swarthy small son Pedrito.

From the royal palace at Monterey every courier carried overland letters to Doña Eulalia, still lingering in Spain:

Beloved, come. I cannot leave these Californias. Alta California especially is most important strategically to His Majesty King Carlos III. It is coveted by both England and Russia. Do not delay, *carita*. Bring our Pedrito. I yearn to see him playing in the *palacio* courtyard. He must have brothers and sisters—all little Californians. *Querida,* do not fail your husband. My arms, my heart long for you both. Love of my life, I will scorch you with kisses.

Imperious young Doña Eulalia Celis de Fages felt that she had conferred distinction on young Lieutenant Pedro Fages in becoming his wife while he was on a furlough from Mexico, and she refused to depart from the stately Celis dwelling at Barcelona. To her husband she reiterated:

Pedro *mio*, let England and Russia have the entire American continent, if they are such imbeciles as to want leagues of wild lands with Indians. I will not go to your savage Californias. Months of sea sickness would kill me. Leave your post to other officers who prefer to be separated from their wives. Come back to Barcelona and civilization.

Don Pedro Fages was a dynamic Catalonian. He had pioneered fifteen years in Mexico and the Californias. Refinement of living charmed him little. The sprawling whitewashed adobe royal residence at Monterey, its crude furnishings, talk in the barracks with rough men like himself, hunting antelope and bear, dominion over a province, hope of advancement, held him on the far frontier. Days were not long enough for Fages. He planted orchards; he supervised the garden and vineyard; he stored away brandy. When he rode to Mission Carmelo for Mass he argued with zealous *Padre* Junípero Serra about founding the Mission at Santa Barbara Presidio in the south. Thinking of his own son Pedrito in faraway Barcelona he emptied his pockets of *dulces* into the hands of soldiers' children and little Indians. To his wife he dispatched another letter:

Eulalia *mia,* I must have you and our son. Your misfortune is never to have seen this paradise California. We have gigantic trees such as man has never beheld, and also palms, pomegranates, olives, and oranges of Europe. Even our vegetable garden is bordered with wild azaleas. You will live like a queen in the Governor's *palacio* here at Monterey. Pedro Fages is a humble peon with his eyes turned toward his mistress in Spain. Your kingdom awaits its first great lady.

After the fashion of her time that autocrat, Doña Rosa Celis, Doña Eulalia's mother, decided her daughter's future. "It is indecent for a young married woman to live apart from her husband. Pedrito needs a father. You married a soldier. His Majesty and the Viceroy of Mexico appreciate Pedro Fages. They have made him Governor of California. You alone ignore him, Eulalia. Behave like a soldier's wife. Join your husband."

And so, in the spring of 1783, His Excellency Don Pedro Fages rode southward from Monterey toward the ancient city of Loreto, presided over by Our Lady with her necklaces of pearls, to meet his beloved Eulalia. Sixteen years of soldiering, Indian fighting, trail-breaking, founding Missions and pueblos, had tanned Fages' skin, grizzled his unkempt beard, lined his face, thickened his waistline;

but they had given him new strength and authority. To the rugged brown soldiers who rode with him in worn leather jackets His Excellency was another Cortés.

Fages had little pleasure in Baja California with its gray desert and cacti, but he seemed to have been reborn in the rich mother earth of Alta California. Even the yellow pathway over which the Governor and his train passed, *El Camino Real*—the King's Highway—had allure. Had he not been one of the trail-breakers through the northern wilderness fourteen years gone, when he came to San Diego with Father Junípero Serra? His own sturdy hands had helped mark the path with crosses and had heaped up the crude cairns pointing the path from San Diego to the iris-blue Bay of San Francisco. The Missions at which he paused gave the Governor their benediction. Fages was far from devout, but they were part of him, as were the Presidios and pueblos that had come into existence since his arrival. He was one of the founders of this civilization. As his cavalcade jingled Loreto-ward he felt in truth that he was going to bestow his own kingdom of California upon Eulalia, his wife.

By the shark-infested waters of the Vermilion Sea, the Gulf of California, Don Pedro and his men pitched tents in the hot July sun to await Doña Eulalia, California's first great lady from Spain. A feast was prepared—antelope, venison, *tortillas, frijoles,* dried fruits, wine. Guitars were strummed and Fages chanted Indian songs.

In the last moment anxiety beset His Excellency. His friend, *Capitán* Joaquin Cañete, had been commissioned to escort Doña Eulalia and Pedrito to the meeting-place. Had they lost their way? Were they ill? Had they been attacked by Indians?

But finally Don Pedro saw approaching on burro-back a man in black and red uniform. *Capitán* Cañete was leading the way. Doña Eulalia and Pedrito, also mounted on little burros, followed. Behind them came a train weighted down with bags and boxes. Don Pedro's world, his Spain, was coming to him—his wife and son! His heart hammered against his scarred leather jacket as he rollicked forward, teeth chattering with joy. He nearly crushed his wife in his arms.

She was the same Eulalia with long Grecian eyes, soft skin, and masses of fair hair like heaped-up sunshine. He was drenched through with her loveliness. "My beautiful, my beautiful!" He seized Pedrito like a bear, eyes atwinkle he shouted, "Sugar plum! My little soldier!" In gratitude he kissed both cheeks of his friend Cañete for having brought Doña Eulalia and Pedrito safe to him.

Young Pedro munched the *dulces* bulging from the Governor's pocket. *"Padrecito!* At last I have a father!"

Doña Eulalia still had the grace of a breeze in her movements, but as she looked at her mantle and gown torn by brambles and thorns she said, "See what this California has done—those hideous cacti! Your paradise, Pedro!—rattlesnakes, tarantulas, screeching night owls!"

Fages' hungry lips silenced her carpings. *"Carita,* this is Baja California. Wait till you see the California of the north!"

One of Doña Eulalia's many boxes was opened. She put on a fresh gown, bathed her face in cologne and brightened when Fages wound round her neck a long strand of pink Loreto pearls. *"Querida,"* he said, "precious—Mother Eve!"

During the feasting by campfire Don Pedro listened to family news, gossip of Seville and Madrid. The soldiers gazed at Doña Eulalia in awe. They treated Pedrito as a princeling. The Governor and *Capitán* Cañete emptied horns of wine, drank to His Majesty King Carlos of Spain and to Doña Eulalia, Queen of the Californias. By starlight the desert rang with their songs echoing the days of the Moors. Even Doña Eulalia sang. Fages' hopes rose. Ah, Eulalia would like California.

When the tempestuous husband held his wife in his arms that night in the tent, he retasted honeymoon sweets with his long-awaited bride, who protested, "My great handsome bear."

At San Diego *la Señora Gobernadora* Fages set foot in her kingdom. California's first Mission was in *fiesta.* Bells pealed welcome; guns volleyed salute; friars paid Doña Eulalia reverent homage, and children looked with wonder at velvet-clad Pedrito. Soldiers, gazing on Doña Eulalia's brilliant face with its creamy skin half concealed by a mantilla, recalled the women of their own homeland, Spain, and the Indians marveled at the first fair *señora* they had ever beheld.

Don Pedro washed the dust out of his throat with San Diego's famous wines and graciously praised them. He distributed *dulces* among the children. He told his wife how he had entered the harbor in 1769 on the *San Carlos* with most of his men dead or dying of scurvy. At the Santa Barbara Presidio the Governor found his old friend Sergeant José Francisco Ortega, now *Comandante*. They spoke of the time when they lost their way seeking Monterey and had to live on mule meat, and of that memorable moment when they first beheld the Bay of San Francisco.

Doña Eulalia was not entertained by these pioneering reminiscences, but she was pleased when Santa Barbara Indians offered her their rarest artistry—a long mantle of sea-gull down.

Governor Fages and Doña Eulalia proceeded north over a spring carpet of orange poppies, blue and yellow lupines, wild cyclamen and canary-colored violets. The Governor halted the cavalcade to pluck wild roses for his re-found bride. At Mission San Luis Obispo grizzly bears crashed through the brush in the night, and Fages told Doña Eulalia how even before a Mission had been built here, when supplies from Mexico failed, he and his soldiers hunted bear in this vicinity and saved Monterey from starvation with their pack train of meat.

January saw Fages with his wife and son at Monterey. On the day preceding their arrival the sun was shining over the crescent-shaped blue bay. Montereyans brought forth from chests their *fiesta* garments. Children were smartened; women braided men's hair in queues—and then a winter storm boomed in from the southeast, swaying the tempest-twisted cypresses and lashing the cobalt waters of the bay to purple black. In this storm Doña Eulalia arrived.

But guns volleyed. Bells rang. At the Presidio entrance facing the ocean men in black and red uniforms saluted. An awed soldier's wife curtsied and kissed Her Excellency's hand. Drenched to the skin, Doña Eulalia coolly commented, "Paradise!"

"Carita," apologized the Governor, "this rain makes our lovely flowers."

Horrified Doña Eulalia observed a group of naked Indian women in the shelter of a high wall surrounding the royal residence. "Pedro, do women wear no garments in Paradise—not even in rain?" She halted the procession. "Open my boxes. Get clothes for those poor naked creatures. Make haste, Pedro."

"Not in the rain, *carita*. Wait till we reach the palace."

"Pedro, you like naked women!"

In her chagrin Doña Eulalia did not notice the adobe wall nearly half a mile in circumference, nor the barracks built into the wall. She did not see even the small Royal Chapel. The Governor's party crossed the sandy parade grounds and Indian hostlers took their horses. Doña Eulalia wondered why they were stopping before a low rambling building. Could that be—the palace!

A few whitewashed rooms with no glass in the windows! Blue wooden shutters to keep out wind! Windows barred with rough grills to ward off Indian attack! The long *sala* floor was of earth baked hard but clean swept and partly concealed by bearskin rugs, trophies of Fages' hunting expeditions. This bleak *sala* was faintly warmed by a brazier of red coals. Doña Eulalia summed it up: "There is hardly room in this house for my boxes."

Suddenly the great *Señora's* presence seemed to pervade the Presidio. "Now," said a soldier in tattered black and red uniform at the thatched barracks, "a lady has come. She will change Monterey."

And she did.

At first Doña Eulalia did not notice silent Dolores, the little Indian maid who was everywhere in the royal residence. In a coarse gray smock Dolores went barefoot from room to room with a tarweed brush flicking dust from the long heavy sycamore tables and the chairs with rawhide seats. She was in *sala*, dining room, kitchen, and outbuildings. She made ready Doña Eulalia's spacious bed with soft, fine, hand-drawn linen. Always looking demurely downward, she placed flowers before holy pictures. She seemed never to see His Excellency, but he scarcely completed an order before she fulfilled his wishes. She was, however, the only one at the Presidio who gave no sign of rejoicing when the Fages arrived.

From the confusion of clothing, draperies, silver, linen, Doña Eulalia appealed to Dolores, "What shall I do with my treasures in this hovel?"

Dolores devised clothes presses of leather chests and lacquered red boxes left at the Presidio by Manila galleons. Finally Doña Eulalia's belongings were housed.

Of all the Presidio Indians Dolores alone spoke intelligible Spanish. "Where did you learn, child?" questioned Doña Eulalia.

"Dolores hear *padres—Señor el Gobernador*. Dolores hear *Señora la Gobernadora.*"

Doña Eulalia condescended; "Dolores, you are no fool. Bring those Indian girls from the corridor. They disgrace the capital. I wish to dress them decently."

"Bronco Indians, Excellency," replied Dolores. "Not go Mission. They say Mission Indians traitor Indians. We must go mountain— live free mountain Indians."

"All the more reason why I must clothe these mountain Indians, Dolores. I can't have the creatures at the palace gate. I'm ashamed to have my little Pedrito see them. As for the soldiers— Make haste, Dolores!"

Soon Doña Eulalia was distributing smocks, chemises, petticoats, mantles among Indian women in the corridor. Dolores was her interpreter. "Tell them they are bad girls. Decent girls don't go about the streets naked. They must make dresses for themselves or remain in the mountains."

Suddenly some of the mischievous Indian girls seized an armful of Doña Eulalia's gowns and made off. They also took the Governor's garments.

During the confusion Don Pedro clanked into the Presidio courtyard from Mission Carmelo. He had given Pedrito a riding lesson, his first, on a gentle Palomino horse. Eyes shining, Pedrito announced to his mother,

"*Padrecito* is going to make me a soldier. I'm a Californian!"

"Californians, Pedro!" scoffed Doña Eulalia. "This plan of civilizing Indians! How can statesmen be so imbecile? Of course, the dear *padres*—bless them—what does a friar know about life?"

"*Carita*, what is the matter?" asked the Governor.

"I had to bring all those Indian girls from the rain and give them clothing. Pedro, what have you been doing these fifteen years? Why didn't you get the Indians dressed? Not that they showed gratitude— they stole our clothes and fled. But they must be dressed."

"Slowly, Eulalia," laughed the Governor. "Thousands of Indians are without clothing. In winter they paint themselves with mud or wear a pelt. But there are no shops at Monterey. The supply ship comes only twice a year with goods for the Presidio—coarse stuff for soldiers. After your dresses from Spain are gone—you will be here years."

"*Dios de mi alma!* Not in this huddle of dirty huts."

"Eulalia, it is the capital. After you get over homesickness, you will like Monterey."

Doña Eulalia shivered and flung a brilliant blanket over her shoulders. "This adobe house gives me chills. I'll take the first boat for Mexico, then Barcelona."

"The first boat leaves next year," chuckled the Governor.

"Then I'll go overland. Cañete will take me." Fages smiled.

Unseemly dress was Doña Eulalia's topic the following day when Father Junípero Serra limped into the royal palace, having trudged on his ulcered leg over the four miles of the *Via Crucis* from Carmel to Monterey to bid her welcome. When she looked at this aged grayhabited Franciscan, his intense eyes illumined with the ecstasy of an invisible world, she ceased for a moment to be the spoiled Barcelona beauty and was humbled to her knees.

"*Padre* Junípero," said Doña Eulalia, rising, "I was pained yesterday when I arrived! Naked Indian girls everywhere! You perform miracles, *Padre* Junípero. Can you not clothe these women?"

"My dear *Señora Gobernadora,* if I could, I should be canonized! Blessings on you for coming to California, an example for the lowly. I hope to see you at Mass, Excellency, at Carmelo."

On Sunday morning Montereyans beheld for the first time His Excellency Governor Fages riding with a touch of majesty over the *Via Crucis* to Carmelo. Black velvet knee breeches, a three-cornered hat and carefully braided locks had replaced the coarse worn leather garment and unkempt hair of the Governor that Monterey best knew. In a full black taffeta gown and black mantilla Doña Eulalia was mounted on a small man's saddle at her husband's side. With them were Pedrito and the entire Presidio population—officers, men, women, and children.

Indians of both sexes stood in line at the low Mission entrance, bowing obeisance to their ruler. They were clothed in smocks or blankets. Some had bone ornaments, and gray and white tufts of sea-gull feathers in their hair. Others were smeared with charcoal soot or nightshade juice; still others were tattooed or were painted red and white. Shaggy black hair hung across their foreheads and to their waists.

Father Junípero greeted the Governor's family at the church door. Before an altar illumined with candles and bedecked with his favorite wild roses, Serra offered thanksgiving for the safe arrival of their Excellencies. Little Dolores had brought prayer rugs for the Fages, but most of the congregation knelt on the dirt floor of the crude whitewashed church. Monterey numbered only a few Spaniards. Many of the worshipers were soldiers and their Indian wives.

Suddenly turning her head, Doña Eulalia recognized one of her stolen garments. A bare-shouldered Indian was clad in her own red velvet dress once worn at a court ball in Madrid. Another native had donned a purple brocade mantle—but no skirt. Still another wore Don Pedro's black and red coat without a nether garment. Doña

Eulalia shook with laughter. "I am Queen—of the California Indians!"

Her mocking mirth was checked by Father Junípero in the pulpit, exalted beyond himself. Holding a stone in his hand, he beat his scarred breast. With flaming candle he seared his own flesh. For the hour Her Excellency ejected trifles from her mind.

Again Doña Eulalia was about to become a mother and her complaints increased. "It is inhuman to expect me to endure exile among people who do not speak my language. I hate California, Pedro. You love the province more than you do me."

"Not jealous of California, Eulalia?"

But it was true! Fages carried stones and shells of California in his pockets. The province was a siren enchaining him—as if she were that Queen Califía for whom California was named.

Don Pedro made a compromise. "At San Francisco Don José Darío Argüello is in command. He and his wife are gently born Spaniards. There is an excellent surgeon at the Presidio. Let us go there for the birth of the child. Some of the *rancheros* near San Francisco have interesting families. That will be a distraction."

When the Fages set out from the royal dwelling for San Francisco, little Indian Dolores turned away her face and silently wept. Doña Eulalia was touched. As gifts for the Argüellos, the Governor put aboard ship olives he had pickled, almonds he had grown, fruits he had dried, a barrel of his wine and skins filled with brandy—his California pride! Despite the possible peril of the journey Doña Eulalia thrilled when the long-boats made their way among spouting whales, from the shore to the packet for San Francisco.

"To get away from Monterey! I am so happy. If only this ship were going to Spain!"

Alone at the royal residence Pedrito hilariously disobeyed Dolores. He milked the goats; he acquired a pet lamb. He helped Indian girls dig weeds in the vegetable garden. He ran with the Indian boys through the orchard frightening away bandit birds with miniature bows and arrows.

A week after their departure from Monterey the Fages rode over the sand dunes to the high presidio dwelling of *Comandante* José Darío Argüello which, among the scrub oaks, resembled a comfortable German farmstead. They looked off on the Golden Gate and purple Tamalpais beyond. *Señora* Argüello was just recovering from the birth of her son Luis, a future Governor of California. Her daughter Concepción, who would be California's first nun, was yet to be born.

Maternal *Señora* Argüello volunteered as assistant midwife at the accouchement, and later went to the Mission Dolores where Father Palóu christened the newest California baby María del Carmen. Later there was a great celebration at the *Comandante's* residence with the heavy Moraga silver called into service. Doña Eulalia especially welcomed the little María del Carmen; the infant would be a lever to assist her return to Spain.

Suddenly the Fages were summoned to lamenting Monterey. Father Junípero Serra had died in his small cell and was already entombed at the foot of the altar. Spaniards, Mexicans and Indians had battled to obtain a fragment of his habit. But Serra's spirit seemed to shimmer in the air.

With Father Junípero gone Doña Eulalia clamored daily, "This place is killing me. Pedro, if you do not take me to Spain, I will never kiss you again." She drove the Governor from her room and barred the door.

Tempestuous Fages returned. "Eulalia, *carita,* this is cruelty. I am no Franciscan."

"I am no Indian. It is cruel to keep me here among the Indians, to bring up our children as savages. I am no Fages. I am a Celis of Barcelona. I will write my mother. She will present my wretched situation to the *Audiencia.* I will have you ordered away."

"Fatuous woman! Leave me alone. I may be Viceroy."

"I don't wish to be Vicereine over Indians. Mexico City is only more refined exile. I'd as lief be a peon. Barcelona—I must go home!"

Stormy Don Pedro no longer resisted banishment from Doña

Eulalia's embraces. Her monotonous existence was broken by the first foreigners to visit California. Count Jean François Galaup de La Perouse and his men entered Monterey Bay on two French frigates. Doña Eulalia brought out her silver, her brocades and her Barcelona linen. Catalonia was near France, and she spoke French as she did Castilian. Monterey made *fiesta* for the Frenchmen.

"Won't you tell me about Europe, *Monsieur le Comte?*" implored the Governor's wife. "Civilization—"

"Dear Madame, we came to flee civilization," laughed La Perouse. "In this distant Monterey I may say discreetly the King is vacillating, the Queen is silly. We have reverted to the Indians—to nature."

At once La Perouse and his men set up a laboratory on the white sanded beach. They made notes of flowers, rocks, and native customs.

Doña Eulalia saw in La Perouse an opportunity to escape. *"Monsieur le Comte,"* she begged, "do give me passage in one of your frigates to Europe. California is killing me. My children will die in this cold adobe house."

"Dearest lady," replied La Perouse, "if conditions do not grow better, many will die in Europe. I am leaving His Excellency a bag of that new South American vegetable—potatoes. They are quite delicious. Raise potatoes. Remain at Monterey with your admirable Fages. It is far safer than the South Seas into which we are sailing, not to mention Europe. As for Indians, they alone are followers à l'américaine of France's most popular philosopher, Jean Jacques Rousseau."

La Perouse's frigate sank near the New Hebrides, and within a few years the vacillating French King and his charming Queen lost their heads. California recalls La Perouse for having introduced potatoes at Monterey, but Doña Eulalia abominated the new vegetable because the explorer would not further her escape.

To her mother, Doña Rosa Celis, Doña Eulalia appealed:

Help me, *cara Madre*. I am in rags. The Indians have taken all my clothes. Have Pedro transferred from this terrible California. Intercede with the *Audiencia*.

Before an answer came Doña Eulalia surmised the sinister reason for Don Pedro's acquiescence in their quasi-separation—Dolores! The Indian girl's glance seldom met Doña Eulalia's penetrating eyes; she trembled when Fages entered the room and Doña Eulalia determined to find out why.

Fages never failed to rise early, but Doña Eulalia was up before him. In winter darkness she tiptoed about the *palacio*. At last, he came—Pedro, the heavy brown bear, rumbled through the dark hall and across the courtyard. With Catalonian fury Doña Eulalia burst upon the Governor and the Indian girl in Dolores' neat little room.

"In the name of God!" protested Fages.

"Aren't you presumptuous to mention God, Pedro? You, disgracing your King, your country, your family!"

"Eulalia, you drove me away!"

"Now I know why you remained in California. You're one of those white men who have become part Indian!"

"And you are one of those wives who think they can hold a husband at a distance of seven thousand miles!"

With both hands Doña Eulalia pulled his beard. Dolores flung herself at her mistress' feet, entreating, "Please, *Señora la Gobernadora*."

"Little fool."

"I go back Colorado, *Señora*."

"No, Dolores," said Fages.

"An Indian Paradise!" accused Doña Eulalia.

"Dolores asks nothing. She gives everything. You ask everything. You give nothing." Heedless of the cruel stab to the Indian girl, he added, "Eulalia, why do I adore you—hellion?"

Fages followed his wife to her room.

"Divorce! Divorce!" threatened Doña Eulalia. "I'll go to Carmelo. I'll tell the *padres* everything. We'll see who rules California!" And like a maniac she shouted to listeners, "Pedro Fages sleeps with Indians! Divorce I will have!"

Doña Eulalia aroused a drowsy Indian hostler, mounted a horse and rode over the sandy *Via Crucis* while gray rags of fog still clung to the pine trees. She stumbled into the missionaries' dwelling at Carmelo just as Father Paterna and Father Pieras were about to say Mass.

"Pedro Fages has an Indian mistress—that Dolores from the Colorado! Both admitted it in Dolores' room this morning."

"That poor child of the wilderness!" pitied Father Paterna.

Doña Eulalia felt magnanimous as she said, "*Padre,* I don't blame the Indian girl. She hasn't dared look me in the face since I came. But may the devil carry me off if ever I live with Pedro Fages again! Divorce!"

"Divorce! *Señora!*" protested Father Pieras. "Such a thing has never been heard of on the continent."

"Today this continent hears of something new! The California Governor's wife demands divorce. By the Blessed Virgin, I'll leave this vile Fages, this barbarous province. I'll stand on the Presidio wall and scream till you give me divorce."

"*Señora,* marriage is a sacrament."

"This shameless man, father of two children, imprisons his wife in miserable Monterey, humiliates her by living with an Indian! And I can't be divorced?"

"Calm yourself, Doña Eulalia. Divorce in our Church is virtually impossible."

"It will be possible in California, or the Santa Barbara Mission will not be built. My mother, Doña Rosa Celis, has great influence with the *Audiencia.* No more Missions will be built. My mother made Fages governor. She will unmake him. She will cut off Mission supplies."

"Sacred Heart of Mary!" protested Father Paterna with whitening cheeks.

The friar laid a calming hand on Doña Eulalia. "My dear *Señora la Gobernadora,* perhaps it is all a mistake. We will investigate."

"Investigate, *padre mio!* Everyone knows but you!"

Back at the royal residence Doña Eulalia heard Don Pedro say, "By the holy bones of Saint Bartholomew, I have fought Apaches, but they never fought like you."

She kept up her warfare until Father Matias Antonio de Noriega was summoned to Carmelo to take testimony in California's first divorce case. After examining Doña Eulalia's witnesses Father Noriega returned his decision, "There is no ground for divorce."

The case was reported to the Bishop. Doña Eulalia received the order from the Fathers, "Remain in your apartment. Do not repeat your charges throughout the capital."

But this fiery Catalonian was not to be subdued by an order from humble Franciscans. Doña Eulalia refused to remain at the royal residence—"that hovel!" She rode back to the Mission and made outcries during Mass. Even Franciscan patience was exhausted. The Fathers sympathized with Don Pedro when he dashed from the Presidio to Carmelo frowning and plucking his beard.

"*Jesucristo!* My wife is driving me mad. I'm trying to write a book on California. I cannot. She behaves like a lunatic. I cannot leave this province. It is the home of my heart. I am going south with Pedrito—to save my reason. Manage Doña Eulalia if you can. *Padres,* tie her hands; silence her! Good luck to you. *Adiós!*"

Doña Eulalia carried on the battle—the State warring against the Church. For the dignity of the rulers Father Noriega sent an officer to effect the removal of the First Lady of California to Carmelo.

"Take me by force!" defied Doña Eulalia.

And that is precisely what happened. Her hands bound, Doña Eulalia was transported to Carmelo. There she received what she considered the culminating indignity. She was placed in the *monjério,* the building where Indian women were kept. She shouted. She screeched. Furiously she kicked! With such lack of control there was nothing to be done.

"*Señora Gobernadora,*" the Fathers warned, "restrain your wrath, moderate your behavior. Otherwise you will be bound and put in stocks."

"You fight women! If *Padre* Junípero were not dead—"

Doña Eulalia wrote to her mother, Doña Rosa Celis:

My husband has made me prisoner with Indian women. If I remain in California, I will die. If I do not die I will kill myself. If you wish to see your daughter again, go to the *Audiencia* and request that Pedro be removed from office. The climate is injuring his health.

At last the First Lady triumphed over California. When the overland courier brought the news from Spain, Don Pedro broke in grief over his violated career. Doña Eulalia took him tenderly in her arms and said,

"Ah, Pedro, you have worked too hard, done too much. It was not appreciated. I forgive you for behaving so badly. The rest of our lives will be one long honeymoon. In Barcelona we shall be happy, happy."

Then Doña Eulalia sailed with her two children from Monterey. Fages remained for a time to adjust his affairs. He had starved, his men had died to create California with its eleven missions, its four presidios, and its three pueblos. He had ruled the province from Cape San Lucas to the Bay of San Francisco. That was ended. Over were the great campaigning days! Never would he have another adventure such as these rich twenty-one years in this province had given him.

Fages was the sort of man who could adore a mountain, a seashore. It was near death to him to look for the last time at the blue Monterey Bay with white sands, the windswept cypress, the cactus hedges bright with fruit, the little fluttering gray olive leaves. He could not turn to glance at the garden, the orchard, the vineyard he had planted. He did not attempt to take leave of Dolores. With him he carried too many memories of her devotion. Never could he forget the trails he had made, the glory of saving starving Monterey, the joy of helping to create a new Paradise. On that May day in 1790 when the *San Carlos,* the same brave ship that had brought him to San Diego, swung out on the tide, Fages did not look back. He held his stern soldier's eyes steady toward the sea and Spain.

No one noticed a slender round-faced Indian girl slip from her smock and swim after the disappearing ship. She tossed for a time in the waves plowed up by the *San Carlos,* and then was no more.

III

AMATIL AND OLANA

1799

GOVERNOR PEDRO FAGES wrote that the Indians of Mission San Buenaventura on Santa Barbara Bay were of unusual civility and intelligence. Zuzu was the name of their village of eighty-four rancherias, *but Portolá who was with Fages on their march northward in 1769 renamed the place* La Asunción de Nuestra Señora.

Already the Portuguese Cabrillo, first European to land here, had called the village the Pueblo de las Canóas, *because the Indians had spacious, efficient canoes. Later, when the gray-robed Serra passed along the shore, he named the village* La Asumpta, *saying, "The site of Mission San Buenaventura has been found."*

As early as 1768 Don José de Galvez, Visitador-*General of Mexico, had planned Mission San Buenaventura. "My Mission," he called it as he himself packed church goods for the establishment and laughingly boasted to Serra, "I am a better sacristan than you,* Padre." *He ordered the Mission to be founded as soon as Serra reached California, but Indian uprisings caused delay.*

At last, in 1782, the establishment was made, but not, however, with the splendor that had been planned to honor the presence of Governor Felipe de Neve. Impressively arrayed, His Excellency had set out from San Gabriel with Serra, but couriers halted him with the news of a Yuma uprising. Neve turned back and joined forces with Fages to battle with Indians, but Serra went on with Lieutenant José Francisco de Ortega, discoverer of San Francisco Bay, and a few score of soldiers. After planting the Cross, he celebrated the first high Mass in a brushwood shelter. At last Galvez's Mission was founded.

Flowers, fruit and grain grew in the lush black soil of the Mission ranchos, *delighting Captain George Vancouver, the first Englishman to visit California, when he came on the* Discovery *in 1793. He reported that the buildings at San Buenaventura surpassed those of other establishments. Converts, however, were not numerous. Pagans fought those who accepted the new faith, and in one of these battles were a classic pair of lovers, Amatil and Olana.*

AMATIL, the dreamy-eyed daughter of Chief Matilija, first beheld Olana on the eastern peak of the San Cayetano Mountains, the sacred place of the Chumash tribe. He was from the country of wild lilacs and wild walnuts to the north, and she was from the sunny canyon of Matilija in the south. Tribesfolk had assembled on this height to pray to I-shoi-esh for bountiful harvests. Around the black totem pole bedecked with wings of crow and buzzard, the people of Chief Matilija and Olana had offered acorns, plumes and trinkets, for two days. They had feasted on dried fish and piñons, praying, "Do not fail us, Great Captain of Captains."

The last prayer died on the air. I-shoi-esh must be satisfied. Olana, a wreath of golden-brown feathers on his head, rotated fragments of dry willow between his palms. A spark flashed. He caught it up with a feather. Dried grass was lighted. Small branches kindled. I-shoi-esh was a tower of flame! Fish, acorns and befeathered baskets were cast into the fire. The encircled Indians intoned a sad deep chant as the flames took their cherished possessions. Devoutly they believed I-shoi-esh would reward them with abundance.

After the sacrifice the Indians went down the mountain side in reverent silence. Amatil walked with Olana, whose loins were bound with black condor plumes. When they reached the turning on the trail which Chief Matilija took to go to the peaceful fertile canyon where he had his lodge—Ojai, the Nest—Amatil said to Olana, in a voice as sweet as a thrush's note, *"Kaie-kiwa-na-alt,* good-by."

Without speaking he turned abruptly and sped fast toward the country of wild lilacs and wild walnuts. A cloud shadowed the eyes of Amatil as she went into the canyon of Matilija which hitherto had held for her all beauty—sage-covered slopes with tangled yellow love vines, tall spiky white yuccas, wild fruit, grain, game; and fish in the river.

After Amatil's pilgrimage to the sacrifice of I-shoi-esh on the peak of the San Cayetano Mountains, some of the rich warmth departed from the air of Ojai, the Nest. But she dried fish. She cured acorns and cooked them with venison. She roasted toyon berries. She gathered *mej-me,* rushes, in the river for making *coras,* baskets. She cured them in ashes, bleached them white and dried them in the sun. But her thoughts were in the northern country of wild lilacs and wild walnuts.

Soon strange tales came to Chief Matilija's canyon. Pallid gray-robed men had arrived at the village of canoes on the Big Water, a day's walk from Ojai. They had built dwellings of mud and logs, quite different from the conical Chumash houses. These men were not guests. They refused to depart.

Chief Matilija's father had heard of white men who, centuries before, had arrived over the Big Water at the village of many canoes. They had left a new substance, iron, valued by Indians more than their own flint weapons or their most precious treasures. Those men of the past had departed over the Big Water in the vast canoes that had brought them. From the Sierra peaks the Indians occasionally beheld them sailing proudly past on the Big Water.

These gray-robed newcomers were called by the Indians *Taquimine,* or Christians. They boldly snared fish in the Big Water. They reared their own totem pole, a high Cross. They unfolded a banner. They placed it over a white scarfed altar. They lighted candles before a beautiful Lady holding in her arms an Infant. "Worship the Virgin. Worship her Son!" commanded the gray-robed men. "Destroy I-shoi-esh!"

The simple natives of the village of canoes at first did not understand why the white men had killed their God. Chief Matilija, however, interpreted faith—all men killed their god! Had not the Indians sacrificed I-shoi-esh? The Indian god promised only abundant fish, singing, dancing, and eternal playing on elderwood flutes. But the God of the *Taquimine* of the village of canoes, these gray-robed Christians, promised eternal life.

Soon *Padre* Antonio, a gray-robed sandaled friar, brought the new teachings to Ojai, the Nest. He was guided by a tribesman who had accepted the faith of the beautiful lady. Chief Matilija scorned the neophyte of Mission San Buenaventura. He dressed like a woman; he covered his naked body, pride of the Indian. Not only had he new garments, but a new name—Juan. Both Chief Matilija and Amatil, however, liked the gray-robed friar wearing a broad-brimmed hat and, at his waist, a string of beads with a shining Cross bearing a suffering figure of the new God.

Padre Antonio brought bright-colored beads, scarfs, handkerchiefs, chocolate, a mouth organ. Juan, the neophyte, had dazzling tales of Mission San Buenaventura and of the deeds of the pale men who had traveled many moons across the Big Water in giant canoes to bring the new faith.

Clearly these strangers were mighty medicine men! The *Padre* unrolled a scroll on which was pictured the beautiful Lady. Even Chief Matilija had never seen a painting; he knew only those figures graven on tree bark with crude stone implements; or mere outlines of the sun and the moon or coyotes and cougars stained on cave walls with dyes from blossoms. All the Indians in Matilija Canyon hurried to see this magical work shown by the man in the gray robe. It alarmed Chief Matilija that sorcerers should dwell near. So potent were they that without doubt they would remain forever.

Making strange gestures in the air, chanting awesome words, *Padre* Antonio departed from the canyon, but he left many gifts with Chief Matilija, Amatil, and their tribesfolk.

Long the Indians spoke of the beautiful Lady, of the music, of *Padre* Antonio and his new world only one day's walk from Ojai, the Nest. Amatil often talked of venturing to the Mission between the two rivers now called San Buenaventura and Santa Clara. It alarmed Chief Matilija to hear her say, "When days are longer I will walk to the village of canoes."

Chief Matilija shook his head and sternly grunted, "Forget the new God. I-shoi-esh is not to be angered. We have prayed for abundant harvests. If you enter the house of the new God, I-shoi-esh will turn the hills brown; he will cause fish to die."

Again and again *Padre* Antonio returned to Ojai, the Nest, and with each visit Amatil's eagerness to see Mission San Buenaventura increased.

In grass-sprouting-time Olana came from the country of wild lilacs and wild walnuts. With him were his parents and tribesmen, all bearing wedding gifts to Chief Matilija and Amatil—otter skins, obsidian arrowheads, feathers, baskets of fine weave.

Amatil's heart stood still. She had thirsted for the sight of Olana ever since he had gone northward. She knew that he had come to take her to the country of wild lilacs and wild walnuts. Would Chief Matilija accept the gifts?

With his own flint adze the chief felled the first dappled gray sycamore tree. To his tribesmen he said, "Build a tepee for Amatil and Olana."

The tepee completed, all gathered in the round feast house. A fire was lighted, the smoke passing upward through the hole in the top. Arrayed in furs, flowers, feathers, shells, the shaggy-haired natives formed a circle against the wall while Chief Matilija told tribal tales of centuries gone.

Then Amatil and Olana stood forth. They gazed at each other but went in opposite directions. Their feet barely left the earth as they danced while musicians beat time on rawhide stretched on a heavy brown frame. All night they danced without touching each other, yet they seemed to come nearer and nearer, to blend and be one in the air of flame. Olana whispered, "Fire-maiden!"

At sunrise, when Amatil and Olana went to their tepee of sweet-scented brush, terrifying sounds boomed into the valley. The earth seemed to tremble. Strange animals appeared at the canyon entrance

—neither deer, bear, elk, nor antelope. Not one of the Indians had ever seen a horse and some of them fell in fear before the wild rushing animals carrying riders of the race of *Padre* Antonio. But no gray-robed men did the animals bear; they carried angry-eyed men in blue and red, brandishing muskets, lances and knives. Mission San Buenaventura had been attacked by Indians and soldiers had come to Matilija Canyon to make reprisals.

Chief Matilija drew his bow; but Sergeant Carlos rode him down and left him bleeding. Muskets and lances laid Indians low. Women and children were seized by soldiers. Amatil was bound to a horse by burly Sergeant Carlos, the man with bold dark eyes and a scar on his left cheek burning red. She was carried sobbing out of the canyon and she thought each moment her last as she rode *reata*-bound on this strange new animal, the horse. Whither she was going, she knew no more than the screaming captive children, but after hours of riding in the hot sunlight she reached the village of canoes by the Big Water. It was the Mission of San Buenaventura.

In a square surrounded by log and adobe buildings, new and rough-finished, they stopped. Before the largest structure stood the gray-robed friar who had borne gifts to Chief Matilija. "*Padre* Antonio," said Sergeant Carlos, "we have brought you some Christians."

"I trust, Sergeant, that you used no violence."

"*Padre,* you can't put down revolt with prayer. At least, a soldier can't. Here is Amatil, Chief Matilija's daughter. Make her a Christian if you can! The bitch scratches. Look at my face!"

Amatil flung herself to her knees before gaunt *Padre* Antonio. Benign and gentle, he loosed the *reata* binding her and, touching her head, he said, "Child, have no fear." He led her toward the sobbing Indian children who had been brought to the Mission by soldiers and were huddled in the Plaza. His manner was a blessing to Amatil and the children. He gave them chocolate and *dulces.* Amatil ignored the gifts and the food brought from the neophytes' long table. She continued to sob.

Doña Rosa, a large maternal woman who spoke all idioms of the neighborhood tribes, led Amatil to the *monjério* or nunnery with whitewashed walls where were lodged Indian women and children who had been baptized.

"Ojai, the Nest! Poor, my father! Poor, my Olana!" moaned Amatil. "Take me to Ojai, the Nest."

Doña Rosa tried to soothe her. "Amatil, life is better here at the Mission. See this nice house, always dry in the rain and warm. You will have pretty clothing, plenty to eat. Say your prayers and go to Mass every day. You will never die, but go to Heaven. If soldiers had not brought you here, you would never have heard of Heaven."

"What Heaven?" wondered Amatil.

"A happy place. Love God and ask Him to take you to Heaven."

Amatil ceased sobbing. "Ask God take Amatil to Ojai, the Nest."

"*Carita,*" said Doña Rosa, "you wear pagan dress, grass garments. We'll put them away." She brought forth a white cotton blouse with a red petticoat and a blue striped blanket. "Wear Mission dress. We'll go see God."

Amatil dropped her grass skirt, wrapped herself in a blanket and said, "Amatil go see God."

"Not yet, Amatil. Put on this cotton blouse first, then the petticoat. Stay here at the Mission. You'll learn how to weave pretty garments."

Docile with fear Amatil permitted Doña Rosa to dress her. "Too hot," she said fanning herself with her petticoat.

"Don't do that, child," protested Doña Rosa. "Your petticoat is to cover your body."

"What for?"

"God does not like naked bodies in church."

"Amatil like God. God take Amatil to Ojai, the Nest."

Doña Rosa led the wondering Amatil from the nunnery through the Plaza. To the girl each building seemed more awesome than the other—the great log granary, the soldiers' houses, the missionaries' dwelling of adobe with tile roof. They stood at the entrance of the long wide porch with its tower and pealing bells. To Amatil the tower seemed to reach the sky.

In the church entrance were many women and children dressed in garments like hers. *Padre* Antonio passed among them and came to her, saying in Chumash, "Welcome to San Buenaventura, Amatil. Be happy here." When *Padre* Antonio and Doña Rosa led her into the church, they both made the sign of the Cross.

"Amatil," said the *Padre,* "make the sign of the Cross."

"God give me what I like?"

"If you are good and obey him."

Amatil blessed herself and said, "Great Captain of Captains, take Amatil to Ojai, the Nest."

"Amatil, stay at the Mission where people know God," said *Padre* Antonio. "Ask your friends to come here."

"Bad blue-blanket men kill my friends."

Doña Rosa was leading the girl toward the altar when suddenly Amatil beheld the image of the Virgin, in Her arms the Infant.

"Beautiful Lady! Beautiful Baby!" she cried, rushing toward the altar on the right where stood the Virgin with the Infant. Amatil had her arms around the Infant. "Amatil baby."

"Amatil, do not touch!" said the *Padre,* "That baby is God."

In ecstasy she gazed at the Infant, reluctantly removing her hands from its face. So absorbed was she by the image of the Virgin and Child that at first her eyes did not lift above the altar. Suddenly she beheld the figure of Jesus on the Cross and she moaned, "Dear, my father! Blue-blanket man kill dead."

Padre Antonio comforted her. "Amatil, that is the image of God who died to make us happy, to prove to us how much He loved us."

"Poor, my father—Matilija!"

"God is your father. He wishes you to stay at the Mission. He asked us to protect you. This is your home."

After instruction Amatil was baptized Ana, but she asked to be called by her tribal name. For weeks her sobbing could not be quieted, so great was her longing for Ojai, the Nest. Then followed outward content. Music, ceremonies, ritual, evening games, her own small duties crowded her days. No neophyte fingers were so deft as hers weaving baskets. Only she understood the legends she threaded into the baskets. Each was different, each marked with the first letter of her name, and the words Mission San Buenaventura. *Padre* Antonio sent them as gifts to the Viceroy in the City of Mexico.

With the passing of time Amatil's countenance altered. Some visitors who came to the Mission on great foreign ships said that she resembled the *señoritas* of Spain more than the Chumash women. Faith she accepted, prayers she repeated, hymns she chanted; but her spirit longed for life without Mission duties, unfettered by the white man's law.

One day a tribal runner from the north whispered in her ear, "Olana still lives in the country of wild lilacs and wild walnuts."

At acorn-time when the runner went speeding northward she murmured to him, "Tell Olana Amatil waits."

In the days that followed magic seemed in Amatil's fingers as they wove baskets in the colonnade of the *monjério;* her eyes lighted up all that her gaze fell upon.

"My child," said the *Padre,* "the time has come for marriage."

Amatil shook her head—no. "*Padre* Antonio, please—"

"An officer—Sergeant Carlos."

Amatil burst into sudden weeping. "No, *Padre* Antonio. Please no! Sergeant Carlos kill Chief Matilija."

"Amatil, marry anyone you wish at the Mission. Choose."

"Make plenty baskets, *Padre* Antonio. No marry, please."

"Sergeant Carlos wishes—"

"Sergeant Carlos marry—not Amatil."

Padre Antonio ceased from urging and Mission San Buenaventura throve and was blessed with peace. But at the time of the east wind, on a solemn feast day, after Padre Antonio had finished the sermon and intoned the *Credo,* wild Chumash cries rose in the Plaza. Painted for battle, Olana headed a force demanding the Indian women.

The *Padre* led the neophytes and women from the church to safety.

Yelling neophytes beat off attackers with heavy clubs, while large guns on high ground back of the Mission boomed. Olana's men seized muskets, swords and lances, and hand to hand fought the guards. A corporal lay dead in the Plaza. But soon the soldiers regained their weapons and pursued Olana who was in flight. Wounded pagans were placed in chains in the guardhouse. *Padre* Antonio himself remained near the *monjério*. The Mission was without other guard.

That night the *Padre* returned to the missionaries' quarters to rest, and Doña Rosa was left to protect the *monjério*. She slept as heavily as the neophytes she guarded.

But for Amatil there was no rest. Stealthily she stole from her rawhide bed and went barefoot into the jasmine-scented night of Mission San Buenaventura. The only sound was the surf breaking on the near-by sand. The only light was the never-extinguished altar candle.

Amatil could not depart without invoking the beautiful Lady. Before the altar where a candle flame flickered she knelt. For the last time she looked upon the dying figure on the Cross. Then quietly she went out, the fog shielding her like a celestial cloud.

At last she was a *cimarone,* a runaway. That night she lay by the trail side waiting for the light in the east. She rejoiced in the fog on her face, the wind blowing through her hair. For the first time since leaving Ojai, the Nest, she felt free.

At dawn she followed the footprints left by Olana and his men in their flight. There were brown stains on the ground. She flung herself prostrate on the earth—the stains had blood-scent. Up and down hill she sped, never far from the Big Water. No runner of her tribe had fleeter feet. At last, the leaves of every sycamore and oak had a familiar look and sound; they sang welcome with the birds. She was at the mouth of the sunny Matilija Canyon, whose slopes were covered with gray sage and white yucca blossoms. The joy of it choked her with tears.

Distant fires were burning. It was her father's *ranchería.* Chief Matilija's spirit still presided over Ojai, the Nest. Never again would she leave this canyon. There was deep-toned chanting. But as she drew nearer it was not a dance of joy she beheld, but a dance for the dying. Olana lay on a blanket stained with blood from the wounds that had guided her from Mission San Buenaventura. Flinging herself at his side, she sucked the blood from his wounds. Now always they would be together!

Swift riders surging into the canyon brought Olana to his feet. His men sprang to his side, all twanging arrows. With wild shouts they met the Spaniards at the canyon entrance. Muskets dispersed arrows and many Indians fell.

When Olana failed to return to the *rancheria*, Amatil again followed his trail. Up the mountain she traced his bleeding footsteps toward the summit. There she found him fallen to the earth. From a near-by spring she brought him water in a vessel fashioned from tree bark. They spoke of life eternal that *Padre* Antonio had taught her at the Mission.

When Olana's lips moved no more, and his eyes stared straight upwards, the moaning Amatil cut off her hair with a sharp stone and scratched and blackened her face with mud. With sticks she hollowed a shallow earth-house for Olana. In his fingers she placed her rosary and covered him with her Mission garments. Breast to breast she lay with her beloved. Then, fearing that pitiless night birds and prowling cougars might disturb her dead, she heaped high stones over Olana.

Far below the river wildly reveled toward the sea, urging her to renew life, but she remained as if awaiting the Resurrection promised by *Padre* Antonio at Mission San Buenaventura.

So it was that Sergeant Carlos and his soldiers found them. And this is why a cross above Matilija Hot Springs near Ojai, the Nest, marks the spot where Amatil and Olana died.

It is said that after the passing of the lovers the gray sage disappeared from the canyon slopes. And now they cradle the majestic Matilija poppy named for the chieftain, with its robes of snow and its heart of gold.

IV

REZANOV AND CALIFORNIA'S
FIRST NUN

1806

AS the Missions grew more numerous, Indian revolts were less violent. Spanish governors, however, knew increased anxieties from without. Fages departed from California, to be succeeded by Don José Antonio Romeu, the invalid governor who soon died at Monterey. Temporarily his place was taken by the bachelor, Don José Joaquin de Arrillaga, almost as saintly in his life as the padres. He held office until the arrival of the jovial Governor Diego de Borica with his wife, his daughter and a train of servants.

The Governor was a California enthusiast and he wrote to his friends, "One lives better here than at the most cultured court of Europe. The climate is so good that we are all getting to look like Englishmen." Borica established a new scale of living at Monterey for rulers of the province. Again he wrote, "To vivir mucho and without care come to Monterey, it is a great country." He avoided controversy and devoted much time and energy toward developing California and strengthening her fortifications. From his private fortune he gave generously and even contributed toward sustaining wars in which Spain was engaged.

At the turn of the century the able Borica was obliged to leave on account of his health. Governor Arrillaga, his successor, was as eager as the padres to protect the Missions, of which California now had eighteen. There had also been established the pueblos of San José de Guadalupe and Los Angeles de Porciúncula as well as the Villa de Branciforte at Santa Cruz. The great days of Mission-founding were over; in 1804 Santa Inés was established, the last Mission to be founded in southern California.

The Missions were at the height of their prosperity when rumored threats of invasion by England and Russia disquieted the remote province. It was said that the English had a score of frigates in or about the Gulf of California, and Comandantes *were instructed to use double precautions. Everyone who could shoulder a musket was drilled; even neophytes were told to prepare to defend the territory. Suddenly a royal order closed every port to all but national mail vessels, and a sentinel ship patrolled the coast.*

Apprehension was tense at the Presidio on San Francisco Bay, and at Mission Dolores one league distant. In 1806, Comandante *José Darío Argüello was summoned to Santa Barbara, and with some trepidation he rode south, leaving his son, Don Luis, in command.*

During his absence began California's most cherished romance.

DOÑA MARÍA CONCEPCIÓN MARCELA ARGÜELLO little resembled a nun that day. She looked like a gorgeous poppy, in her scarlet and white dress, as she stood on the thick adobe wall of the Presidio. Her tone was that of defender of this northern frontier of Spain as she called, "Luis! Luisito!"

With strong bare arms and heavy braided black hair hanging below her waist she seemed more than her scant sixteen years. Panic-pale she peered into the fog veiling Tamal Mountain on the far side of the narrow mouth to the great Bay of San Francisco. Certain that she saw a ship moving wraith-like toward Fuerte San Joaquin de San Francisco, she repeated, "Lu-i-i-s!"

With the agility of a Californian her brother Don Luis was at her side. He wore a *caballero's* wide felt hat, striped shawl-like poncho and gaudily embroidered spurred boots. Anxiously he asked,

"What is it, *carita?*"

"Look!" The ship was moving toward the fort.

"It must be English, Concha."

"Those cruel arrogant English—last month's courier said England had attacked Spain. Oh, why did Papa go to Santa Barbara! Luis, sink that English ship."

In absence of his father, Don José Darío, Don Luis was acting *Comandante* this April of 1806. He knew that the guns of the fort were decrepit. "Concha, go into the house."

"No, Luis, here I stay with you." Her tone and manner were from the Spain of her ancestors. "We command San Francisco."

Luis' eyes so intently followed the ship in the fog that he had no time to subdue his sister. This California beauty ruled her parents, the *Padres,* and even the bachelor Governor Arrillaga. Don Luis hurried to the soldiers' quarters for a trumpet and called to the strange brig sailing through the Strait of Yulupa—later rechristened by Frémont the Golden Gate. His voice seemed to sound over the entire Bay of San Francisco, to the near-by Mission Dolores and even to Missions San José and Santa Clara. "What ship?"

"What ship?" Concha called after her brother. He smiled with male superiority when her voice rang out alone, "Surrender!"

"Hush, little sister!" commanded Don Luis Argüello with the authority of a future governor of California. With rising wrath he thundered, "Anchor, *Capitán!* Anchor!"

While the young *Comandante* stood trumpeting his order to the intruder from the sea, the entire San Francisco army of thirty soldiers grouped around him. Only forty soldiers defended the three northern Missions and Fort San Joaquin against five thousand imperfectly Christianized Indians and twenty thousand hostile pagans, to say nothing of foes such as this mysterious ship defying the *Comandante* and the laws of Spain by entering unbidden the port of San Francisco. Even Doña María Ignacia Moraga de Argüello, alarmed, came from the low whitewashed *Comandante's* dwelling, and half a hundred ill-clad wondering Indians followed. Just as *Padre* de la Cueva emerged from the small chapel near the house where he had been saying Mass, Don Luis gave his final command:

"Anchor, *Capitán.*"

At last the strange commander trumpeted, "Si, *Señor!*" The ship ran the Boca desperately, passed the fort, entered the bay and anchored.

"What ship?" demanded Don Luis.

"*Unona!*" replied the battling foreign voice.

Padre de la Cueva, the Presidio chaplain, enlivened the grave situation with a jest. "My children, why is my delicious breakfast chocolate delayed? Why these strange cries?"

"*Padrecito,*" replied Concha, "do not laugh. These Englishmen come to kill us. They are more savage than Indians, even Tulares."

Don Luis and his company hastily flung themselves upon horses.

"Let me go with you, brother mine," pleaded Concha.

"Remain with *Mamacita,* sister."

In spite of gray habit and sandaled feet, *Padre* de la Cueva rode a prancing stallion like a Californian. "I may be no soldier," he exclaimed, "but I can shrive souls. Spaniards must not die unshriven. That is for Protestant English." From his saddle with a gallant gesture the *Padre* spoke, "*Señoras,* I have had no breakfast, but for you and Spain we perish!"

The lion of Castile fluttered protectingly from the flag pole over the *Comandante's* adobe house, the chapel, and the tree-bordered wall of the San Francisco Presidio which had been commanded for nearly two decades by Don José Darío Argüello. While Doña María Ignacia and her daughter Concha knelt before a little shrine in a niche in the long *sala,* Don Luis led the defenders of San Francisco over the sand dunes to confront the strangers.

Doña María Ignacia invoked, "Mother of Jesus, guard my son! Guard California!"

Sometimes, as today, Concha tenderly scolded Saint Francis, patron of the port of San Francisco. "Dear Saint, I shall never pray to you again unless you save us. You are stronger than England. You can perform miracles."

Indeed, a miracle it seemed when, after three anxious hours, the fog lifted and Don Luis led a joyous cavalcade from the port over sand dunes covered with blue and gold lupine and pink verbena. The day seemed to laugh over the poverty-stricken Presidio, the glittering bay and Tamal Mountain across the Boca.

Doña María Ignacia and Concha hastened to the narrow veranda. *Padre* de la Cueva arrived ahead of the others. Smiling jovially, he slipped lightly from his saddle and said to the anxious women, "The visitors are not English but Russians—distinguished *señores*. Everyone has heard of the Russian Columbus, Nikolai Petrovich Rezanov."

Don Luis presented the visitors, all in black and red uniforms. Rezanov, pallid, with deep-seeing eyes and sensitive mouth, had so vital a presence that when he bowed low over Doña María Ignacia's hand and raised it to his lips, he brought to this simple dwelling the imperial St. Petersburg of Alexander the First. Rezanov's myopic physician, the naturalist Dr. Georg von Langsdorff, was obscured by his splendor, as were two young naval officers, Lieutenants Gavril Davidof and Alexander Khvostov.

In Rezanov's presence Concha was no longer the Presidio's Joan of Arc. She became tongued-tied sixteen until Luis said,

"*Mamacita,* our guests are thirty-three days from Sitka. They are perishing for fresh fruit."

Then Concha became her natural, artless self. "Strawberries! Let me fetch them!"

"Where will you find them, *Señorita?*" asked Rezanov.

"Here at the Presidio—wild!"

Rezanov spoke Spanish slowly but distinctly. *Padre* de la Cueva laid a friendly hand upon his shoulder, saying, "*Señor,* you speak Spanish. You had no need of my babbling Latin with our good friend, Dr. Langsdorff."

"*Padre,* I prefer your Latin to my Spanish."

Langsdorff's hands were filled with wild flowers gathered on the half-league ride to the Presidio. In Latin he was interrogating *Padre* de la Cueva as to their names. Rezanov, man of action, felt Langsdorff overdid his love of nature. So occupied had the physician been with bird and sea life during the voyage that several of the depleted *Juno* crew had died.

Doña María Ignacia appeared with chocolate and cakes that enhanced Concha's heaped-up bowls of wild strawberries, and food disappeared with such abashing rapidity as to make the Argüellos realize they were hosts to starving men. Davidof and Khvostov drank so much brandy punch that they burst into Russian folksong.

Concha finally found courage to address Rezanov, "We feared you were English, *Señor*. We are happy to find you Russian."

"Bless one Englishman, Captain Vancouver," replied Rezanov. "In that fog his chart saved us and brought us to this happy haven."

"It is a pleasure to have guests," said Concha frankly. "You are the first visitors I recall, except Spaniards."

"You are most kind, *Señorita*. We realize we are violating Spanish law, but our ship was damaged by the storm and we had to enter the port or perish. As soon as the *Juno* is repaired we shall leave. Meantime, I shall send a messenger at once to Monterey to inform the Governor of our enforced entrance into your port."

Aware that Spain desired no strangers to see the feeble California fortifications, Don Luis quickly said, "Excellency, I've already sent a messenger."

"You are more than generous. I shall write His Imperial Majesty, our Emperor, and ask him to thank you for giving us this refuge."

With equal graciousness Don Luis replied, "Excellency, His Majesty of Spain would be greatly displeased with any discourtesy shown a representative of the great Alexander on this continent. Remain in our port until it is safe for you to sail north."

As the day passed the Spaniards and Russians outdid each other in amiability. Doña María Ignacia brought forth the best wines from Mission San José and Baja California. At dinner in the *sala* she served fowl, asparagus and peas from Mission Dolores only three miles away. Seated at the crudely carved table with its strangely contrasting handsome silver service, Rezanov feasted on the first good food he had eaten in two years. "Forgive me if I seem a glutton, but the Czar's chef never prepared such a dinner."

"Will you not take vegetables to the ship for all the crew?" asked Doña María Ignacia.

Rezanov knew how to touch a woman's hand. His fingers lightly on those of his hostess, he lifted them to his lips. "My mother could not have been more kind, *Señora*. You live so graciously. In this unconquerable Nueva California you cannot imagine last winter at Sitka —massacre and counter-massacre. Men almost ate each other."

"And your wife—" asked Doña María Ignacia. "How did she bear it?"

Rezanov seemed stabbed with pain; it filled the room. No one had dared mention his wife to him since her death long years before.

At last he spoke, "My wife, *Señora*—fortunately she was spared seeing human beings starve. She had all the greatness of her father Gregory Shelekhof, founder of Russian-America. Perhaps she was too sensitive for the world. She lived only a few years after I married her. Since I have lost her, my personal life is of no consequence. I live for Russia's glory. I have carried the Russian Eagle around the world. Now His Majesty wishes me to go to India and found a trading company similar to the East India Company. It sounds fantastic— so do all great undertakings, on paper. I shall go."

How different was Rezanov in his high energy, compared with sandaled Franciscans and pleasure-loving, bullfighting Californians! Concha was a girl of ambition. Her mother's family, the Moragas, had founded presidios and missions in California. She was stirred and dazzled by Rezanov. His scale of life made her realize how provincial had been her own existence—sixteen years in this modest adobe house! For travel she had gone to Santa Barbara. Her opera had been the Indian orchestra and dances at Mission San José. To be sure she had all the grandeur there was in California, but in presence of one who had been the friend of Catherine the Great, of dull Emperor Paul, and especially of Alexander the First, it seemed insignificant. When Rezanov spoke of his dreams for Russia she seemed to become Russian. When he recounted his effort of the previous year to open Japan to

Russia, she was indignant because he had been thwarted by the Mikado.

"His Imperial Majesty sent gifts and personal messages. Barefoot, without my sword, I was obliged to speak with the Mikado's representative—I, the personal ambassador of Alexander the First! The Mikado dared refuse us entrance. We sailed away, but I will go back. I will blockade the country. Two hundred thousand people may starve, but Russia shall yet enter Japan."

Under the thrall of Rezanov's eloquence Concha was breathless. "How magnificent to have such a life!" And Don Luis Argüello also fell under the spell when the Russian added:

"Russia and Spain should never permit the Bostonians to acquire the Columbia River country in the north. They should be kept on the Atlantic side of the continent where they belong. Russia and Spain should rule this country, *amigo*. You and I can bring it about."

The acting *Comandante* suddenly seemed host to a statesman. Young Don Luis was flattered, as Doña María Ignacia had been when her dinner table was compared with that of the Czar's, and as *Padre* de la Cueva had been when his Latin was praised. "Whatever my father and I can do—" promised Don Luis.

Before he rode back to the *Juno*, Rezanov spoke to Doña María Ignacia. "*Señora*, will you graciously permit me to come daily for the sake of speaking Spanish with you and your delightful family? Spanish is the most beautiful of languages and I wish to speak it well. It is my highest ambition to make allies of Russia and Spain."

"This poorest of houses is yours, Excellency," replied Doña María Ignacia. "While you are in port, come always to dine with us."

Rezanov then made his adieus; to Concha he offered only a low salutation.

The best Presidio horses were put at Rezanov's service and Don Luis gave him a dragoon as guard. The following day Rezanov led the Russians back to the Presidio laden with gifts. Although he and his crew had been starving, their offerings revealed the incredible riches of their country. During its twenty years of existence this frontier Presidio had never seen such splendor. *Padre* de la Cueva was delighted with the bell for his chapel—so massive that he must send an ox team and a *carreta* to transport it. There were rich vestments studded with gold for the chapel, and also for the Mission Dolores. Don Luis rejoiced in a fowling piece and a Swiss watch. Impressively Rezanov offered Doña María Ignacia a large silver crucifix. "It belonged to my mother-in-law, Natalia Shelekhof, a superb woman. She went through Siberia with her husband, colonizing Russian-America, and for years after his death she carried on the work brilliantly. She would wish you to have her crucifix. It was given her by the great Catherine."

For Concha's small sisters there were laces and shawls. There were gifts for the servants, bright colored gewgaws from the Orient; there were even large boxes of beads for the Indians. Concha felt strangely ignored.

Suddenly her gift appeared—sable scarves so wide and long that they might have served as robes. In the chill Presidio fog Concha draped herself from head to foot in what Rezanov called "God's sables." Her dark grave beauty enveloped in soft brown fur made her seem a woman of a different world. New blazon illumined the girl and Rezanov's eyes lighted up. Until this hour his wife's face had always fallen between him and any woman. Suddenly it lifted. He saw Concha Argüello, her high color, dark hair, smiling lustrous eyes, carmine lips revealing white teeth. His manner flattered her as he said, "You look like the women of Russia."

Concha felt herself important—important to Rezanov. She breathed with new buoyancy. Into this modest house he had brought his own great world. She wished passionately that her existence might harmonize with these regal sables.

During the next few days Rezanov and his company hunted bears and wolves with Don Luis Argüello. They rode over the sand dunes to Mission Dolores, which was in a sheltered locality at the base of two peaks called the Indian Maiden's Breasts. *Padre* Ramón Abella, who had lived at the Mission eight years, served his visitors with chocolate. He showed them the orchard of peaches, pears, apples, and apricots, the weaving establishment, the *jaboneria* where soap was made, the huts of twelve hundred neophytes, the new chapel with a painting of Saint Francis. Langsdorff rejoiced over a specimen of blue lilies in the *laguna* near the Mission. The naturalist's great day came when he beheld redwood trees growing on Argüello's Pilar *Rancho,* south of the Mission. In presence of the great trees he all but knelt, and Rezanov remarked to Don Luis, "Peter the Great said that the destiny of the Russian Empire was the American continent."

"Excellency," replied Langsdorff, "that redwood tree was alive at the time of the Roman Empire. The tree still stands!"

Later Rezanov impatiently remarked to Don Luis, "Langsdorff is a stuffy old fogy, but one must have a physician and a valet."

Afternoons and evenings Rezanov spent at the Presidio. The Castros of San Pablo and the Peraltas of San Antonio came across the bay in straw canoes for dancing. The Russians sang songs of their own country; the Spaniards played their guitars and violins. And in this new land Rezanov no longer clutched at the old dead life. He shook himself free from the past, and danced with Concha. Better than anything else she liked dancing. She taught him the dances of California and he taught her those of Russia. When he swayed with her to music she possessed for him charm greater than all the intriguing women of the court. Her naturalness and sincerity, and her interest in his achievements, strengthened the union between them.

Rezanov thought he had no illusions. He neither liked nor disliked people save only as they served Russia. An impoverished noble, he had been courtier to three Russian rulers. He had served not only at foreign courts but among uncouth natives in the north. Now he entered into a new world—the world of Concha Argüello. Each detail of her life interested him, all her desires and ambitions. She wished to go to Mexico City, she told him; to Madrid, to Rome and to Athens; to Persia, Bagdad, Constantinople—

And she was under a spell almost hypnotic when he replied, "I will take you."

At a *merienda* that evening, bathed in the amber sunset glow, he gathered fragrant yellow roses from the hedge near the Presidio wall and, as he placed them in her hair, he kissed her lips. At that voluptuous Russian court where a sixty-year-old Empress spent sixty million dollars on lovers, Rezanov had lightly kissed women for fleeting excitement, but seldom had he encountered real emotion. Once more he was young, trembling as if with first love for Concha Argüello.

Next morning the cannon of the fort and presidio saluted. His Excellency, Governor Don José Joaquin Arrillaga, rode in from the south. With him came *Comandante* José Darío Argüello. Serious men, these two, rulers of California, fagged by the long ride from Santa Barbara. Sixty-year-old "Papa" Arrillaga was especially weary, too weary to call on Rezanov, as was also *Comandante* José Darío Argüello. The Governor and the *Comandante,* friends of many years, had brought up the entire Monterey garrison and stationed it at Santa Clara to be summoned in the event of Russian attack. They felt safer with the Monterey troops only a few hours' ride distant. When they discovered how completely the Russians had captivated both the Presidio and Mission Dolores they congratulated themselves on their farsightedness.

Rezanov called upon the Governor at the Presidio where he was stopping. He brought paintings of the royal family for "Papa" Arrillaga, and books from the Czar's library for the *Comandante.* After speaking French with the Governor he remarked to His Excellency, "Your accent is like that of the Ambassador of France to Russia."

"Papa" Arrillaga was so exhilarated by the compliment that he ventured to dance with Concha, in spite of his rheumatism!

To the tall dark *Comandante* José Darío, Rezanov remarked, "How did you manage, *amigo,* to make this port of San Francisco into Utopia? Not even a jail for all these natives! It's your kindness. But for your noble family every man on the *Juno* would have perished off the coast. No wonder that even the Indians are subdued by your goodness."

"Excellency, I quite agree with you," said the Governor. "I call our friend Argüello, *El Santo*. The *padres* do not lead holier lives."

Gradually, at the daily Presidio dinner, Rezanov disclosed his plans to the Governor and the *Comandante*. "Our Russia is so rich and strong that we can be frank," he said. "We desire no new territory. All we wish is the furs of the north. They will last for centuries. Spain should have the Pacific Coast, perhaps the continent; but we should like food. China can supply it, but China is too far away. If you will permit us to buy food here, *Señor Gobernador,* Russia can bring California a million rubles annually."

The blue-eyed gentle Governor belonged to the Third Order Secular of Saint Francis. "I've lived sixty years without reproach," he answered, "and rubles do not tempt me."

"*Señor Gobernador,*" Rezanov persisted, "the Bostonians are every-where in the Pacific. Twenty ships a year come from Boston to Sitka. I bought the *Juno* from a Bostonian. The Bostonians are a menace. Spain needs Russia's friendship. Spanish-America may be taken by the Bostonians. They are as greedy as Jews. Keep them on the Atlantic Coast where they belong."

"Papa" Arrillaga, however, was not dazzled by Rezanov's vision of ruling a continent. For his few remaining years he asked only tranquillity. "Excellency, I am sorry, but we cannot change the laws of Spain." And with the Governor stood the *Comandante*.

But *Padre* Abella at Mission Dolores was a realist. His Indians were dying; they must have clothing against San Francisco fogs. Over many cups of chocolate he said to Rezanov, "I have no desire to barter illegally, but the government does nothing for the Mission; it does not even supply clothing for the garrison. I will see that the *Juno* is filled with food, if you will bring my children, the Indians, manu-factured goods."

Rezanov and the *Padre* embraced. "We will explore California together, *Padre;* you have saved my countrymen at Sitka."

The *Padre* smiled. "Let us say that Saint Francis has performed another miracle!"

Rezanov envisioned the dying Russians in the north. He must sail immediately with supplies. So back to the Presidio he rode with renewed buoyancy. Would Concha go with him? Could he ask a young girl to share his life of peril?

It was *siesta*-hour in the Presidio garden. Concha was seated in a rawhide chair on the low narrow porch. Her gown was the color of Castilian roses. The first oleander was blooming on the south side of the house. Rezanov's heart was thundering. He thought of the harsh life in the north. He would have known what to say to a woman of his own world. But to Concha he could only stammer,

"Has Langsdorff returned from Mission San José?"

"He hasn't been here," she replied.

"As soon as he comes back, we sail for Sitka."

Never had he seen such passion in a countenance. Concepción Argüello flung herself upon her knees and kissed his hand. "Will you not take me?" she whispered.

"Beloved! Forgive me, I am an old man—forty-two!"

She clung to him. "I love you."

"I have lived a century, Concha."

"So have I—since you've been here. Kiss me again."

He held her close. "Concha, the *Juno* is a leaky brig. Can we ever reach Sitka? If we do, what will there be? Revolt, massacre! Natives in the north are not like docile California Indians. Even if Sitka is quiet, there is Siberia. Only the utterly reckless dare Siberia."

"I am reckless—"

"You are no Natalia Shelekhof."

"What any woman has done, I can do with you, Nikolai."

Aroused from their *siesta,* suddenly Don José Darío and Doña María Ignacia stood in the deep doorway. Don José was a stern *Comandante* but a devout Roman Catholic.

"Concha, go to confession," he ordered; then, he turned to Rezanov. *"Señor,* I am pained. You violate our hospitality."

"Don José, Doña María, forgive me," replied Rezanov. "Concha and I ask nothing dishonorable—this is love. I am not insignificant.

I am the representative on this continent of Alexander the First—his Chamberlain."

Doña María Ignacia was all mother. "Señor, you are a heretic, of the Greek Catholic Church. Not a friar in California would marry you. Go immediately!"

"I cannot leave until Dr. Langsdorff and Lieutenant Davidof return from Mission San José."

"Never come here again," ordered the Comandante.

"Papa," protested Concha, "then I shall go and never return."

"Child, marriage with a heretic is no marriage."

Rezanov returned to the Presidio, however, again and again. As much energy as he had employed in trying to open Japan to Russia he summoned for breaking down opposition here to his marriage with Concha. But the resistance against it was solid as the wall surrounding the Presidio. All were against the lovers—the Argüellos, the padres, even gentle Governor Arrillaga. Doña María Ignacia pleaded,

"Go, Señor, it is useless to persist."

"You have a wonderful daughter, Doña María Ignacia. She belongs to the great world," urged Rezanov.

"We can't give her up. She is too young. Señor, go quickly."

"Perdón, not without her, Señora. Concha has given me new life."

"Señor, your faith is not ours. To us faith is everything."

It was a week before Langsdorff returned from Mission San José. Sometimes Rezanov wished that the naturalist would never come back! Boldly he besieged the Presidio. Together he and Concha rode to the Presidio to beg Padre Abella to marry them. All in vain!

At last Langsdorff and Davidof returned. No one listened to their experiences among the fire-eating, dancing Indians at Mission San José. No one was interested in hearing that they had been lost three days and had had to live on bread, cheese and brandy; no one was interested in the story of their struggle with wolves and wild cattle.

But jovial Padre de la Cueva had a solution for the lovers' difficulties. "Amigos, we have forgotten the supreme wisdom of Rome. Let the Holy Father decide! Do not resist human nature. Let Concha and Señor Rezanov be betrothed. Let us give the Russians all the food they ask and send them north as quickly as possible. Let *Señor* Rezanov go to Rome. If the Holy Father grants his permission, I will marry them. Then poor Concha can live at the North Pole the rest of her life, instead of in sunny California. But," he smiled, "destiny or the angels will intervene."

Rezanov and Concha accepted the compromise. The Russian insisted upon formal papers of betrothal being drawn up, and the *Juno* was filled with supplies. On the last day before his departure, Rezanov and Concha knelt for an hour at Mission Dolores, their hands clasped in rapt ecstasy. "This is marriage, Concha," her lover murmured.

"Forever," she vowed, while the sacred images looked down upon them.

On that May day when the *Juno* sailed out of the Gate of the West, the Governor, the Argüellos, and the *padres* waved farewell from the Fuerte de San Joaquin de San Francisco. Concha alone had no doubt that Rezanov would return. He was going out with the tide, but another spring tide would bring him back. The seven volleys from the *Juno* were the promise, the truth, of his spirit; and the promise and truth of her spirit spoke in the nine volleys from Fort San Joaquin. She could not see Rezanov's face, but she knew that his eyes were looking into her eyes, and that his lips were on her lips.

As the *Juno* sailed straight into the westering sunset, Concha knew that Rezanov could not fail. From mighty powers he would bring back permission for their union. Some driving force within him would batter down any obstacle.

Later, by way of a Boston ship from Sitka, she heard that Rezanov had saved his countrymen. And then the white north closed over him. Spring came, many springs, but no Rezanov. *Comandante* José Darío Argüello became Governor of California and Governor of Baja California. Don Luis Argüello also was California's Governor. To Concha it mattered nothing where she lived; she looked always to the silent north.

Some said Rezanov had died. Some declared he had married. Men sought Concha's hand, but she waited for Rezanov. Always serving the lowly, the Indians, she was called *La Beata* at Santa Barbara. Half a lifetime she waited, her face ever more like a mystical flower turned toward the silent north.

At last a traveler, Sir George Simpson, brought word of Rezanov to Santa Barbara. Eager to reach Rome, after relieving his countrymen in the north, he had pushed on across Siberia. He was drenched in rivers; he tented in storms; he fell from his horse. Finally at Krasnorarsk in the beautiful fertile valley of Yeniseí he died. Sir George had visited his tomb, fashioned like an altar.

As Concepción Argüello listened to the traveler's words her dreams died; her life that had been Rezanov's died, and Sister María Dominga was born; Concha became California's first nun. The only picture of Sister María Dominga in existence is said to be in the cornerstone of the convent at Benicia where she served and died.

On another May morning, when everything was clamoring for life, I took some yellow roses to her grave where she sleeps with other white-robed Dominican religionists on the hillside looking off on Benicia Bay. One hundred and thirty years had passed since Rezanov sailed from California, but Concepción Argüello's earth-home was covered with the flowers of those who still remember.

Gertrude Atherton has told her story in the splendid novel *Rezanov;* and Bret Harte celebrated her love in a long poem which has these concluding lines:

> *Two black eyes in darkened orbits*
> *Gleamed beneath the nun's white hood:*
> *Black serge hid the wasted figure,*
> *Bowed and stricken where it stood.*

> *"Lives she yet?" Sir George repeated.*
> *All were hushed as Concha drew*
> *Closer yet her nun's attire.*
> *"Señor, pardon, she died, too."*

V

GUADALUPE'S PIRATE

1818

BEFORE his death Rezanov dispatched to his government a plan for making a settlement in northern California and gradually extending the Russian boundary line to San Francisco Bay.

In 1809 Ivan Kuskof on the Kadiak *entered Bodega Bay in northern California, making off with twenty thousand otter skins. Back he came the following year with ninety Russians who built cabins and erected a fort. In spite of Governor Arrillaga's demands, they declined to depart from Spain's California. Arrillaga himself died in 1814 and was buried at his beloved Mission Soledad. There in its ruins his grave lies unmarked together with that of his best friend,* Padre Florencio Ibáñez.

Don José Darío Argüello, father of Doña Concepción, ruled California until the arrival in 1815 of Governor Pablo Vicente de Sola, who was greeted at Monterey by President Senan with twenty padres and thirty native singers. Lovely Magdalena Estudillo came from San Diego and offered the only address of welcome made by a woman in Old California, as she led twenty señoritas to kiss His Excellency's hand and present him with flowers, fruits and wine. For days festivities continued, concluding with the fandango and a bull fight.

Tumult followed soon. Privateers were coming from South America! Panic-stricken Sola found California defenseless, Comandantes *were exhorted to gather bows and arrows and heap up red-hot balls to cast at the invaders.* Padres *were ordered to furnish vaqueros armed with reatas. But the buccaneers did not appear.*

Finally, in 1818, the pirates arrived at Monterey and for a day ruled

64

California. Under the black flag of Bouchard, the buccaneer, came an astounding lover.

A PIRATE he came to Monterey—Bouchard's "Blond Joe." Doña Guadalupe Ortega, hair parted Madonna-like under her white *rebozo*, long black braids to her waist, first saw him in the Royal Chapel. Half-naked, pike in one hand, torch in the other, he profaned the deserted holy house with drunken English words she did not understand: "I am George Washington of Boston. Burn the damned church."

California's dread, Bouchard, was here—the South American buccaneer! A sail had appeared off Point Pinos flying an unknown flag, and an arrogant voice trumpeted, "Surrender, California!"

The *Comandante* defied. "First we die."

Monterey, the peaceful Capital on the blue oval bay rimmed with white sand, was terrified. Its defense was feeble—a fort with eight guns, a garrison of twenty soldiers, some neophyte archers and a few lancers. But Montereyans thrilled to the *Comandante's* sonorous "Soldiers of Cortés, brave sons of Mars, let us shed our last drop of blood for God and the King and California!" On this Indian summer morning in November, 1818, they prepared to die like *caballeros*.

Bouchard's black frigate, its deck swarming with men, opened fire. The shore battery answered. For two hours the battle went on. Several died like *caballeros,* but they didn't matter; they were only Indians.

Bouchard sent giant Blond Joe Chapman ashore with two sailors under a flag of truce. "Surrender, California!"

"Not while a Californian lives!" was the *Comandante's* ultimatum.

Drummers rushed forth beating drums around the Presidio Plaza. Troops mounted horses; artillerymen ran to the fort; stock were driven to the mountains. Sacred vessels, vestments and valuables were loaded into ox carts and sent with the Vallejo, Pico, Estudillo and Rodríguez families to Mission Soledad and Mission San Antonio.

Guadalupe Ortega of the *Rancho El Refugio,* guest of the *Comandante's* family, refused to flee in fear. A descendant of the pathfinder,

Captain José Francisco de Ortega—who guided Serra into California, discovered the Golden Gate, commanded San Diego, Santa Barbara, Monterey, founded Santa Barbara Presidio and Missions San Juan Capistrano and San Buenaventura—Guadalupe felt herself California. This Royal Chapel, with only the Stations of the Cross remaining, was her fortress. Before its altar she sank to her knees.

Plundering went on. These creatures from the sea were beings of another world—Bouchard the Frenchman, Irishmen, Spaniards, South Americans, Mexicans, Hawaiians, South Sea Islanders, Chinese, Negroes; some naked, some clad in rags, carrying picks, lances or guns. Scum of the scum! Blond Joe Chapman, with red flag and torch, led. With a band of music he advanced to the Presidio Plaza, straight to Governor Solá's residence. It was abandoned. His Excellency had named as his successor, in the event of his death, Don José de la Guerra of Santa Barbara, and had ridden away to the *Rancho del Rey* at Salinas. Bouchard had Monterey.

Wild Tulare Indians would have been more merciful. The buccaneers destroyed Governor Fages' beloved orchard. They ravished Indian women. They gave Presidio houses to the flames. They rolled guns from the fort down to the black frigate.

Into the Royal Chapel staggered Blond Joe Chapman with torch and pike. At first he did not notice Guadalupe with her head enhaloed by a white *rebozo*.

When he shouted, "Burn the church!" Guadalupe looked up from her prayers for the safety of Monterey. She did not understand the language of the stranger, but his torch and pike made her realize that the Royal Chapel founded by Padre Junípero Serra was doomed. "*Señores,* spare this house of God, for Christ's sake!" she begged.

Reeling under Governor Solá's brandy and wine, Blond Joe looked at the girl as though he had seen a vision. His Irish companion, Carney, exclaimed, "The Blessed Virgin!"

A new brightness illuminated Guadalupe as she said, "*Señores,* the Holy Mother will bring you every blessing—spare the chapel!"

Awestruck Carney whispered, "Sure, Joe, it's an angel."

Blond Joe laughed, "An angel!" He seized one of Guadalupe's long braids and burned it off with his torch. As Guadalupe fled his words followed her in a hoot, "An angel!"

But later she was to learn that the Presidio Chapel was the only Monterey building except the Custom House to stand before the torch of Bouchard.

Guadalupe Ortega, the "angel," burst out of the Royal Chapel. Humiliated, she touched the hair burnt close to her head. In her nostrils was the scent of the singeing she had received at the hands of Blond Joe. She felt herself violated.

The Plaza was a litter of uniforms which the buccaneers had stolen from the garrison. In dread lest she again be attacked by a pillager, Guadalupe quickly bound the one remaining braid around her head, put on a ragged felt hat left in the street, drew on a pair of dragoon's breeches, flung herself into the saddle of a horse she found tethered to a cypress, and was off riding like a *vaquero* toward Soledad Mission on the *Camino Real*.

Her first thought was of flight from the man who had degraded her by burning her braid. Then she remembered California to the south, unwarned and unarmed. Her family *Rancho El Refugio* on the coast lay unprotected. She must warn the south!

Through the oak-dotted valley along the Santa Lucia Mountains she rode. On her way to Soledad Mission she overtook refugees in creaking *carretas,* and was received with embraces and prayers of gratitude.

Señora Vallejo begged, "Do not go south alone."

"Refugio must be saved!"

"Then Paulino shall go with you, Lupe."

Old Indian Paulino had once been the body servant of *Padre* Junípero Serra—the founder had baptized him at San Carlos. Even on this desperate journey Paulino tried to tell Guadalupe of his love for a corporal's wife. He recited verses he had written to her and Guadalupe smiled as he naïvely added, *"Padre* Junípero would have liked my poetry."

Speed, speed, speed! Guadalupe rode on. Mission San Antonio was warned. So was San Miguel where she rested a few hours. At San Luis Obispo *Padre* Martínez rose from his sick bed, saying, "I have only two soldiers, but I'll burn this Mission before I surrender to Bouchard!"

Next day they reached Purísima by the sea, and *Padre* Payeras began his defense. At Mission Santa Inés frail *Padre* Ullibarri had a hemorrhage of the lungs when he heard that Bouchard was coming.

All the way, as her horse's hoofs hammered through the valley from *rancho* to *rancho,* and over mountains, from Mission to Mission, Guadalupe raged at memory of the drunken giant speaking the strange tongue, who had dared burn off one of her long black braids of hair. She was riding not only to warn the south but to ride away from that stranger, to obliterate her shameful memory of him.

At last she reached the Ortegas' *Rancho El Refugio* with its twenty miles of coast line. The one-story rectangular house—the patio with pomegranates, dates and palms, red peppers hanging from hand-hewn posts, bake oven, deep-recessed windows, cool walls hung with pictures of saints, chairs plain and straight with rawhide seats, rawhide beds with embroidered linen, braziers of burning coals, leather-covered chests bound with iron, and her warm welcoming parents, Don Antonio Maria Ortega and Doña María—all this, the most conspicuous ranch in all Southern California, was indeed Guadalupe's refuge.

Here dwelt those vital pioneers—the Ortegas, beloved of Serra, asleep for nearly half a century at San Carlos—the Ortegas, pathfinders and smugglers! For years they had carried on daring contraband trade with men from the sea, especially with Boston traders, the *Yánquis.* Tales were told of the Ortegas' fabulous wealth. El Refugio was said to be richer than any other California Mission, except San Luis Rey.

And *Rancho El Refugio* was Bouchard's objective. Eleven days after he appeared at Monterey, his black frigate anchored off the Ortega *rancho,* northwest of Santa Barbara. But the buccaneer and his men found the low house empty. Vanished was the Ortega treasure, concealed in leather-covered chests. Embroidered linens, laces, sacred pictures, satin counterpanes, had been carried to Mission Santa Inés for safety. With them had gone guitars, violins, flutes, and dresses of *fiesta*-time. There remained only the pictures of saints and battered furnishings. On the hills ranged the cattle.

Bouchard jeered to Blond Joe, *"Pase Vd, Señor—la casa es suya!"*

"Gracias, Excellency," jeered back Blond Joe, who understood many languages.

The buccaneers found the wine barrels and Bouchard shouted to his men, *"Pase Vd, Señor—la casa es suya!"*

Flames took the Ortega residence. Only the four-foot adobe walls remained. Those pillagers who had not fallen into a drunken stupor went into the hills above the ranch house and made targets of the cattle. Blond Joe led.

The slaughter of cattle ceased when suddenly Don Antonio Maria Ortega, with his sons Pedro and Francisco and some *vaqueros,* rode out from the hills. Before the buccaneers could take aim, a *reata* tightened around Joe's neck and cold steel seemed to pierce his heart. He was dragged to Mission Santa Inés, where, in the courtyard, he came back to consciousness, half alive.

"That is the man!" he heard a woman's voice say. "He burned off my hair!" Her head was bound with a bright kerchief to conceal the degradation.

Don Antonio Maria was for revenge. "Let the Indians drag him to death."

Guadalupe intervened. "Why not send the pirate to Governor Solá at Monterey? He should be shot publicly in the Plaza—as a warning to pirates."

Blond Joe's eyes were like blue steel. He looked straight at *Padre* Ullibarri and spoke words understood only by himself: "That goddam priest will want me dragged to death by Indians. I'm sorry I saved that Monterey church. Churches! They ought all to be burned, especially Baptist and Catholic."

But to his amazement *Padre* Ullibarri said in Spanish, *"Amigos,*

I don't wish to interfere with justice, but we need workmen to complete this Mission. One white man is worth ten Indians." Barefoot Indians wearing smocks were treading clay and straw, making adobe brick in the Plaza. "Why not consider this man as ten Indians? I'll keep him here at work—as long as he behaves."

Guadalupe was alarmed. She removed the bright kerchief from her head and disclosed her hair half singed off. "*Padrecito,* do you realize what this man did? He attacked me in the Royal Chapel while I was praying for Monterey. He tried to burn me alive."

Joe laughed with gusto. "Listen, *señorita,* Pat Carney said you were the Virgin Mary. I wanted to show him you're just another woman." Guadalupe was glacial.

The *Padre* explained, "*Amigo,* naturally Doña Guadalupe is indignant. In California we disgrace women by cutting off their hair. Probably you never lived among Christians."

"Hell, no! I was born at Boston, Mass."

"Have you ever been baptized?"

"Not as I know. I always went to the Baptist Church."

"*Misericordia!*" said the *Padre.* "Boston—Baptist—both benighted! *Amigos,* it is unchristian to reproach the man for being a pirate. Remain at Santa Inés, my son."

"*Padre,*" urged Guadalupe, "Californians will fear to come to the Mission if you keep this man here."

"Guadalupe," replied the *Padre,* "we have twelve hundred neophytes. I'm afraid many of them have taken life. Why not let this *Yánqui* remain a few weeks? If he misbehaves, then we can send him to the Monterey firing squad."

And so Blond Joe Chapman became California's third American pioneer.

But Guadalupe was vexed. *Padre* Ullibarri was protecting a man who had burned off half her hair. It was slow in growing, and she was obliged to wear it bound round her head as though she were married. So the Ortegas now attended Mass at their own private chapel, happily undisturbed by pirates.

José *el Americano,* as Blond Joe was called, was a joy to *Padre* Ullibarri. During his wanderings the pirate had learned many crafts. He built ships, made furniture, fashioned inlaid cabinets, grafted grapevines. The *Padre* tried to conceal Joe's talents, but all the southern Missions borrowed the *Americano.* His reputation was established at Santa Inés when he built a gristmill, the finest in California. And thereupon the San Gabriel *Padres* petitioned the Governor that "the pirate prisoner, José Chapman, be permitted to come to San Gabriel to build a gristmill like that he had built at Santa Inés."

While at San Gabriel the *Americano* made a large fountain for the Indian washerwomen and launched a small boat on its waters. "I'll name it the *Guadalupe,*" said Joe, "the prettiest word I know."

"My son," approved *Padre* Sanchez, "that shows you intend to accept the true faith. The Virgin Guadalupe—your unconscious devotion!"

Padre Sanchez determined to keep the *Americano* at San Gabriel, and a great rivalry developed among the Missions to obtain Joe's services. The San Buenaventura *Padre* resorted to strategy, "*Padre,* do you not fear to have the *Americano* at San Gabriel?"

Jovial *Padre* Sanchez closed both eyes and laughed until his rotund stomach shook under his brown habit. "I fear not to have him. I have seen worse Christians among our own people. Who can be surprised that a Baptist turned pirate?"

Joe continued to curse in English when he was emphatic or enthusiastic, but *Padre* Sanchez closed his ears—the *Americano* was his favorite, was almost a magician. Joe brewed herbal teas and relieved the *Padre's* indigestion. He massaged the nerves of the priest's head and cured his insomnia. He became an amateur surgeon and treated even the Governor. Many called him "Doctor."

During this period Guadalupe Ortega was thrown onto a rock from her Palomino horse while riding him into the sea at Refugio. Her arm was broken and it was clumsily set by a midwife. Soon it seemed that the arm might be permanently deformed. Her family made novenas to Saint Roch and Saint Anne and Guadalupe moaned over her misfortune.

"Lupe, you shall go to the City of Mexico," declared Don Antonio Maria. He himself had never been out of California. He rode to Santa Barbara to consult the *Padre,* who advised him,

"Send for the *Americano.* He is the best surgeon in California."

"That buccaneer shall not come to El Refugio," declared Guadalupe.

In desperation Don Antonio Maria hastened over the mountains, past the shimmering Nojoqui Falls, to obtain the judgment of the Santa Inés *padres.* There again he was told,

"*El Americano* is the only surgeon."

So at last Don Antonio Maria rode to San Gabriel. "*El Americano* is a wonder worker," said *Padre* Sanchez. Hesitatingly, therefore, Don Antonio Maria approached the *Americano* whom he had once ordered dragged to death by Indians.

"Don José," he began. Then he changed to "*Amigo,*—Doctor—*Señor,* my daughter Guadalupe has a broken arm, badly set. We have made many novenas—" He shook his head despairingly. "*Padre* Sanchez says you can help. Bring back the use of her arm and you shall have half a league of land."

The American was embarrassed. "Did Doña Guadalupe ask you to come?"

Don Antonio Maria evaded. "Not exactly—but my leagues of land are a desert if my daughter is crippled. Anything I can give you—"

"Hell! I'll do it for nothing, Don Antonio Maria."

Without sleep the clock round Don Antonio Maria and Blond Joe rode toward El Refugio. At Mission San Buenaventura and again at Mission Santa Barbara they changed horses. The little silver and blue cove smiled when they arrived at El Refugio early the next morning. But Blond Joe saw other things—saw Bouchard, the black frigate, the savage crew, the drunken looters, the wild pillage, the cold *reata* around his neck—all this came back to him. Never again had he thought to see El Refugio; but now he looked upon its reroofed house, its vines grown again during the two intervening years, and its pomegranate trees fruiting in the patio.

In spite of his blue eyes the American resembled a son of California when he arrived wearing a silk kerchief on his head, a broad-brimmed hat, scarlet-trimmed jacket and deerskin boots.

Anxious Don Antonio was almost abrupt. "Lupe, your new doctor."

Guadalupe adjusted her lace-trimmed white blouse. *"Padre mio,* I would rather not have my arm set again."

Doña María held her daughter's hand. "Poor baby, let *el Americano* make your arm well. Unless he does you can never ride—"

"No, no, *Madre mia."*

"—never play the guitar—you will dance awkwardly—"

"Say, Doña Guadalupe," began Blond Joe as he looked at her braids bound round her head with a bright ribbon, "I'm goddam sorry about burning off your hair."

Guadalupe lay on the long rawhide couch. She turned away her face and said, "Please go."

"It's hell that you should be sick. I can make you well, but first I must make you sicker."

"Go, *Señor."*

Not until the *Padre* came from Santa Inés did Guadalupe yield to the family urging and permit Joe to treat her arm. The American's hands were like rock. Under his touch she felt weak, unresisting. "The bones have grown together wrong, Doña Guadalupe. Can you stand pain?" His hoarse deep voice, his touch, his strength, was like an anesthesia, but she moaned.

"Shut up!" he ordered. "Stop crying! Damn it all, I can't stand hurting you! It won't pain much. I broke Padre Sanchez's dog's leg the other day. He didn't whimper—licked my hand."

Doña María was saying a prayer. Guadalupe's lips murmured another. There was tearing pain—then complete numbness. "It's all over," said Joe. "Now the splints." He worked rapidly.

Guadalupe felt like *Padre* Sanchez's dog. *"Gracias,* Don José."

"Call me Joe. Hell, I'm no Don—just a Boston sailor. I don't know how I escaped hanging."

"The *padres* say you have done much good at the Missions."

"They say a Yankee works better than an Indian," he said as Doña María fetched linen. He finished binding up Guadalupe's arm.

"*Gracias, amigo,*" said Don Antonio Maria. "Whatever I have—"

"May all the saints bless you, *Señor,*" went on Doña Maria, serving chocolate. Joe abominated chocolate but he drank.

After a second breakfast Blond Joe said conclusively, "*Adiós, Señora,* I'll be going back to San Gabriel."

Together the Ortegas protested. "*Señor* Don José! *Amigo,* you will not leave us so soon. *La casa es suya.*"

"*Padre* Sanchez needs me to make the Indians work, my friends," said Blond Joe; but he went down before Guadalupe's "Perhaps we shall need you to re-set my arm," and replied,

"I'm a better dog and horse doctor than a doctor of human critters, but I'll stay tonight."

El Refugio was in *fiesta*—it was the monthly wash day. *Señora* Ortega had pride in the quantity and quality of her embroidered linen. From distant *ranchos* screeched *carretas* filled with soiled garments in charge of Indians. Older women traveled in ox carts, younger ones rode. All day long they soaped and rubbed soiled linen on the rocks along the creek banks. Then they stretched the laundry out on bushes and on the branches of low trees to dry. Men sat in the shade singing as they played guitar, violin and flute. Horse and foot races occupied the afternoon.

Doctor Joe had ordered quiet for Guadalupe, and she lay on the rawhide couch under the grapevine in the patio while he worked mysteriously in the cook-house. After the *rancheros'* wives had served roast beef, chili sauce, and fried red beans, Joe brought forth his surprise—apple pie! The Californians had never before seen the Yankee delicacy. Joe's pies brought him more renown at El Refugio than his treatment of Guadalupe's arm and established him as a skilled *Yánqui* cook.

"That's nothing," he said, but he was pleased. "Next time I'll make doughnuts and mince pie. We have them three times a day at Boston."

Then, north and south, the cavalcade departed with fresh laundry neatly piled on the *carreta* floors, and melodies floated back above the sounds of the screeching wooden wheels. That night Don Antonio Maria called upon the saints "to protect our family friend and bene-factor, José *el Americano.*" In the morning he thanked the saints that "José *el Americano* has passed the night safely and is to remain a part of our household."

Protesting, Joe remained at El Refugio several days. "I feel l.ke a coyote," he said to Guadalupe, "sitting here eating your *frijoles* and drinking your chocolate. If your arm doesn't knit right, send for me. *Adiós!*"

Instead of shaking hands he fumbled with his sash. She offered him her left hand and as he bent over she stared amazed. Projecting from his shirt was the end of her braid of hair that he had burned off in the Royal Chapel! Without a word she drew it forth.

"Forgive me, Doña Guadalupe," apologized the abashed Joe. "Why did I do it? Goddam it, I couldn't help it. When I saw you I wanted to carry you away. I had to have that braid. That's why I didn't want to come here—you hating me. You'll never see me again—unless you're dying."

Her soft fingers clung to his hard hand. "Don't go away unless you promise to come back. I'm glad my arm was broken."

"Guadalupe, I'm only a pirate."

"You're everything!—that's why the *padres* love you."

"No, you're everything, Guadalupe."

"*Querido,* wind that braid around my head—tighter!" He stood clasping her fingers with both his hands. They gazed at each other in blind intensity.

Don Antonio Maria entered. "*Amigo,* you have earned your half league of land."

"I'm sorry, Don Antonio. It isn't enough."

"That is what my wife thought. Doña María wishes to give you half a league also."

"I don't want land, Don Antonio. I'm a pirate. It's Guadalupe—"

"Let Guadalupe decide," replied Don Antonio Maria.

"I'm a pirate too," she smiled. "I want José." Don Antonio Maria and Doña María gave their grateful blessing, and Joe measured Guadalupe's foot so that he might make her six pairs of slippers, according to the California custom.

On returning to San Gabriel, Joe said to *Padre* Sanchez, "I don't want to be a goddam hypocrite, but I'd like to go to Guadalupe's church and your church and get down on my knees as she does. It's all a bully show—only I don't believe—"

"José, pray for faith—it will come."

"Even to a pirate?"

"After you are baptized, my son, the good God will forget—even though you were a pirate."

Blond Joe forgot that he had been a pirate—cursing churches, burning and looting—when the bells at Mission Santa Inés rang for his wedding in 1822. Governor Solá already had granted amnesty to one José Chapman for having entered California as a pirate! The Governor was grateful for José's surgical services at Mission San Gabriel, and he sent Doña Guadalupe as a wedding gift a long string of pink pearls from Loreto. She wore it over a jacket of yellow satin with a green *sarga* skirt and silk stockings. On her feet were silver-buckled slippers which Joe had made.

For a regretful moment the cream lace mantilla on her head recalled to the bridegroom the white *rebozo* he first saw her wearing in the Royal Chapel at Monterey. But it was his wedding day; he rejoiced in his yellow satin jacket buttoned with Mexican *pesetas,* and the breeches and buckskin boots fastened with *pesetas;* and all his regrets vanished in the *fiesta.*

Santa Inés was a laughing California carnival when Pirate Joe and his bride rode over the Gaviota Pass to Santa Barbara, to San Buenaventura, to Los Angeles, and on to San Gabriel. Guadalupe scarcely knew where she was going, and she cared little. All seemed pre-arranged by some unseen destiny.

At San Gabriel new stature came to Joe. So much of the Mission was the result of his imagination, energy and skill in directing work-men, that Guadalupe realized she had married an unusual man, even though he had entered California as a buccaneer.

Blond Joe did not tell his bride what was awaiting her at San Pedro ten leagues distant. Later she would know that, upon returning from El Refugio, he had gone with half a hundred Indians into the mountains and there had hewed timbers. She would learn of the months of work with the Indians in the San Gabriel shops. For later, when they rode out to San Pedro, he was to prophesy, "This will one day be a great harbor," and was then to point out to her a ship with dazzling sails and fresh paint, and say, "I built this boat for you. Guadalupe I named it for you."

Blond Joe and his wife sailed away on their wedding journey aboard the *Guadalupe*, the first ship built in Southern California. To the bride it seemed as large as the ship which brought Columbus to America—as indeed it was. Their long happy life together had begun. Later Pirate Joe would return to become one of San Gabriel's most important and respected citizens.

VI

SAN DIEGO'S RUNAWAYS

1829

"VIVA la independencia! Viva el Emperor Augustin I!" shouted Californians in 1821 when the flag of Castile was lowered over the Capitol and the Custom House at Monterey and the standard of Mexico broke to the breeze. Mexico had declared her independence, Iturbide was Emperor Augustin I.

Ambitious Sola, Spaniard that he was, accepted the altered political situation and became California's first Mexican governor. He remained in office only one year and was succeeded by Don Luis Argüello, brother of Doña Concepción and California's first native son to rule the province.

During the second year that Argüello was in office California's last Mission, San Francisco Solano [Sonoma], only a few hours' ride from Fort Ross, was founded, to warn Russia against further encroachment.

The news crashed in from Mexico, another revolution. The Emperor had been executed. Unrest seized even the Indians; revolt broke out at Missions Purísima, Santa Inés and Santa Barbara.

Don Luis Argüello was glad to be relieved of office when, in 1825, Governor José Maria Echeandía was appointed governor of both Californias by the Viceroy. To the indignation of northern California, Echeandía paused at San Diego and established his executive residence. There he met Señorita Josefa Carrillo, granddaughter of that disturbing widow who set out with the Anza Expedition in 1775, but left it at San Gabriel to marry. Governor Echeandía's decision to remain at San Diego precipitated an elopement which is not forgotten even after a century.

HIS Excellency Don José Maria Echeandía, Governor of California, arrived in San Diego on his way to the capital, Monterey. He was a purposeful man, and his plans for California were revolutionary—he would seize the Missions for the government of Mexico!

At Don Juan Bandini's *tertulia* in his honor, His Excellency met Doña Josefa Carrillo, loveliest member of the handsomest family in California, and granddaughter of charming Doña María Feliciana Arballo de Gutiérrez of the Anza expedition. Doña Josefa was tall, with level-looking dark eyes, a classical chin line, and hair banded with pearls of Loreto. Her grace in dancing carried the Governor back across the sea to Mother Spain.

After His Excellency unbent from his gaunt professional dignity and danced with Doña Josefa at the Bandini *tertulia,* he was no longer eager to press on to Monterey. San Diego climate he found enchanting. The Governor erected a large adobe residence in the center of the presidio Plaza from which he haughtily surveyed the bay, the town, and even the residence of Don Juan Bandini. A sentinel with musket, slouch hat, deerskin leggings and spangled garters guarded the mansion. From the executive abode the Governor emerged at midnight to serenade Doña Josefa with his guitar and his admirable tenor voice. He developed a slight cough and determined to transfer the capital from Monterey to San Diego.

Over this decision Northern California was wrathful. But Southern California was delighted, especially the politically-minded Carrillos. And Don Joaquin, father of Doña Josefa, was gratified over the possibility of acquiring the Governor as son-in-law.

One afternoon when hollyhocks were nodding to drowsy four o'clocks, the Governor called at the Casa Carrillo. After many ceremonious inquiries concerning the family health, he began, "Doña María, may I have the honor of your daughter's hand in marriage?"

"Your Excellency," replied Doña María Ignacia, "you have my permission to speak with Josefa."

Later the *señorita* laughingly described the scene to her parents. She mimicked His Excellency's precise Castilian accent, his pomposity.

"The Governor was like a wooden statue talking. *Por Dios!* What a beard! I would rather be a spinster like Doña Concepción Argüello, dreaming of a lover in Russia and teaching Santa Barbara Indians, than marry the affected Governor! She waited twenty years for Rezanov. A lifetime is not too long to wait for a man I can love."

Unlike many fathers of Old California, amiable Don Joaquin Carrillo did not lash his daughters into marriage. He was more adroit. He liked to play the violin, he would give a *tertulia* for the Governor! He would bribe Josefa with gowns bought from the Boston ships. So at chocolate hour he said to her,

"*Carita,* you need a new silk dress for the *tertulia.* Make haste to buy one. The *Maria Ester* is in the harbor." In those pastoral days California had no shops, only trading ships. "*Capitán* Enrique Fitch, the Boston trader, sells everything. Perhaps the *tertulia* will last two days. Buy two silk gowns, with red silk stockings!" A woman in red was ever irresistible to smiling Don Joaquin, but he always returned to his fat comfortable wife who wore black.

"No girl in California has such a father," said Josefa, embracing Don Joaquin as she set out with her cousin, Don Pio Pico, for the New Bedford brig, the *Maria Ester,* an alluring floating shop anchored on that great sheet of turquoise, San Diego Bay.

Josefa thought it an adventure to be escorted by her gay cousin, clad in velvet with gold buttons. Baubles, women, and life Don Pio loved. How exciting to ascend the rope ladder! In the effort the wild rose in Josefa's cheeks deepened. She adjusted her *rebozo,* her short-sleeved white chemise and green satin jacket. In silver-buckled slippers she stood face to face with Captain Henry Delano Fitch, smiling master of the *Maria Ester,* his blue American sailor suit Californianized by a serape over his shoulder and a broad-brimmed black felt hat on the back of his head. Josefa's Andalusian eyes looked into the incredibly violet eyes of Captain Henry and Moorish Spain smiled with white teeth at fair New England.

It was the first time Josefa had met a Yankee. His Boston world seemed foreign and romantic. A music box on deck was playing

Yankee Doodle. The United States flag with red and white stripes and twenty-four stars on a square as blue as the San Diego sky, topped the mast. Powder was noisily exploded. The War for Independence was not half a century gone—and this was July Fourth, 1827.

Of the daring seafaring Delano family that later produced Franklin Delano Roosevelt, Captain Henry Delano Fitch, tall and genial, had a sailor's—and also a President's—gift of making friends.

Since the reign of the eagle and nopal, and while California had been under Mexico's green, white and red, no trader had been more popular than the Captain. In all weather good and bad this smiling seaman sailed up and down the Pacific Coast offering for sale everything from red silk stockings to the banned books of Voltaire and Rousseau. Displayed on the decks of the *Maria Ester* were Boston groceries, calicoes, and furniture. Old Mexico sent shawls, serapes, silk yardage, inlaid tables, pearl necklaces, rice and *panocha.*

In Spanish Mexicanized and Bostonized Captain Henry began with an engaging smile, *"Señorita,* stockings, slippers, shawls, mantillas, dresses, combs?"

Josefa ignored red stockings, cream lace mantillas, striped *rebozos,* embroidered shawls, buckled slippers, but she was captivated by a tortoise-shell comb. Such a comb she had never seen, large as two hands, of mottled shell carved and banded with gold. She removed her *rebozo,* held up the comb to the sunlight, coquetted before a gold-framed oval mirror, placed the comb in her hair, left, right—right, left!

Captain Henry stood smiling at Josefa. *"Señora* Estrada of Monterey bought one. So did *Señora* Vallejo of Sonoma."

"She is my aunt."

"I have only one left."

Fascinated by the comb, its unique size, color and carving, for the first time Josefa understood theft. Nervously she asked, "The price, *Señor Capitán?"*

"Six hundred hides, *Señorita.* It is a great deal of work to cure six hundred. I've done it myself."

"If I could have that comb," thought Josefa, "I would give a thousand hides." She had no desire for the trader's silk stockings, dresses, mantillas or pearls. She readjusted the comb and called to Don Pio Pico, "Cousin, look." Don Pio applauded.

"In all California," cajoled Captain Henry, "I've never seen anyone wear the comb so well." Josefa recalled the price—six hundred hides! —and with a sigh she returned it. But—"Take it with you, *Señorita,*" urged the Captain. "Show it to your parents. They will let you keep it."

"I fear not, *Señor Capitán. Gracias.*" As she went down the rope ladder her dark eyes smiled in farewell, *"Hasta otra vista!"*

"Six hundred hides!" exploded Don Joaquin Carrillo to Josefa when she came back from the *Maria Ester.* "Such a price! It has never been asked."

"Si, si! Señora Estrada. *Tía* Vallejo—"

"Rich! Preposterous! Six hundred hides! Boston robber!"

All agreed with Don Joaquin—his motherly smiling wife and his father, Don José Raimundo, founder of the family. Therefore, in the shadowy *sala* of Casa Carrillo, Josefa was in tears.

Don Joaquin despaired. "What notions these trading ships bring! An eighteen-year-old girl with six hundred hides in her hair! That Boston! No wonder the *Padre* says it is the center of hell."

Josefa gathered courage. "If I can't have that comb, I'll not go to the *tertulia.*"

Music-loving Don Joaquin avoided the discord of disputes and turned for comfort to his violin. Suddenly he ceased playing and presented a political compromise:

"Querida, you shall keep the comb. Wear it to the *tertulia.* Tomorrow I shall tell our friends that you are to marry the Governor. This comb will be your betrothal gift."

Upon his first words Josefa had embraced her father, but now the rose left her cheeks. She flung the comb across the room and spoke with the disdain of eighteen for forty years. "The Governor is an absent-minded old professor. He even forgets his name before he signs letters. When you give the *tertulia* for the Governor, I shall have a headache."

Not since the flag of Spain had fallen four years before over San Diego had Don Joaquin received such a shock! Again he took refuge in his violin. He sent the tortoise-shell comb back to Captain Fitch by Don Pio Pico, and related his troubles to his brother, Don Guillermo Carrillo, who rode down from Santa Barbara to play the guitar at the *tertulia*. Doña María Ignacia went on placidly assembling olives, chili sauce and cheese for the supper. In their own quarters the Indians were making ready for the dance. It was in the air that His Excellency, the Governor, and Doña Josefa were to be publicly betrothed. The Carrillos prayed to San Diego that nothing should intervene.

As Don Joaquin and Don Guillermo, returning from a ride, tossed their horses' bridles to the Indian boys, they saw a foreigner appear, clad in a blue seaman's suit, with a serape carelessly flung over one shoulder and a broad-brimmed black hat. Smiling engagingly he began:

"Don Joaquin Carrillo? I am Captain Fitch of the *Maria Ester.*"

Don Joaquin thought he understood. "*Capitán,* you are a very smart Boston man. My daughter told me about the comb—"

"Your daughter likes it—"

"She likes pretty things, but she has many combs. An eighteen-year-old girl in California does not wear six hundred hides in her hair."

"Don Joaquin, may I speak with your daughter?"

"Why encourage folly? I am sorry, she is a little stubborn. We Carrillos—soldiers—"

Josefa, sad-eyed, entered the *sala* and Captain Fitch lost his genial poise. Embarrassed, he opened the silk-encased parcel half concealed under his serape. "Don Joaquin, if you permit—*Señorita,* if you will accept—" Like an awkward boy he held out the comb to her.

"*Señor Capitán!*" exclaimed Josefa.

Don Joaquin protested, "*Capitán,* only a relation may give such a present—"

"That's just what I mean, Don Joaquin." He turned to Josefa, "You understand?" He offered her the parcel. "No one can wear the comb like you, no one from here to Cape Horn or from Cape Horn to Boston." He placed it in her hand. "I go with the comb."

"*Gracias! Gracias, Capitán* Enrique. What you say sounds too beautiful, even if it isn't true."

"It is as true as that I am standing here. Keep the comb." Josefa despaired. "*Capitán* Enrique, you are so good. Why don't you Boston men believe in God?"

"*Señorita,* if God is all that stands between us, I'll fix that up. I believe in any God you do."

"*Capitán* Enrique, have you ever been baptized?"

"Not lately, *Señorita.* But the San Diego *padres* baptized thousands of Indians. I guess a New Bedford sea captain is as good as an Indian. Fix it up! I don't mind the Catholic Church. More trimmings than my New England Unitarian, but I like trimmings. I'll be tickled to be baptized."

Don Joaquin was grave. "*Capitán,* it is more than religion. It is against the law for Californians to marry a foreigner."

For more than ten years Captain Henry Delano Fitch had been battling with tides and storms and he met Don Joaquin's objection with super-amiability.

"Doña Josefa's flag is good enough for me. I'd be a Hottentot for her. Runaway sailors have been naturalized—Irishmen, Englishmen, Russians! Why not a Yankee? I'd rather live in California than anywhere—San Diego preferred. Can't it be arranged?"

Defying remonstrating parental glances, Josefa placed the comb coquettishly in her hair. "Come to the *tertulia* tonight, *Capitán.*"

Don Joaquin was polite but formal. "The Carrillos are hosts for San Diego."

With the scent of Castilian roses in the air Southern California danced to music of guitar, violin and flute in the long *sala*—all save Governor José Maria Echeandía. In sinister silence he watched Josefa Carrillo dancing farther and farther from him into the life of Captain

SAN DIEGO FROM THE OLD FORT [From *Notes of a Military Reconnaissance*: Lieutenant-Colonel W. H. Emory, 1846].

MISSION SAN JOSÉ INDIANS, ALLIES OF YOSCOLO [From a drawing by Langsdorff, 1806].

Henry Delano Fitch. They danced till lights were dim and tallow dripped in the sockets of the high candlesticks lining the walls. The comb in Doña Josefa's hair told the story of the betrothal of the Californian and the American.

Finally His Excellency burst out to Don Joaquin, "Why does our Republic allow Boston traders to enter our ports?"

"We should keep them out," agreed Don Joaquin.

"My first act shall be to expel foreigners."

When the ball concluded with the *canastita de flores*, Captain Henry's eyes were like blue flame. The dancers circled round singing and on the last word each man rushed forward to embrace his best beloved. His Excellency, who hated foreigners, remained to see Josefa Carrillo in the arms of an American!

San Diego shared the Governor's consternation. What would His Excellency do? *Quien sabe?*

After the *tertulia* was over and the last guest had departed, Captain Henry Delano Fitch rowed Josefa Carrillo out to the *Maria Ester*. In moonlight they stood together on the deck of the brig, wrapped in the American flag.

"Nothing can separate us now," vowed the sea rover.

"I love your Stars and Stripes," she said.

Later these rash lovers scandalized San Diego by stealing past the Presidio sentinel asleep on a musket in his blanket, and by singing *Yankee Doodle* under the window of His Excellency, the Governor, at four in the morning.

Don Joaquin and Doña María Ignacia Carrillo were reluctant to yield. They cajoled, they reasoned, they implored Josefa to become *la Señora Gobernadora*. But they had no desire to see their daughter brood in melancholy, so in the end youth triumphed over middle-aged wills.

Don Joaquin and Doña María Ignacia signed the marriage agreement of Captain Henry Delano Fitch and Josefa Carrillo. But Governor Echeandía smiled sardonically. He defied Josefa to marry a Protestant born in Massachusetts, U. S. A.

Would the lovers marry? Dared they? California thrilled to the province's newest high romance.

With a directness of a man of the sea, Captain Fitch approached the Governor. "I wish to become a citizen of California. Doña Josefa Carrillo and I intend to be married."

"What a pity," sympathized the Governor. "Your marriage will be null and void."

The Captain defied His Excellency. "Who says so?"

From friar to friar went Captain Henry Delano Fitch, at his side Doña Josefa Carrillo. "I intend to become a citizen of California, *Padre*. Will you baptize me? Then will you marry us?"

The Franciscans promised to baptize the Captain, but they knew that the Governor was threatening to seize the Missions, and they would do nothing to precipitate the overthrow of those establishments which the Franciscans had spent more than half a century in building. They would baptize the Captain, but they refused to perform the marriage ceremony.

Finally Captain Henry and Doña Josefa sought out a Dominican, *Padre* Antonio Menendez, the Presidio chaplain. Franciscan Missions were no part of *Padre* Antonio's pride. "Have pity on us, *Padre* Antonio," implored Josefa. "Governor Echeandía is determined to keep us apart. Marry us."

Captain Fitch reinforced his betrothed. "I earnestly wish to become a Catholic, *Padre*. Do not treat us as though we wish to live in adultery. Marry us."

After instructing Captain Fitch in Church Doctrine, *Padre* Antonio baptized him, at the Presidio Chapel, Enrique Domingo Fitch. The Captain laughed, "I like my new name Domingo."

Soon *Capitán* Enrique was burning candles in the Presidio Chapel to his parents and all his dead friends. He filled the poor boxes. For an hour *Capitán* Fitch, with his bride-to-be, was on his knees before the altar. His non-Catholic muscles ached from the unaccustomed posture, but he laughingly said to Josefa, "After a few years I'll get used to it."

Padre Antonio made the lovers happy with the assurance, "You shall be married as soon as you come with your witnesses." All San Diego—the Bandinis, the Argüellos, the Estudillos—assembled at the Carrillo adobe residence for the wedding. Doña Josefa and *Capitán* Enrique knelt long before the altar especially erected in the *sala.* The bride's four sisters exclaimed over her new Parisian bonnet, shaped like a basket of flowers—a gift of the *Capitán* together with pearls and bright silk handkerchiefs. So delighted were they with the gifts that they ceased wondering whether Josefa could be happy with a foreigner.

With mischievous quips and laughter Cousin Pio Pico appeared. The first witnesses arrived, Captain Richard Barry, and *Capitán* Mariner Beristian. But where was Uncle Domingo Carrillo, aide to the Governor? No Uncle Domingo! Josefa was in despair. Uncle Domingo was her godfather. He represented the Carrillo family.

"Why wait?" urged the impatient bridegroom. So the ceremony began without Uncle Domingo. Vested in white, *Padre* Antonio Menendez was reading the required ritual, when Don Domingo arrived. Josefa turned and clutched his hand.

"I'm sorry to bring a bride bad news," he told her, "but I can't be a witness, and the Governor forbids *Padre* Antonio to perform the ceremony. He will prosecute anyone assisting at the marriage. *Capitán* Enrique, it is unfortunate—you're not a citizen of California."

"Godfather, godfather," implored Josefa, "don't desert us."

She realized that her Uncle Domingo was a politician before he was her godfather when he added, "His Excellency will report any one aiding the marriage to ecclesiastical authorities."

Dominican *Padre* Antonio tried to comfort them. "My children, I will marry you anywhere beyond the bounds of California. But in this province the Governor is absolute."

Capitán Enrique became the grim man of the sea as he stormed, "Josefa's parents have given their consent. Tell the Governor we shall be married in spite of him."

The guests departed. With the desertion of her uncle, Josefa felt desolate. All powerful forces were combined against her and the Yankee *Capitán*. From beneath her Parisian flowered bonnet she looked up and said,

"Why don't you carry me off, Enrique?"

Quickly and softly he answered, "Tonight."

Cousin Pio Pico, a man of unashamed passions, was their sole supporter. "Let me attend to it," he urged. "You can't be married in California. Go to your ship, *Capitán*. We'll tell everyone the marriage has been abandoned. Get ready to sail. Secure your papers for sailing to South America. I'll bring Josefa to you."

So the lovers said a mock farewell. Fitch, once again at sea, ordered the anchor raised and the ship put in readiness for sailing. At nightfall, with four strong oarsmen, he entered his best boat, and was rowed to the shore where, landing, he concealed himself behind a boulder long to be known as Fitch's Rock.

Don Pio was always ready for any recklessness. Often he wagered a basket of uncounted gold on a horse. He especially enjoyed hoodwinking the Carrillos who lamented, "Josefa will be another spinster like poor Concepción Argüello." So, with a sly pleasure, he called to take Josefa for a ride.

"*Gracias*," said Don Joaquin, "the poor child is in despair after that hideous humiliation."

Josefa did not return in good time from the ride. "No matter," said Don Joaquin, "she is with Cousin Pio, probably dancing at the Bandinis."

"Dancing will make her forget," agreed Doña María Ignacia. "But I wish she would return."

For a year Josefa did not return from that ride! At eleven that night Cousin Pio and she met Fitch, who was awaiting them. *Capitán* Enrique led her to the boat and commanded the oarsmen, "Row for your lives!"

In two hours they reached the *Maria Ester*, and out from the Bay of San Diego Josefa sailed with *Capitán* Enrique Domingo Fitch for South America. Two months later friendly winds had wafted the lovers to their port.

At Valparaiso, on the evening of July 3, 1829, Henry Delano Fitch of New Bedford, Massachusetts, U. S. A., was married to Josefa Carrillo of San Diego, California. The next day Valparaiso saw its first American Fourth of July celebration—arranged by the bride and bridegroom aboard the American ship.

Vainly Don Pio Pico tried to explain Josefa's flight. The weeping family abused him; Governor Echeandía clutched his scraggly beard, and his rage brought on indigestion. "That American smuggler has abducted poor Josefa. If he comes back he shall be punished. He shall not live in California!"

But in the following year Captain Fitch proudly sailed into the port of San Diego on his brigantine with his twenty-year-old wife and their laughing, kicking son Henry. They had gone as far as New Bedford, Massachusetts. They were at San Diego for the Fourth of July, but the Carrillos did not welcome the runaways.

Rage still possessed, held sullen, pallid Governor Echeandía, and soon his invisible power began to move. It was felt first at Mission San Gabriel when *Capitán* Enrique and his bride sailed up the coast on their trading ship. There, *Padre* José Bernardo Sanchez of Mission San Gabriel ordered Fitch to present his marriage certificate for inspection. The *Capitán* sent the required paper to the Padre and continued northward.

At Monterey Governor Echeandía ordered husband and wife torn apart. Alferez Nieto took *Capitán* Enrique from his ship and transported him to San Gabriel. Doña Josefa and little Enrique were imprisoned in a house at Monterey, still standing, which belonged to Captain J. B. R. Cooper.

"I'm being taken from my ship, from my business," protested *Capitán* Enrique. "It will ruin me. Imprisonment will break my wife's heart."

But *Capitán* Enrique's business was no concern of the Governor,

nor Josefa's heart! "Once the American ran away," said His Excellency. "He shall not again escape. He kidnaped Doña Josefa."

Fitch was incarcerated in one of the rooms at Mission San Gabriel, and for five months Josefa was held as the Governor's prisoner at Monterey. Vainly she wept. "Let me go to my husband. I shall die. My baby will die."

At last she made a personal appeal to the Governor. His Excellency replied with a magnificent gesture. "Of course, Doña Josefa, go to San Gabriel."

But even at Mission San Gabriel Doña Josefa was not permitted to live with her husband, only to be near him. She had a woman jailer.

Meantime *Padre* José Bernardo Sanchez of San Gabriel was tormented day and night by fear that the Governor would seize the Mission. Finally an ecclesiastical tribunal was set up and the culprits were brought before *Padre* José Bernardo as judge.

Together and separately *Capitán* Enrique and Doña Josefa were questioned. Were they legally married? Their marriage certificate was inspected. It was blotted, torn. Why? The certificate was not viséd by the Chilean Minister of Foreign Affairs. Why? *Padre* Orrégo of Valparaiso had no dispensation to marry the American Captain and the Californian. Most suspicious! The certificate contained no statement of the city or church where the ceremony was performed. Had the couple really been married at all?

Fitch realized what Echeandía was trying to do. Before the ecclesiastical court the sea captain became his own defender: "You're trying to ruin my business. You blast my wife's reputation. You make my son illegitimate. *Bien!* Declare our marriage null and void. Marry us again."

For months the trial proceeded. At last the judge rendered the decision: "The Valparaiso marriage is valid. *Capitán* Fitch shall be set at liberty. Doña Josefa shall be permitted to live with her husband, but on Sunday next they shall be *velados* and receive the sacraments that ought to have preceded the marriage ceremony at Valparaiso. The couple shall also present themselves at San Gabriel Church holding lighted candles to hear High Mass for three *días festivos,* and recite together for thirty days the Rosary of the Holy Virgin."

The crux of the judge's decision was, "Considering the scandal which Don Enrique has caused in the province, I condemn him to give as penance in reparation a bell of at least fifty pounds in weight to the Church of Los Angeles, which barely has a borrowed one."

One hundred and eleven years have passed since the married lovers knelt holding lighted candles for three feast days in the church at Mission San Gabriel, and devoutly performed acts of penance. Ten children and all good fortune came to the pair. Today the sweetest sound in Los Angeles for lovers of Old California is the pealing of the ancient bell in the Plaza Church, given by Captain Henry Delano Fitch of New Bedford, Massachusetts, U. S. A., as penance for his runaway marriage with Doña Josefa Carrillo of San Diego, California.

VII

YOSCOLO AND PERFECTA

1829

WERE California Indians weaklings left behind in the great migration from Asia to Mexico? So some writers have asserted. But Serra at San Diego in 1769 found them fierce and militant. During his first month at the Mission he himself barely escaped death. Later the Indians swooped down upon San Diego, burned the Mission and clubbed to death Padre *Luis Jayme, who died saying, "Love God, my children!"*

In the first days San Gabriel Indians also savagely fought the Mission founders, and Mission San Luis Obispo was set on fire several times, bringing about the introduction in California of roof tile.

For a month Pacómio, an educated neophyte, with four hundred Indians, took possession of the church at Mission Purísima and made prisoners of Padre *Blas Ordáz and* Padre *Antonio Rodríguez.*

No Mission suffered more from Indian attacks than San José de Guadalupe. Several times soldiers were summoned from the Presidio at San Francisco for protection from the Indians. Most formidable of the rebels was Alcalde Estanislao, who finally surrendered, but he was the pride of Padre *Duran, who obtained a pardon for him from Governor Echeandía.*

Indian wars were usually fought over food or women, and it was for a woman that Yoscolo, last rebellious Mission chieftain, but a favorite of the padres *at Mission Santa Clara de Asis, battled so desperately but to so little avail.*

IN the somber redwood-covered mountains lying between Missions Santa Clara and Santa Cruz by the sea, *Padre* José Viader, a gray-habited Franciscan friar, clashed with Yoscolo. A demon of an Indian, full-blooded, exuberant, was the great man of the wild tribe on the far Laquisimes River. In a mood of God-almightiness he flung himself upon *Padre* José. Force met force. The *padre,* a huge Catalonian, was never without a large Cross on the rosary at his waist. He cast it aside, disarmed Yoscolo, bound him with willow withes and brought him captive down the mountainside and through the valley to Mission Santa Clara.

Head high, like a superb animated figure of bronze, Yoscolo's glance missed nothing: the impressive towered church frescoed with the All-seeing Eye, the mighty Cross, the long dwelling of the missionaries, the substantial building housing Indian girls, the neophytes' houses, the great kettles for cooking *atole* and *pozole,* the long tables, the Plaza where the converts played games in the evening! All this Mission built in honor of Santa Clara of Asis seemed to Yoscolo to be a part of *Padre* José, the "gray-blanket man," his conqueror.

Yoscolo was certain that he was to die, but the Indian came of a tribe that knew how to meet death with dignity and in the gloomy guardhouse, his prison, he resignedly awaited the end.

But to the chieftain's astonishment, instead of being pinioned to be shot down by the boom-boom weapons of the soldiers in red and blue who paced up and down before his prison, the *padre* came bringing strange foods—corn porridge, peaches, pears. Thought Yoscolo, "Bloodless death!" and declined the supposed poison. He preferred to die in the grand manner, with noise and fury.

But *Padre* José himself partook of Yoscolo's food. The Indian was astounded. Was the gray-blanket man a sorcerer? Or was the stranger with the new faith offering mercy? At last he shared the repast with the *padre* and in friendship he took his conqueror's hand. When the chimes sounded he entered the beautiful church. In awe he gazed at the ceiling frescoed by his own tribesfolk. Suddenly he realized the quality, the imagination, the achievement of these gray-habited men of fair skin who planted tall Crosses, chanted strange words and distributed food and clothing to the red men of California.

Like the natives of the Santa Clara Valley, Yoscolo was a sun worshiper. He also believed in transmigration of souls, but he abandoned his faith for that of his merciful conqueror *Padre* José. Before many months passed Yoscolo, the vanquished, was in charge of the Santa Clara neophytes, an *Alcalde* at the Mission. Administration of authority became him. The gentle valley neophytes usually obeyed him, but with granite sternness he punished the insubordinate. Quickly he mastered Mission handicrafts—the tile and brick making necessary to enlarge and embellish the buildings. Scrupulously he distributed rations, *atole* and *pozole,* as well as smocks and blouses.

Yoscolo's lavish presence gave new impetus to Mission Santa Clara, which had been built up largely by *Padre* José Viader and that miracle-worker *Padre* Magin Catalá. The zealous neophyte guided friars and soldiers to the river land and hills where his tribesmen dwelt. To the natives he interpreted the *padres'* teachings and brought many of the curious to be instructed in their doctrine and manner of living.

On one of these journeys Yoscolo found on the trail a sobbing lost Indian girl of dusky loveliness and brought her on his shoulder to the Mission. Perfecta of Dolores, the *padres* christened the child. Her warm smile was like new sunshine in the valley of the oaks and after her coming Yoscolo had little desire for roaming. There was new music in the chimes, new beauty in the ceremony around the altar. Existence at Mission Santa Clara was rich and deep.

Perfecta lived with the other Indian women in the nunnery. Gladly she put away her *tule* skirt and the little mantle of coney skin. Her obedience was cited as an example to the Indian girls who frequently cast off smocks given them by the missionaries and unashamed flaunted their coppery bodies in the courtyard. Perfecta liked Mission garments. She even embellished them with embroidery and dyes from roots of herbs. Her hair was burned off evenly over her forehead, and the braids hanging down her back like those of *señoritas* gave her a young dignity befitting one who rang bells for meals and at night turned the nunnery key. Yoscolo's eyes gleamed as if for the first time they beheld beauty. Even Corporal Antonio Soto, when he looked at Perfecta, adjusted his blue and red striped *poncho* to heighten his soldierly air.

Soon every flower in the valley of the oaks was known to Perfecta and decorating the altar was her especial delight. All growing things were precious to the girl. She delighted the *padres* by bringing back wild rice from far marshes. She sweetened their food with sugar which she extracted from an olive-like fruit. She knew where there was an unending supply of wild onions, watercress and garlic for salad. She brought medicinal herbs for the afflicted.

Perfecta began teaching the girls to spin and weave. She presided over grain grinding as well as the boiling of maize and beans in great iron caldrons over the courtyard fires. She taught other Indian maidens how to roast grain in bark baskets over small lighted coals— how to shake the baskets so rapidly that the seeds swelled and burst without igniting the bark. At mealtime she quieted disputants. It was she who decided which children had learned their catechism best and should be rewarded with scrapings from the iron caldrons.

Demure little Perfecta gave even the friars a lesson in self-denial. Some Franciscans turned nostalgic eyes toward faraway Spain; they brooded in their austere adobe cells and shivered while at prayers in the church. But Perfecta never complained of the rude shelter in the nunnery. She seemed always near the new God whose martyrdom was daily celebrated on the candlelit altar guarded by Santa Clara.

But suddenly Perfecta became another Helen. One day Corporal Antonio Soto appeared at the missionaries' quarters in his bravest blue and red uniform. *"Padre* José," he said in his staccato military manner, "I'd like to marry Perfecta."

"Bien!" replied gaunt *Padre* José. "I'll send for her!" From the beginning of Spanish occupation of California the *padres* had encouraged soldiers to marry Indian girls. When the girl answered the summons, the *padre* said:

"Three days from now, Perfecta, at ten in the morning, put on a clean smock and come to the chapel. Corporal Antonio will become your husband."

After a long pause Perfecta lowered her eyes and half-whispered, "*Si, Padre* José."

Romance was not in the vocabulary of Corporal Antonio, builder of a new civilization on Spain's northern frontier. The rugged soldier held Perfecta's slim young body in rough embrace as his wide mouth bestowed upon her several resounding smacks.

"Perfecta, you be a good girl—my wife. I'll be a good husband—never beat you." And he gave her another bearlike hug.

"*Si*, Corporal Antonio," whispered Perfecta.

Corporal Antonio was a rough-riding trail-breaker, one of California's Indian fighters. The scars on his body were scars on his memory also. Mountain Indians had twanged arrows at him and hurled rocks upon him; but unfailingly he brought back scalps of the broncos to the *Comandante* at San Francisco, and the blood of his foes stained the sienna-colored mountain soil. Sobbing Indian women and children herded by him into Mission Santa Clara were trophies of his victories. *Padre* José felt that the Corporal's marriage with Perfecta would guarantee peace. Instead, it resounded through the establishment like infrequent California thunder.

For Yoscolo stormed into the doorway of *Padre* José's narrow cell, eyes black as death; and stood there with folded arms, his long smock sleeves rolled up as were his trouser legs. "*Padre* José," he began, "Yoscolo good Christian?"

"*Si*, Yoscolo," replied the wondering missionary.

"Yoscolo do good work?"

"None better."

"Yoscolo marry Perfecta, *Padre* José?"

"I'm sorry, Yoscolo. Corporal Antonio is to marry Perfecta."

Suddenly every coarse black hair in Yoscolo's broad head seemed alive. "Perfecta, Indian girl. Yoscolo marry Perfecta."

"Too late, Yoscolo, I'm afraid," said *Padre* José. "Perfecta is promised to Corporal Antonio."

"Yoscolo find Perfecta in mountain. Yoscolo bring Perfecta to the Mission. Indian know Indian heart. Corporal Antonio not Indian. Yoscolo marry Indian girl."

Padre José placed a quieting hand upon Yoscolo's shoulder. "My son, you shall have Juana."

"Yoscolo no like Juana—too fat."

Padre José became gently insistent. "Juana, she likes Yoscolo."

"Yoscolo like Perfecta." He pointed to the towered adobe church across the Plaza. *"Padre* José, three days ring bell in morning. Yoscolo make Perfecta wife. If Perfecta not Yoscolo's wife, Yoscolo go mountain."

Yoscolo's threatening face made *Padre* José's heart stop beating. Once again he relived his first conflict with the tumultuous *Alcalde;* but he remonstrated, "Yoscolo, we'll find you a good wife."

The Indian's words were like falling rocks. "Yoscolo go mountain!"

In hasty conference the missionaries decided that Corporal Antonio and Perfecta should be married immediately. Then revolt rushed through the Mission. In midnight blackness guards were bound. Locks of the *monjério,* or women's quarters, were broken and hundreds of girls were freed. Neophytes burst open the Mission stores, seizing all they could carry. They hacked the giant Cross from the altar in the church and trampled upon it; they insulted the guards and defied the *padres,* crying, "We go mountain—free!"

On Yoscolo's black horse Perfecta rode away. The rebels drove the Mission cattle down the Santa Clara Valley across the pass to the east and into the wide Valley of San Joaquin to join another renegade Christian Indian, Estanislao, who had fled from Mission San José.

Few California establishments ever suffered so devastating a revolt as Yoscolo's rebellion at Mission Santa Clara. *Padre* José opposed violence, but he said to the soldiers, "Follow Yoscolo. Frighten him with fireworks display. Assure him that he will not be punished, and bring back the poor misguided children."

From their hiding place in the willows, sycamores and poplars on the Laquisimes River, Yoscolo and his followers jeered at the

Spanish soldiers and their childish fireworks. "You fight like old women! Put on skirts!"

Corporal Antonio thundered, "Surrender!"

"Kill Indians, if you can!" taunted Yoscolo. "Cowards! White hearts!"

At Mission Santa Clara the *padres* despaired as they received the woeful tidings and they appealed to *Comandante* Sanchez at the San Francisco Presidio for aid. The *Comandante* himself, splendid in blue, gold and scarlet, and white-feathered hat, headed a force armed with a swivel gun, and faced Yoscolo's barricade in the thick wood along the river.

Muskets attacked, and a cloud of arrows answered. It was an all-day battle between arrows and muskets. The swivel gun was soon crippled; then bullets gave out and the guns were loaded only with powder. When their store of powder was exhausted, the soldiers, at sunset, withdrew.

In the torrid heat of the following day they returned to fight. Several were killed. From the thicket Yoscolo shouted, "Indian die! Indian no give up!"

Taunted by the *Alcalde's* voice, "Yoscolo no give up!" the soldiers tried to hew their way with great axes to the foe. The *Comandante* returned with reinforcements and three-pounder guns. The soldiers burned the forest and shot naked Indians fleeing from the flames. After the blaze died down the attackers found the bloodstained barricade empty, and they pursued.

On the heels of the Indians were the soldiers. Next morning they surrounded Yoscolo and his followers in the distant thicket. Soldiers pressed forward through the chaparral, discharging muskets and field-pieces. "Surrender!" called Corporal Antonio. Again the ammunition of the besiegers gave out, and some Indians escaped; but the barricade filled with bodies disclosed that many of the natives had died rather than yield.

Three women had remained with the Indian wounded. One of them was Perfecta, and Corporal Antonio succeeded in bringing her back to Mission Santa Clara. Bleeding profusely from an arrow wound in his throat, he rode through the Pueblo San José de Guadalupe. Then, in the Plaza, he toppled from his horse and was no more.

Perfecta wandered down the *Alameda* to the Mission Santa Clara and humbly said to *Padre* José, "Sorry heart." Once more she took up her tasks. But youth seemed to have departed from her eyes.

Word came on the winds from the Tulares in the south that Yoscolo was there, hiding with other renegade and outlawed Indians. But in the quiet that once more reigned at Mission Santa Clara, Perfecta again went about her daily tasks. She taught the neophyte children obedience. From her they learned their first prayer, and how to make the sign of the Cross.

By fire Yoscolo had been defeated and with fire he fought when he came back to Mission Santa Clara, at the head of his followers on their splendid high horses.

Padre José was offering Mass. He was elevating the Host when Yoscolo and his men, torches in hand, dashed from building to building, savagely shouting, "Yoscolo come back! Yoscolo!"

As swift as Yoscolo, *Padre* José rushed from the altar, seized the *Alcalde's* torch, and made a bonfire of Yoscolo's arrows in the Plaza. The Indians menaced the *padre,* but he held up the crucifix of the great rosary at his waist. So like a prophet was he that the Indians shrank from violating the tall, gray-habited figure. At last Yoscolo and his men retreated toward the mountain forest where the redwood trees were so large that eight warriors holding hands could not encircle them.

The Pueblo San José de Guadalupe, only one league distant from Mission Santa Clara, was beset with panic. In every bush and tree of the *Alameda,* the Holy Way to Santa Clara, lurked Yoscolo and death. *Rancheros* and *pueblaños* rode their swiftest horses fifteen leagues to the San Francisco Presidio, seeking aid from the soldiers there in the task of conquering Yoscolo. All California north of Monterey united to put down the Indian. So long as Yoscolo lived, there could be no safety for the six northern Missions.

With muskets and lances they came, the defenders of California, and assembled in the Plaza of Mission Santa Clara. An avenging deserter from Yoscolo's band guided the force through the valley to the mountain thicket where the *Alcalde* and his men fortified themselves behind great trees and rocks cemented with adobe clay. Those who attacked vastly outnumbered the Yoscolo force. They could not fail! From dawn until sunset purpled the eastern foothills the soldiers' guns cracked and boomed to avenge the defeat on the Rio Laquisimes. Indian arrows whizzed back their reply. Many soldiers fell. Suddenly the arrows ceased to blacken the air. Was Yoscolo's force weakening?

The Indians had formed a hollow square and were fighting lying down. Most of them lay on their own graves. Desperately Yoscolo alone rose to his feet. For a moment his daring stunned the white men. Over the barricade he sprang toward the soldiers.

With his lance Anastasio Mendoza rushed forward. The white man and the red met in a death duel. There was a desolate cry like that of a maniac coyote. Yoscolo was stretched out lifeless!

With his lance Anastasio Mendoza severed the great Jovian head of Yoscolo from his body. It was like cutting granite. Then in triumph the shouting victors rode into the Pueblo San José de Guadalupe.

Nearly a century later a tottering Spanish-Californian, Doña Luisa Sepulveda Mesa, with a face like brown wrinkled parchment, described to me the scene that was burned into her childhood memory. *"Muy mal!"* she called it with rueful shaking head. "Oh, very bad!"

Anastasio Mendoza led the death procession. Swinging from the pommel of his saddle, suspended by long coarse black hair, was the blood-stained lion-like head of Yoscolo. Through the Pueblo, to music and cheers, marched the victors with their gruesome trophy of conquest. In gratitude to these destroyers of Yoscolo, *señoras* and *señores,* the aged, even the children, followed shouting, *"Vivas!"* Each of the defenders was a hero. At last the Pueblo San José de Guadalupe and Mission Santa Clara were saved.

After the Pueblo had ended the *fiesta* of victory, Anastasio Mendoza, still carrying Yoscolo's head, led the rejoicing band out upon the wide willow-bordered *Alameda*—the Beautiful Way—laid out by the Holy Man of Santa Clara, *Padre* Magin Catalá, and his neophytes to smooth the road to eternal life. Before Mission Santa Clara, Yoscolo's head was hoisted high on a tall redwood timber where for three days it remained as a warning to rebels.

For Perfecta alone the dread head of Yoscolo had no terror. In prayer she prostrated herself at the base of the timber and looked up at the chieftain's head. There for three days she remained. The silent Mission Santa Clara seemed to have no lights on the altar, no supreme presence to worship. Even the incense had lost its fragrance. Would the sun ever rise? Would the stars ever shine? Would Yoscolo live again? Would Yoscolo and Perfecta be reunited?

VIII

LARKIN'S ROMANCE OF THE SEA

1831

EVEN while the flag of Spain was flying over California, permanent American settlers were arriving. As early as 1816 Boston contributed the first American resident, Thomas W. Doak, who was to make an offering to art and religion little to be expected from a sailor coming in on the Albatross.

Shortly after his arrival Doak was baptized Felipe Santiago at Mission San Carlos. Later, in 1818, he journeyed to Mission San Juan Bautista where the padres *were completing a new church. Just before Doak arrived, the painter Chavez, who was working on the altar, had cast aside his brush and was demanding increased pay. The* padres *were in despair. Six reales a day! The Mission could not meet the demand, and the church must be consecrated in November! What should they do?*

Modestly Doak undertook the task of finishing the painting. Padres and neophytes gazed admiringly at each stroke of the volunteer artist. It is recorded by the padres *that Doak, "the Anglo-American, with the aid of God and some* muchachos" *succeeded in embellishing the altar with beauty. The church was duly consecrated, and after more than a century Doak's work is still admired. His achievement established him in the community. Soon he married Señorita María, daughter of Don Mariano Castro of the great Rancho La Brea near Mission San Juan Bautista.*

The sea continued to bring interesting strangers, especially from New England. In 1830 the white people in northern California numbered three thousand, about three hundred and eighty being foreigners. One of the best known was Captain John Bautista Roger Cooper from Boston, master of the Rover. *He had married Doña Encarnación Vallejo, sister of General Mariano Vallejo, and was a conspicuous trader at Monterey; and so he sent for his half-brother, Thomas Oliver Larkin.*

In 1832, while Pio Pico was Governor, Larkin arrived from Massachusetts. When he sailed out of Boston harbor for Monterey, California, six months before, although he had not realized it, his ship was freighted with romance. It brought not only him, but the first American woman to California.

AT sea they met and at sea they were married, Thomas Oliver Larkin and Rachel Hobson Holm, the first American couple to settle in California.

Born in Massachusetts, only a few miles apart, these young people had not met when they took passage on the *Newcastle* in Boston harbor that cool September morning in 1831. Fair-haired, hazel-eyed Rachel, wearing a mauve bonnet and a sedate brown gown, was sailing alone on the brig to faraway Hilo in the Sandwich Islands. There she was to meet her husband, the Danish Captain John Holm, master of the *Catalina,* then plying the Pacific. Larkin was bound for Monterey, California, to engage in business with his prosperous half-brother, Captain J. B. R. Cooper.

When the hoarse-toned boatswain called, "A-a-ll ha-a-nds! up anchor, a ho-oy!" Rachel excitedly waved farewell to her family and friends, and then gladly turned her eyes seaward. At last she was escaping from Ipswich where she was born; she was bound on a long voyage; and she floated off into a new world of dreams, scarcely conscious that she was the only woman on the *Newcastle.* What a great adventure to be sailing on this brig laden with furniture, cotton, calico, boots, shoes, cutlery, tea, coffee, sugar and molasses—all products of Massachusetts—for the Sandwich Islands and California!

On the very first day the sea began to alter the life of Rachel Hobson Holm. The rain beat down; the great sails filled out, making a thunderous noise as the *Newcastle* pitched and the sea rolled heavily. Rachel's high spirits were subdued—and then she was tossed across the cabin straight into the arms of Thomas O. Larkin. A wave broke over the ship, immersing them both. They laughed at their unceremonious introduction, and for a bewitching second she felt herself held by the dark, gray-eyed young stranger. He was not tall, but he had sturdy shoulders and a high head with a cleft square chin—he was someone to whom she could look for protection.

When Rachel revived after a brief seasickness, the *Newcastle* had entered the calm wide waste and Larkin was at her side. "I'm still glad I came," she said. "I hope there are cannibals at Hilo. It would be nice to see one."

He smiled at her carefree humorous outlook. "I think you'll be disappointed. They say the missionaries have cured the natives of cannibalism."

"I hope the missionaries haven't taken all the romance out of the island," she replied. "This going to sea is fun—just like a Fenimore Cooper novel." She hugged a Cooper volume.

Her eagerness for life, her unafraid inexperience aroused Larkin's instinct to protection. She asked him to tell her about himself, and she learned that Charlestown was his birthplace; that seven Larkins had assisted at the Boston Tea Party; that Brown Bess, the horse of his ancestors, had been borrowed by Paul Revere when he went on his famous ride. With a smile Larkin added,

"Revere forgot to return the horse. The Larkins were either very rich or very poor. My folks were poor. I want to make money in California. My half-brother, John Cooper, does. He's a retired sea captain at Monterey, and he has a good business. I'll go in with him. I'm pretty lucky."

"I'm sure you'll succeed," she said, "but there are more flowers in the Sandwich Islands. I never had enough flowers in Ipswich."

"Oh, there are plenty of flowers in Hilo, but business will be better in California."

"I don't worry about money. Food is very cheap, and they say we don't need much clothing. If only I can see those trees of yellow and red flowers, I'll be happy."

Larkin felt that the tropical flowers enticed young Mrs. Holm even more than her husband. She had scarcely known him when he had sailed away five years before, leaving her with her parents at Ipswich. Each year he had intended to return, but he was held by the sea. Now he had written her to come to him. It scarcely seemed that she had been married at all. The Sandwich Islands should be a nice place for a honeymoon.

The *Newcastle* crossed the equator. Together Rachel and Larkin beheld the Southern Cross—never had they seen so brilliant a constellation as those four stars. Ninety days from New England the *Newcastle* met and exchanged greetings with a whaling ship homeward-bound, and suddenly both Rachel and Larkin were swept with an agony of longing for their native land. She dashed tears from her eyes, but Larkin tried to smile as the ship disappeared in the dark horizon.

The grim moment was prolonged when Cape Horn moved toward them. Slate-covered clouds blackened the heavens. Rain, sleet and snow drove in upon them, making night of day. Half of the ship was under water. In the peril Rachel turned to Larkin.

"What will happen?" she asked.

His firm handclasp reassured her. "Cooper's sailors enjoyed these terrible storms off Cape Horn."

They forgot Cape Horn when they touched at Juan Fernandez, Robinson Crusoe's mountainous, rocky island over which floated the flag of Chile. "How romantic," she said, "actually to see Robinson Crusoe's island!"

"Now it's a sort of Botany Bay for the Chilean government," he told her.

With several of the *Newcastle* crew Larkin pulled ashore to fill the ship's water casks. He brought Rachel a few blue flowers and some strawberries wrapped in green leaves. "I'll keep the flowers always," she said. "This is a classic land. It shouldn't be a Chilean prison." And long after the *Newcastle* had tripped anchor and stood out to sea, Larkin and Rachel were feasting on strawberries.

Six months from Boston the *Newcastle* sailed into the crescent-shaped bay of the New Moon, Hilo, whose dense dark green foliage opened the portals to the romantic interest of the big island. Here Captain James Cook had been killed by cannibals—now it was a missionary center! And here ended the happy six months during which Larkin and Rachel had been shut off from the past and future as if living on another planet.

While the ship unloaded its cargo and Larkin assisted Rachel in claiming her boxes, she rejoiced in the beauty of the scene, even in the shadow of the volcano. The flower trees were no fable. Coppery-skinned natives came aboard, their arms filled with brilliant leis of flowers.

"Oh, I never could have believed it!" exclaimed Rachel. "I hope I don't wake up and find this fairy land isn't true. Why doesn't everyone in New England come here? To think of living here," she added, burying her face in the flowers around her neck.

As they were being rowed ashore by natives bedecked with brilliant blossoms, the missionary church bells sounded.

"New England!" said Larkin, "you can't escape Ipswich!"

"It's sweet to hear the bells." They had landed. "My husband, I wonder where he is," she said anxiously.

"I'll find out if the *Catalina* is in port." And Larkin left her to make inquiries while she sat guarding her boxes. After a few hurried questions he returned, "The *Catalina* is late."

With an alarmed look she said, "There's nothing wrong, is there?"

"Nothing. The *Catalina* may come into port any day."

She brightened up. "I'll see the flowers. I'm glad I have plenty of books to read."

Larkin saw her safely installed in the house of a missionary family at Hilo. Just before the *Newcastle* sailed, he said to her,

"The *Catalina* may have gone to California. If I hear of it, I'll get

PORTRAIT OF THOMAS OLIVER LARKIN.   PORTRAIT OF MRS. THOMAS OLIVER LAR-
KIN.

THE FOUNDING OF LOS ANGELES WITH GOVERNOR NEVE, SEPTEMBER 4, 1781 [From a painting by Alson Clark].

in touch with your husband and send you word. If anything happens and you need me, I'll be at Monterey."

"Thank you, but nothing will happen," she said with the blind confidence of youth.

"But if it does, remember that you can count on me for anything." In leave-taking he brought her an armful of fragrant leis; red, yellow, white, blue. She asked him to choose one to wear to California. He selected the red one. In the few hours at Hilo they had learned the Hawaiian word "Aloha," and that was their farewell.

Young as she was, and thousands of miles from home, Rachel did not weep when she found herself alone. Although the *Newcastle* had sailed for California, she had a great sense of security; she had found one who would never fail her. And as Hilo became a distant gray blur on the sea, perhaps Larkin first murmured those words that he was later to write to his wife—words which are now preserved in a letter in the Bancroft Library at the University of California, "I love you more than life."

After delivering its cargo at Yerba Buena—then a small settlement on the bay of San Francisco but the nucleus of the great city to be, San Francisco—the *Newcastle* took aboard hides, tallow and soap, and sailed south. For the first time Larkin beheld Monterey, the old Spanish-Mexican capital with its white plastered houses and red tile roofs, a hundred of them set at random on green lawns among the oaks. From the small square Presidio the Mexican green, white and red flag was flying and soldiers were parading before Governor Figueroa's adobe *palacio*.

Larkin saw it all with Rachel's eyes, which always sought beauty. She would have liked the *señoras,* the *señoritas* with mantillas and gay sashes, and the serenading *señores* in broad-brimmed hats, scarlet-trimmed jackets, velvet pantaloons, and embroidered shoes. Even the half-clad Indians seemed picturesque.

Captain Cooper, Larkin's half-brother, opened Monterey's doors to young Don Tomás. Mrs. Cooper was Doña Encarnación, sister of General Vallejo, California's first citizen, but young Larkin had eyes for none of Monterey's *señoritas*. He lived at the Coopers' hospitable adobe house and found a place at once in his brother's mercantile business. In this land of *mañana* and *poco tiempo* he did not allow "tomorrow" and "after a while" to slow his activity. *Montereños* saw that *el Bostono, Señor Larquin,* was a real *Yanqui*.

Soon he was established in his own business, and he wrote to Rachel telling her what he had accomplished. "Money comes quick —not like Massachusetts. I'm going to sell everything from pins to lumber. I'm glad I came to California. You'd like it—it's a garden country. The Stars and Stripes should wave over California." He told her that he had made inquiries, but no tidings had come from the *Catalina*. The Captain, he hoped, was safe at Hilo.

Months later news came from South America—somewhere between Mexico and Callao, Captain John Holm, a victim of fever, was floating in the sea like a thing that had never lived. Upon receiving this word, Rachel wrote to Larkin. "I'm waiting here at Hilo for a Boston-bound ship."

"You're coming to California," he commanded, "to Monterey— this is where you belong. You're going to be my wife. When you were tossed into my arms on the *Newcastle* it was all prearranged. Consul John Coffin Jones's *Volunteer* will soon sail for California, and I will meet you at Santa Barbara. I love you more than life."

Would she love him? Would the *Volunteer* sink? Would some ghastly catastrophe prevent their wedding? For six months Larkin anxiously wondered. Then he sailed south on a schooner to Santa Barbara to meet his destiny, the *Volunteer,* which had weighed anchor in the Santa Barbara roadstead. Larkin transferred from the schooner to the bark and hurried up the side of the *Volunteer*.

Would Rachel be on board? Yes! There she was, still smiling at life and at him! Under the Stars and Stripes on the high sea Thomas O. Larkin and Rachel Hobson Holm stood on the poop-deck and were married by Consul Jones, the owner of the ship.

Ever-festive Santa Barbara joined in the gay celebration. Few

Barbareños had ever seen an American woman, and they welcomed Doña Raquela to California—the first *Americana* to enter the territory. The *señores* kissed her hand and in the best Mission wine drank the health of *la señora Yanqui* at a *gran fiesta de bodas* in honor of the first American-born couple in California.

During the years following the Larkin thick-walled adobe house at Monterey became a center of hospitality presided over by Doña Raquela, wearing mauve gowns and black velvet slippers. Here their children were born.

Rachel Hobson Holm brought good fortune to Larkin, who became the most important business man in California. He erected the Monterey Custom House and was the only American to serve as Consul from the United States to California; this was in 1844 and 1846. In 1845 he represented the New York *Herald* and New York *Sun* in California. His attitude toward Mexico and the United States alike was so friendly that he did great service in maintaining amicable relations between Americans and Californians. He tried to induce local rulers to transfer voluntarily their allegiance to the United States, in order to counteract the efforts of those favoring an English protectorate.

During the Mexican war Larkin sent his wife and three children to San Francisco for safety. There one of the daughters fell ill and Mrs. Larkin summoned her husband. While hastening to visit his family he was captured by the Californians during the battle of Natividad near Salinas and was held as hostage till the end of the war. They hoped thereby to obtain favorable terms of capitulation. Larkin's daughter died before he was released.

When Commodore John D. Sloat sailed into Monterey Bay, July 2, 1846, Consul Larkin was the first American to greet him. He helped Sloat frame the proclamation following the raising of the flag. After his appointment as Military Governor General Stephen W. Kearny lived at the Larkin house, and Lieutenant William Tecumseh Sherman, the adjutant-general, occupied the small adobe in the garden; so the Larkin house became California's first temporary Capitol. On the arrival of Colonel Richard B. Mason, who succeeded General Kearny, the Capitol was established in *El Cuartel* at Monterey.

Larkin became a member of the first Constitutional Convention. He was one of the founders of Benicia and a San Francisco street bears his name. He acquired large grants of lands in the Sacramento valley and passed his time between San Francisco and New York until his sudden death in 1855. For fifteen years he was survived by his widow.

After the great gold rush in 1849 Larkin disposed of his dwelling to a family connection, Jacob P. Leese. Later the famous adobe was owned and occupied by Mayor Robert W. Johnson of Monterey. In 1919 Mrs. Harry S. Toulmin, daughter of Thomas O. Larkin, Jr., bought the historic residence and there assembled many family heirlooms. Here are the Consul's safe, his desk, his clock, and in the quaint garden is the old well. Sherman's adobe quarters, with the government insignia on the mantel, still stand in the garden. On the walls of the reception room in the large dwelling are the portraits of Thomas O. Larkin and his wife Rachel. Mr. and Mrs. Toulmin have revived the spirit of the period of the Larkin house. They make friendly social contacts, and *Montereños* sometimes feel that once more Don Tomás and Doña Raquela are at Larkin house dispensing the gracious hospitality of Old California.

IX

HUGO REID'S INDIAN WIFE

1832

*FOREIGNERS were permitted to live in California only with per-
mission from the Viceroy, unless they accepted the faith of the province
and applied for citizenship. Even before an American had settled in
California there arrived a Scotsman in 1814, John Gilroy, California's
first foreign settler.*

From the Isaac Todd, *an armed English merchantman bound for
the Columbia River, Gilroy was tossed and left dying of scurvy on
the shore of Monterey Bay. Señora Peralta Bernal, a kindly woman,
took him to her father's* Rancho San Antonio *near Oakland and
nursed him back to life and health. Later at Mission San Juan Bautista
he married Maria Clara Ortega, granddaughter of the Pathfinder of
the Portolá Expedition who discovered San Francisco Bay. All of
Gilroy's acquired lands and cattle were to pass out of his hands, but
the sailor-ranchero lived to see his old rancho the site of the flourishing
town of Gilroy.*

*The most distinguished Scotsman to visit California in the 1830's
was David Douglas, a botanist who came with his dog and spent two
years on the Pacific Coast studying the flora. He sent many beautiful
shrubs and flowers to England, and he wrote that he longed to go
back to the "land o' cakes," but he never did. Instead, he went to
Honolulu to botanize further, and there was gored to death by an
ox in a pit. His dog was found guarding his body.*

*Shortly after the coming of Douglas, Hugo Reid, another Scotsman,
arrived. He also was a man of culture, but he remained in this "savage
land" and, by a curious chain of circumstances, became the husband
of a beautiful neophyte of Mission San Gabriel.*

WHEN you attend the Santa Anita races, or visit the Huntington Library at San Marino, you are treading on the *rancho* of Victoria, Indian wife of Hugo Reid. When that Scotsman sailed northward from Callao, Peru, on the long-nosed brig *Ayacucho,* little did he realize that he was to become Don Perfecto Hugo Reid of California. How could he? Reid was from the University of Cambridge, and in this year of 1832 California was still a savage land, was still using as currency Indian shell money and bullock hides.

Captain John Wilson of the *Ayacucho* was on a trading voyage, and Hugo Reid was the only passenger of the fast-sailing brig, anchored in the stiff mud off San Pedro. *Rancheros* and eager purchasers of the *Ayacucho's* cargo flocked on board from boats plying to and fro. Men, women, even children, crowded the decks. On shore were cattle and carts laden with hides and tallow for barter; and horsemen, excited by the arrival of the *Ayacucho,* were racing over the plains toward the sea.

Bronzed Kanaka oarsmen rowed the tall sandy-haired young Reid in the longboat to a landing place, and barefoot he ventured three hundred yards over the slippery knife-edged rocks to the sandy shore. Quickly the Captain and supercargo transformed the whitewashed adobe Custom House at the landing place into a trading post, and Reid borrowed a mustang from the *ranchero* Don Manuel Dominguez and set out to ride ten leagues to the pueblo of *Nuestra Señora de la Los Angeles Porciúncula.* As he hastened forward the warm land with its grazing herds charmed him. Even the *Palos Verdos,* rolling hills to the northwest, parched yellow-tan like the clay earth, seemed to welcome the Scotsman.

Siesta time saw him at the pueblo making a minor sensation. To the *señoras* and *señoritas,* when a foreign ship arrived off San Pedro, it meant officers, music, dancing and frolic. The sleepy plaza, bordered by low adobe buildings, with a Mexican flag floating from a central pole, suddenly became animated. At sunset Reid sat in the plaza, strumming on a borrowed guitar and singing songs of Mexico and

South America. He even sang of his native Scotland, but all the songs had one refrain—the faithlessness of woman!

For Hugo Reid lived in the time of Byron when men still suffered from and sang of broken hearts. Because of his songs, and not a little because of his pensive blue eyes, he melted into the mellow cadenced life of the pueblo. He became an *hijo del pais,* Don Hugo, and California was anodyne for the pain that for six years had torn his heart. So the *Ayacucho* sailed back to Peru without him.

Soon after Don Hugo had established a trading post in the pueblo, a slender young woman in a black lace mantilla, and holding in her hands the reins of Doña Eulalia Perez' oxen, drove a creaking *carreta* into the plaza. Loiterers dashed off their *sombreros* to greet Doña Eulalia, called the oldest woman in California. The sun had burned her skin to all but the tone of the brown *rebozo* framing her face. Her figure was wasted and her shoulders were bent, but her profile was like that of Dante, and her narrow hands had power. In the province she was a personage—had she not conquered time, made herself almost immortal? Besides, for generations she had been house-mother to the Indian neophyte girls at Mission San Gabriel—one of the builders of that potent establishment.

Few noticed her young companion who so dexterously guided the oxen; only Don Hugo gazed at the girl of such simple dignity and deep mysterious eyes. Later he was to assert that at first glance he thought, "There's a true rose of Castile." She seemed not to see him; in silence she looked straight before her.

Like the other merchants in the pueblo, Don Hugo sought Doña Eulalia's patronage, and so he was gratified when that small but determined *señora* rebuffed those of his competitors seeking to assist her. She stepped independently to the ground from her *carreta* and entered his place of business.

"*Señor,* I have come to see the new *tienda,*" she said.

For her inspection Don Hugo courteously displayed Manila shawls, serapes, candlesticks, and fabrics from the South Seas. She made lavish purchases; Doña Eulalia was not too old to appreciate young *señores* with blue eyes.

But the Scotsman's thoughts wandered to the *señorita* seated alone in the cart gaily upholstered with bright calico and lamb's wool. Who was she? Why did she not come into the *tienda?* How much longer must he wait to see her again? He was, however, the ingratiating host while Doña Eulalia admired the *tienda* and questioned him concerning Scotland, South America and Mexico. Would she never finish?

At last, she turned her steps to the *carreta* and Don Hugo and his shrewd Yankee partners were at hand to aid. They swept her purchases into their arms, but suddenly Doña Eulalia reconsidered. Perhaps she would buy the flame-red shawl instead of the black. She took both. Once more she delayed her departure. She must have another sack of that most excellent Brazilian coffee.

But finally she was installed in her *carreta,* and still the young woman holding the oxen reins seemed not to have moved. In vain Don Hugo sought a glance from the *señorita.* "Come to the *Rancho San Pascual* and have *cha* with us," hospitably urged Doña Eulalia.

"*Gracias, señora,*" replied the Scotsman. "I should be glad to have tea."

"Come soon, before our poppies close their heads for summer. The fields glitter like gold—you can see them leagues out at sea."

"We saw them when we arrived," said Don Hugo, "but I'm eager to get a look at close range. *Hasta la vista!*"

Sombreros in hand, Don Hugo and his partners watched the competent young driver prod the oxen as her firm hands drove them out of the plaza. He gazed at her in admiration and suddenly he felt free of Victoria of Scotland, the woman who had sent him wandering. Never again could she make him suffer! She was shut out of his life by the *señorita* in the *carreta.* But he named the stranger Victoria. To his partner, Jacob Leese, he said:

"That is the prettiest woman I've seen in the pueblo."

"One of the San Gabriel Indian neophytes," replied Leese casually. Reid could not be shocked into a retraction. "No matter."

"She is married."

The eager young man winced, but the next afternoon he mounted his mustang and accepted Doña Eulalia's invitation to *cha* at the *Rancho San Pascual.* Once more he saw the Indian Victoria. Her baptismal name was Bartolomea. Silently Victoria served Doña Eulalia, who had taught her to sew, make lace and embroider.

Again and again Don Hugo returned to Eulalia's hospitable dwelling and she became his first close friend in California. He never wearied of watching Victoria's graceful movements or of admiring the bright boas of wild flowers she wore around her neck. Gradually he entered into her life and heard her story. Married at thirteen to Pablo, thirty years her senior, already she was the mother of four children. Doña Eulalia said that the *padres* had given *ranchos* to Victoria and her husband, although the title was not clear. One was the Santa Anita. "Bartolomea and Pablo shall have those *ranchos,*" declared Doña Eulalia. "They are among the few California Indians sufficiently intelligent to own land."

While Victoria sewed in the pavilion over which gourd vines tumbled, Don Hugo learned from her the customs and religion of her tribe-folk. They had their own heaven, but the Spaniards had brought hell and the devil to California. The Indians had a Virgin Mother, Chukit. She fell in love with Lightning and brought forth Mactutu, son of their god. Wise men burned him alive, but he promised, "In three days I will rise again." When he failed to reappear, "There is no God," declared some. Others had faith. "We destroyed only his body. His soul is in heaven." No one had ever seen the Indian god. "Maybe Indian's god and *padre's* God one god?" said Victoria. She was pleased that Don Hugo set down her words in a book.

One day he asked, "What is the Indian word for love?"

"Indian no love-word."

"I give you love," he said.

She sat staring at her needlework, she embroidered no more. Then she said quietly, "I give you love. Now Pablo, my husband, can kill me."

Again and again Don Hugo's discreet business partners warned him against the savage San Gabriel Indians. Once he had left his native Scotland to wander six years because of a faithless woman. Now, because of a faithful woman, he turned his back on California. He did not even say *adiós* to Doña Eulalia or to *Padre* Esténaga at San Gabriel Mission. Hermosillo, Sonora, became his new home, and there for a year he taught school, with only occasional tidings from the pueblo of *Los Angeles de Porciúncula*.

Then Doña Eulalia wrote, "Death has freed Victoria."

When Don Hugo returned to the *Rancho San Pascual,* Victoria said, "Now I believe Indian god Mactutu will rise again."

The week of the harvest moon in September was set for the wedding. Hugo Reid had been already transformed into Don Perfecto Hugo Reid, a Roman Catholic and a citizen of California. The Scotsman of Cambridge University and the Indian neophyte Victoria knelt before the flower-festooned altar of San Gabriel Mission while *Padre* Tomás de Esténaga united them in marriage, throwing a scarf over their shoulders, yoking them.

Then toward Doña Eulalia's dwelling, the cavalcade set out, the choir boys with flutes, violins and drums, singing merry songs. Don Perfecto Hugo's voice boomed above all, rejoicing, confident of the future. Two white oxen drew the garlanded bridal *carreta;* in another gaily bedecked cart were Doña Eulalia and *Padre* Esténaga. Relatives and friends from the pueblo were on horseback; Indians in gaudy blankets walked. It was the happiest hour in the life of Don Perfecto Hugo and his Indian bride. Arrived at the *Rancho San Pascual* they feasted on hot Spanish dishes, fruit and San Gabriel wine. Then they danced all through the warm night in a pavilion made of the river willows. For a week dancing went on.

Victoria's lowly people became those of her husband; he adopted her children. At times, however, Don Perfecto Hugo realized the difference in race, especially when he began building the Santa Anita ranchhouse for his wife and encountered her protest,

"Please, no high two-story house. I feel the stirring of the seven giants, who are always shaking California because they carry it upon their shoulders. They have even shaken down the bell-tower of San Gabriel Mission. One-story adobe house, please, my husband."

Don Perfecto Hugo tried to laugh away her fears, but Victoria would never set foot on the stairs of the new house. She slept on the first floor, the children and servants occupying the second floor. But Don Perfecto Hugo filled the house with comfortable furniture, precious books and fine linen. Again Cambridge University clashed with native California; the children were taught French, English, Spanish.

"Don't," pleaded Victoria, "you keep the children in the house too much reading. The house is chill; they are not enough in the sunshine."

The husband continued his European way of living and insisted that his native wife should have many Indians to serve her. But theirs was not a happy story. Don Perfecto Hugo lived over-lavishly. He sold the *Rancho Santa Anita*. After the American flag was raised he became one of the owners of Mission San Gabriel; but later that also passed out of his hands. Stripped of his possessions, he sought fortune in the north during the great gold rush of 1849. At Monterey he became a member of the Constitutional Convention of California.

Doña Victoria was alone with her children. Her only daughter María Ignacia, the "Flower of San Gabriel," died before she was twenty. Why Don Perfecto Hugo was absent the Indian mother could not understand. For her daughter's burial she bought white satin, white lace, white ribbons and wax candles. Hundreds of her tribefolk helped her inter the "Flower of San Gabriel," at the Mission's burial place. Long the neophytes lamented.

Black-gowned in grief, Doña Victoria hated her husband. "Murderer! *Asesino!*" Cambridge University was also bitterly reproached. "Books killed my daughter. What a waste of time! Always indoors reading French, English, doing silly sums! Away from the sun she grew weak, unable to fight the dreadful disease. Don Perfecto Hugo with his learning, he murdered her!"

For a time her reason fled. Then chance brought a prairie-schooner drawn by tired oxen to Mission San Gabriel. One of the travelers was a young girl, Laura. Doña Victoria thought that the stranger, Laura, was a reincarnation of her lost María Ignacia, and the new interest restored her balance and sanity.

But her life was laid waste. Don Perfecto Hugo did not live long. He died while he was writing the history of the San Gabriel Indians as related by Victoria, thus giving California one of its most valuable historical documents. A son of Victoria's became a follower of Murietta the bandit. She lost her land and, despite its walls four feet thick, her two-story dwelling built by Don Perfecto Hugo collapsed in an earthquake. At the end she returned to Doña Eulalia Perez and sat in her patio at the *Rancho San Pascual,* with only a colorful print quilt covering her shoulders. Until the last she was protected by that remarkable woman who never failed her neophytes and who was popularly believed to be one hundred and forty years old.

This age, however, has been revealed as an exaggeration. Very recently a memorial garden seat commemorating her life was installed in the courtyard of Mission San Gabriel. She is the only woman so honored for work in developing the Missions. The garden seat is inscribed:

"THIS MARKS THE GRAVE OF
EULALIA PEREZ DE GUILLEN
BORN AT LORETO, BAJA CALIFORNIA, IN 1768
DIED JUNE 11, 1878
14 YEARS MAYORDOMA OF
SAN GABRIEL MISSION
ERECTED BY GARFIELD STUDY CLUB."

X

SANTA BARBARA'S INTERNATIONAL WEDDING

1836

EVEN in the 1820's there were marriages between the California señoritas *and the blue-eyed and gray-eyed strangers from faraway lands who came around Cape Horn riding the perilous sea. Romance ran swift in California—its daughters flashed their black eyes and bewitched lonely travelers.*

Thomas W. Doak, painter of the altar at Mission San Juan Bautista, had pioneered in this field when, in 1820, he married María Lugarda Castro, of the North. John Gilroy had taken his wife, María Clara Ortega, at Mission San Juan Bautista, before her cousin, Guadalupe Ortega, married Joseph Chapman, the reformed American pirate, at Santa Inés. Monterey had become the home of Teresa de la Guerra, daughter of Captain de la Guerra y Noriega, when, in 1825, she married the Englishman W. E. P. Hartnell, California's solid business man. And the province still reverberated with the Fitch-Carrillo elopement from San Diego to South America. In 1827, stormy Captain William A. Gale of Boston had married Marcelina Estudillo, the first California woman to visit New England. She never returned. And Captain William Goodwin Dana chafed with impatience while the vice-regal government was giving him its eventual permission to wed Josefa Carrillo of Santa Barbara, daughter of magnificent Don Carlos, first native Californian to have a book published.

But none of these marriages was on a scale of splendor which equaled that of Alfred Robinson of Boston and Ana de la Guerra at

Mission Santa Barbara in 1836, reported with distinction by Richard Henry Dana in Two Years Before the Mast.

WHEN Alfred Robinson, a Boston youth of twenty-two, sailed into Santa Barbara Bay on Captain William A. Gale's *Brookline* more than one hundred .years ago, he was charmed with the Mission in the background, rising a league on the inclined plane and to the hills beyond. It was as if he had a premonition that there in the Mission town lived his future wife, the *señorita* of the fabulous de la Guerra house.

Of course he did not see the de la Guerras' dwelling with its mysterious attic under the tile roof—the treasure room to which a ladder mounted. Here were dozens of *coras*, compactly woven baskets of large size, heaped up with Spanish and Mexican gold doubloons, all belonging to *el Señor* Don *Capitán* José de la Guerra y Noriega. *El Señor Capitán,* a retired Spanish officer, still wore epaulets on his citizen's clothing, and he had represented his department at the capital, Mexico City. These honors intensified that air of authority sprung from his great fortune, acquired from mighty herds roaming his *ranchos Las Posas, Simi, Callegua, Conejo* and *San Julian,* covering more than three hundred thousand acres.

Unfailingly visitors paid their respects to the de la Guerras, and here Alfred Robinson came—to their *casa grande,* with its arched doorway surmounted by the crest of the Noriegas and the de la Guerras, and presided over by Doña María Antonia, of California's most beautiful family, the Carrillos. She was famous for her dark eyes, her flashing teeth, and her small feet that danced the *contradanza* and the *jota.*

In his book, *Life in California,* Robinson was to describe his arrival at the de la Guerras' stately Moorish dwelling with its courtyard and fountain, and its furniture from Mexico, China and Boston. With Captain Gale of the *Brookline*—called "Four Eyes" by Californians because of his glasses—Robinson paid his first ceremonial visit to the de la Guerras' golden house. The Captain was bearing gifts for the family, and he and Robinson arrived on muleback from the landing place.

At Santa Barbara's great house Gale delivered his gifts while Robinson savoured the delicious de la Guerra chocolate. The *señoras* of the household, in their short embroidered muslin sleeves, flowered muslin petticoats, scarlet sashes and velvet shoes, seemed exotic, and the men with their short scarlet-trimmed jackets, embroidered shoes and beribboned long hair were all in the Santa Barbara mood. Like the other women of Santa Barbara, Doña María Antonia wore a black silk band with a star on her forehead, and her hair was held with a matronly comb. Of her warm hospitality Robinson was to write, "There are two supremely good things in California, '*Señora* Noriega and the grapes.'"

Señoritas Teresa and Augustias, their glossy black hair in long plaits hanging down their back, eagerly distributed the gifts, but little Ana, Robinson's wife-to-be, was too small to appear.

Was it the sunshine? Was it the voluptuous air? Whatever it was, from the beginning Santa Barbara had offered hospitality. Even in 1769 the Indians on the enchanting bay had welcomed the Portolá expedition seeking the bay of Monterey. Natives danced their greetings and saluted the fair strangers with song. They brought gifts and proudly displayed paintings made by them. Modern in every sense, they had a queen ruling over a dozen tribes to the north near Gaviota.

Doña María Antonia perpetuated this traditional graciousness of living. In *Life in California,* Alfred Robinson was to describe the *merienda* given at La Laguna Blanca at which she was hostess. Several ox-carts conveyed the guests to the lake, that of Doña María Antonia leading, arched over and covered with unbleached cotton. Robinson was squeezed in between the hostess and her sister, his legs dangling behind the cart. Ana, a diminutive replica of her mother, in the children's cart that followed, led the gaiety of the shouting youngsters who were guarded by Indian attendants prodding the oxen. Behind was another cart squeaking under the weight of roast turkey, chicken, *tamales* and *dulces*. On horseback followed a score of persons who shared in the feasting, music and games of the *merienda* held in a spacious amphitheater near the lake.

Robinson became the agent of the Bryant-Sturgis Company, the first foreign-established business in the territory. He took up his residence in a building which served also for his business quarters. With him was his servant Harrison, brought from Boston. Young Robinson fell under the spell of the Mission bells and soon was baptized José Maria Alfredo—to Californians he was "Don Alfredo."

Even Don Alfredo's business life had adventure, for he and his servant found it necessary to protect themselves from the lawless with muskets and knives. Up and down the coast Don Alfredo sailed, trading in hides and tallow, and from the bleak Farallones near San Francisco he obtained otter skins for shipment to China.

Among *Barbareños* the friendly and cultured Robinson was much liked—he had had gentler upbringing than the sea captains storming into Santa Barbara. His second home became the de la Guerra dwelling, where he was welcomed as a son by glowing Doña María Antonia.

After Don Alfredo had been in Santa Barbara several years he realized that the youngest de la Guerra daughter was mature. Although Ana María de la Gracia de Dios Leonora de la Guerra y Carrillo was not yet fifteen, it was as if the charm of the mother suddenly appeared in her daughter. This girl with Spanish dreams in her eyes stirred him as he had never been moved by the women of his native Boston. Warmed by the semi-tropical sun of Santa Barbara and speaking the language of the country, Robinson's blood had the same beat as that of Ana's. He felt like a son of California when he told Don José and Doña María Antonia of his wish to make Anita his wife. So it seemed always to have been intended.

Anita's oldest sister, Teresa, was married to the Englishman, William Hartnell, at Monterey, and her brilliant sister, Angustias, had married the government official, Jimeno, at a famous wedding at the Mission the year before. She had ridden on horseback all the way to her new home and was now enthroned as queen of Monterey society.

It seemed fitting that Anita should marry Don Alfredo, an heroic figure, always coming and going in the "house upon the water."

One sleepy Sunday afternoon Don Alfredo and Anita were in the de la Guerra courtyard which was fragrant with the scent of the white bell-shaped datura. Feeling the breeze upon her face, she said, "Don Alfredo, the wind is coming from the southeast. When it comes from there it blows for days and makes the sea rough. Do not go to Monterey. Wait till there is less wind."

"I must sail all seas."

"But you may never come back."

"And if I don't—"

"I shouldn't want to live."

And so they were betrothed. Ana's cousins, the Carrillos, and all the Santa Barbara *señoritas* envied the young girl her "Boston." What a wonderful country that Boston must be to produce men like Don Alfredo.

Before Anita was fifteen, the wedding took place, in January, 1836, just after Richard Henry Dana arrived at Santa Barbara on the *Pilgrim*—a young Harvard student with weakened eyes who had shipped as a sailor, but who was to achieve fame by writing *Two Years Before the Mast*. The *Pilgrim* came riding into port on a furious southeaster, which caused them to slip cable and take to open sea for safety. In his book Dana recorded the festivities of the first great international wedding uniting California and the United States.

The province had never seen such a marriage. At ten o'clock *Señorita* Ana and her sister, dressed in the deep black worn by Californians in church, passed up the long corridor and knelt in the Mission confessional. Beaming, rotund *Padre* Antonio Jimeno, a relation of the de la Guerras, assisted by *Padre* Narciso Duran and other clergy, united California and Boston in marriage. Within an hour the great doors of the Mission church opened, bells pealed, and the bride, dressed in white, came out of the church with the bridegroom, followed by a long procession.

The *Pilgrim* had been ordered to salute Don Alfredo and his bride.

Richard Henry Dana was at the starboard after-gun; the other seamen had matches ready for firing the salute when the flags should be run up. The Captain of the *Pilgrim* gave the signal from the shore to the ship. Just as Doña Ana de la Guerra de Robinson stepped from the church door, a small cloud issued from the bow of the *Pilgrim* and a loud report echoed among the surrounding hills and over the bay. Instantly the *Pilgrim* was dressed in flags and pennants from stem to stern. Twenty-three salutes were given and the ship lay dressed in her colors all day. At sunset another salute of twenty-three guns was fired and all the flags were run down. To add to the gaiety of the scene, from the roof of the de la Guerra dwelling *Capitán* José, the bride's father, saluted by scattering gold and silver coins among the crowd.

Then, what a feast! For an entire day the *Pilgrim's* steward had been making cakes at the de la Guerra dwelling. Supper was followed by a *fandango,* and from both ship and town everyone was invited. All the *Pilgrim* crew rode ashore wearing neat sailor suits. They beached their boat and joined the *fandango* in a tent erected before the de la Guerra house where Santa Barbara danced to violins and guitars. The women remained nearly stationary, sliding about on their feet—invisible because the hems of their skirts reached the ground. Old *señoras* sat in rows clapping their hands to the music and applauding the dancers.

The men danced around the women. Only the aristocracy waltzed. Don Juan Bandini, in white pantaloons with short dark silk jacket, danced like a young faun with Doña Angustias, the handsome sister of the bride. For an hour all dancing ceased but theirs. Old and young applauded, waving hats and handkerchiefs as they watched Don Juan and Doña Angustias dance. The *fandango* became a carnival. Eggs filled with cologne were merrily broken upon the heads of the company. *Señores* tossed their *sombreros* upon the heads of the *señoritas*. Sometimes the hat was cast aside, but if the girl continued dancing it meant that she chose that gallant for the evening. And so for three days on went the *fandango.*

PORTRAIT OF ANA DE LA GUERRA DE ROBINSON.

SENORITA DELFINA DE LA GUERRA (CENTER) IN THE DE LA GUERRA HOME AT FIESTA TIME, SANTA BARBARA.

Alfred Robinson had been absent from Boston for eight years. He had always postponed his return, but through newspapers and magazines he had tried to keep in touch with the life of his native land. Now he had a real incentive to go back—his wife must learn English—must know his country as he knew California. She had been educated by private tutors, but there was much more for a girl of fourteen to learn.

Therefore, after their first child, Elena, was born, Den Alfredo bade his wife make ready to go to Boston. The six months' voyage was too long a trip for the child; they must leave it with the de la Guerras. And they must sail soon, going by way of Honolulu.

Doña Ana had never dreamed this could happen! California women had never traveled. Of course Josefa Carrillo of San Diego had eloped with Captain Henry Delano Fitch; and poor Marcelina Estudillo, after her marriage to Captain William Gale, had gone to Boston but had never returned. Ana shuddered. What if she also should never return? What would become of her baby?

But the de la Guerras calmed their daughter. They would look after baby Elena. Boston must be a wonderful place! It had sent many ships to California manned by hundreds of daring seamen. What a great experience to go so many thousand miles in a "house upon the water!"

Anita knew it was foolish to protest. She must not be a little girl crying at the separation from her parents. Don Alfredo would always be at her side to protect her. This Anita knew, that safety and happiness must be with her husband; so the first Santa Barbara girl sailed around stormy Cape Horn, pioneering to Boston.

And she found that Boston was not Santa Barbara—had nothing of its seductive sunshine and charm; had no tall geraniums, no hibiscus, no oleanders—the Boston spring was like a drizzling California winter. Only in summer was she happy, but that happiness was frozen by the winter. For the first time she touched snow; but worse than family, the restrained Boston manners, the odd Boston customs. And when Robinson broke the news to his bride—that she must go to school—

"To school!" she cried. "Why, I'm your wife! I'm a mother!"

"It's best for you to go to school, *carita*, for I'm going back to California."

"But who will speak Spanish with me?" she wailed.

At first Robinson was frightened by his child-wife's reaction. For a few days she would not eat, and as she said her rosary she looked like a white hibiscus. But he was adamant. Her education must be completed. A few years of schooling and she would be capable of taking her place in any circle.

But what did this Californian care about the schools of Boston? She longed for her baby, her parents, her sisters, her brothers, and the cornflower-blue bay of Santa Barbara with its enchanting life. Worst of all, he had told her that he must return to California—his fortune was there; and that she must remain in a convent in Boston until he returned.

Ana had been taught that a wife must obey her husband; so she wept through two years of schooling, trying to grasp mathematics, geography, rhetoric and, especially, English. In reality, she hated the routine of classes with convent girls. She wished only to say, "I love you, Alfredo and Elena," in Spanish.

Don Alfredo wrote his child-wife by every boat, which took six long months to bring a letter. In two years he himself returned to Boston, but he did not bring her child. Soon there was a real reason for Ana to stay in Boston—the birth of their first son.

Don Alfredo insisted that their children have a Boston upbringing, and that she remain there while he went back to California. Several times he returned, once to bring messages to the government. After four years of separation she had Elena with her. Again Don Alfredo came with gold from the San Francisquito placers near Mission San Fernando, the first great gold strike in California. With more children there were more reasons for Ana to remain in Boston, but Don Alfredo was enmeshed in business. Once he came back to order the construction of three steamers for the Pacific Mail Steamship Company.

Thirteen years passed before the young wife returned to her beloved Santa Barbara. She was not yet thirty and she had the fragility of the white hibiscus. In 1855 she died and she rests under the altar of Mission Santa Barbara.

Alfred Robinson never married again. Most of his life was passed in San Francisco. Only one descendant of his eight children lives. Porter Robinson, a grandson. Recently he told me that he remember. as a child, as late as 1895, seeing his grandfather, a distinguished looking old gentleman in a skull cap, seated in his house on Rincon Hill in San Francisco. He used to ask the little boy to walk past the window that he might see his shadow outside.

At Santa Barbara the de la Guerra house has an aura of romance from its century and more of life. It has been continuously occupied by the same family longer than any residence in California. It still seems the soul of the social life of Old Santa Barbara, although the only person dwelling there today is *Señorita* Delfina de la Guerra, now past seventy years of age. She occupies the one wing of the *casa* which has not been given over to trade. From this dwelling radiate shops, studios, and the gayest and most alluring restaurant on the Pacific Coast—often the center of the annual *fiesta*.

Only the dust of the beautiful de la Guerra women of a century gone still remains, but their beauty is legend in California. The de la Guerra descendants, however, still enchant with their grace and beauty just as when Alfred Robinson came. Of the older generation Mrs. Francis Underhill of Santa Barbara is always admired, and today two of the loveliest de la Guerras are Mrs. Joseph Donohoe IV of San Francisco and Mrs. Alfred Gwynne Vanderbilt of New York City.

XI

LOS ANGELES' INFERNAL COUPLE

1836

LIFE was stormy for Mexican governors of California in the pastoral 'thirties. By an illegal decree Echeandía ordered the Missions secularized, and this was one of the reasons for his downfall.

A new ruler, Manuel Victoria, succeeded Echeandía and tried dictatorship. Echeandía, remaining in the province, stirred up revolt. In a battle near Los Angeles, Victoria was wounded and taken to Mission San Gabriel, where he was cared for by Joseph Chapman, the reformed pirate who was occasionally a surgeon, and by Doña Eulalia Perez, the mayordoma *of the neophytes. After nine months of dictating to California, the wounded Victoria gladly took refuge in a Mexican cloister.*

For twenty days ruled jovial Pio Pico. He had some of the recklessness of his beautiful grandmother, Doña Maria Arballo Gutiérrez de Lopez, whose singing, dancing and flirtations had disturbed the Anza expedition. Ever bedecked with jewels and gold chains, Pico later was one of the most colorful, if not the wisest, of California's governors.

Then swarthy, stocky José Figueroa, an Indian fighter although himself of Indian blood, was sent by Mexico to bring order out of the confusion and to take over the Missions for the government. In spite of his mistresses and his natural children, he is declared to have been the ablest of California's Mexican governors. He brought the first printing press to Monterey and he tried to check the advance of the Russians from the north. Suddenly in 1835 he died, and his remains were taken from Monterey to rest at Santa Barbara.

For four months California was ruled by Nicolas Gutiérrez, a friend of Figueroa; and during that period, by national decree, Los Angeles was declared a city and the capital of California. Angeleños, *however, would not furnish the Capitol rent-free as the government demanded, and their opportunity was lost.*

It was in this era of reckless rulers that a lawless woman and her lover lived a disastrous romance in the new city of Los Angeles.

"THAT infernal couple," the Los Angeles of 1836 called the lovers Gervasio Alípas and María del Rosario Villa de Félix. Even after a century their passion flares scarlet as the poinsettia of Natividad.

Don Gervasio was a *caballero,* a revolutionist from San Diego and Sonora. Doña María was the wife of Don Domingo Félix, the Fortunate. Even his name meant happiness. California had been kind to the Félix. Don Domingo's father was ruler of the Pueblo of the Angels, lord of leagues of land sweeping over what is now Hollywood. Tall and proud Don Domingo walked in the Plaza, his shoulder draped with a Saltillo serape, a sword beneath his arm.

When *Señorita* María became his bride he sent her wedding gifts packed in rose leaves. Like a conqueror he brought her from San Gabriel before him on his saddle. Los Angeles was breathless before the sight of her velvety heavy-lashed eyes, silky black hair, white mantilla with pink rosettes, jonquil crepe shawl, bright shoes, and a sunshade that was a garden of roses and green leaves.

After Don Domingo and Doña María received the paternal blessing there was a great feast in the rear patio. The old Indian cook had prepared chicken colored with sassafras, which was served from large iron pots hanging over fires blazing in stone furnaces. There were *torrijas* and *dulces.* Grandees in broad-brimmed hats, silk jackets, velvet pantaloons and serapes, danced for three days with *señoras* and *señoritas* in satin gowns, bright sashes, mantillas, high combs, necklaces and earrings—as great an occasion, almost, as the wedding of Don Pio Pico and Doña María Ignacia Alvarado.

Life seemed impatient of happiness so flawless. *Los pueblaños* seldom spoke of Don Domingo; they talked only of Doña María, of her grace, and the coquetry in her eyes.

There was always dancing at the Félix *sala,* especially when the stirring drums sounded rodeo time. It was to the spring rodeo that Gervasio Alípas came from San Diego. No one in the south rode so daringly as this follower of Don Juan Bandini, the rebel leader. Fresh from a successful revolt against His Excellency Governor Victoria, Gervasio won new honors at this spring rodeo—three days of riding tornado-like over ranges; three days of rounding up and branding cattle. He threw an unruly bull by a twist of the tail. He rode Don Domingo's wildest horse, standing at his flank, clinging to his belly, astride his neck. He leaped upon a steer new from the hills; three times he rolled to the ground; each time he saved himself.

"Bravo! Bravo! *Viva,* Gervasio!"

With the light of victory in his deep dangerous eyes, he went to the *fandango.* New triumph was his as master of ceremonies in the leafy *enramada* before the low shadowy adobe. Don Domingo was all dignity. The fire and frolic of the music were in Gervasio's blood. He swept the dancers, swayed them, as much at ease at the *fandango* as he had been at the rodeo. He made the evening a night of beauty for all *señoras* and *señoritas* he honored.

Gervasio's triumph became the triumph of Doña María. With her he danced *el borrejo,* the *fandango;* for castanets he snapped his fingers. He was her partner in the *contradanza* and the *jota.* He improvised verse, all in tribute to Doña María. When she danced the *bamba* Gervasio placed a tumbler of water upon her head and spread out on the floor before her his handkerchief with two corners tied together. Still dancing she lifted the handkerchief on her slipper without spilling a drop of water. Gervasio took the tumbler from her and escorted her to her seat. *Señores* applauded and tossed hats upon her head, hurled coins at her feet.

Don Domingo alone was displeased. Never again was he pleased! It seemed to him that María and Gervasio resembled each other. In the eyes of both was the look of some remote Indian ancestor. Don

Domingo saw in María the face of Gervasio; in Gervasio he saw María—he wished that the dance was over. When on bended knee Gervasio paid homage in verse to María, Don Domingo's hand tightened on his sword.

Later he wondered how he had lived through the three days' rodeo and dancing. Especially he wondered how he had controlled himself when, on the last day of the rodeo, María rode back to the *hacienda* before Gervasio in his saddle—her horse had gone lame, she said.

"Lies!" thought Don Domingo. To him the air palpitated with caresses between the lovers. In violation of Spanish-Californian hospitality, even before the rodeo festivity was ended, he gave his hand to Gervasio, saying, "*Gracias,* a thousand times, for your coming and your assistance. What should we have done without you? Do not forget us at the big rodeo. Will you not present our compliments to all our good friends at San Diego?"

Gervasio realized that he was being dismissed. Quickly he sought out Doña María for *Adiós.* Her soft fingers clung, her lips trembled, but she did not speak. San Diego seemed far away—two days' ride!

After the last guitar was silent, and while even the dogs were slumbering at *Rancho Félix,* a distant voice came through the night, singing:

> *Adiós! Adiós, amores!*
> *Adiós, que ya me ausento*
> *Con tanto sentimiento*
> *Que tú me has dado á mí.*

Awake in their high-canopied bed Don Domingo spoke to his wife: "María!" She feigned not to hear but from her breathing he knew she was not asleep. "María, are you awake?" He was sure she was listening breathlessly. "María," he persisted, "did you hear the song?"

She pretended to struggle back to wakefulness. "Which song?" "*Adiós, amores!*" was sounding over the tawny moonlit hills and the hoarse deep voice quickened her heart, but she answered, "*Vaqueros* are always singing."

"That is Gervasio Alípas' voice."

She yawned. "Hasn't he gone to San Diego?"

"Some men would be jealous of Gervasio," said Don Domingo. His very words seemed to smoke.

"Some men are jealous of everyone."

The voice did not come again. The desolate hills burned brown against the hot summer sky. Only an occasional giant oak seemed alive. María felt as lifeless as the lion-colored grass. San Diego seemed as far away as Mexico City. Her dancing feet lagged; her glance no longer invited; and devout Don Domingo approved. He was gratified because she went often to confession at San Gabriel. He wondered what she confessed.

One day, after Mass at Mission San Gabriel in the dead August heat, María in a golden-brown *rebozo* and Don Domingo in black and silver came face to face with Gervasio in snowy silken shirt, red and yellow *bolero* and green *calzones*—all youth! A strange contrast to Don Domingo with power in his shoe-button eyes, power in his scimitar-like nose, power in his narrow jaw—power inherited and acquired.

When María saw Gervasio her lips turned to blood-red jade, but Don Domingo had the self-control to master his emotion. He hastened before María to Gervasio. "Ah, *amigo!* You have come to remain with us, I hope?"

"*Gracias,* no, Don Domingo. I have a *ranchito* in the hills back of San Gabriel—the Governor has been kind. I'm building myself a cabin—only an Indian hut. My dog and I need little. We have a garden, a small herd—very different from the *hacienda de Félix*. But I hope you and Doña María will come there to visit me."

What was there about his voice that made the world vibrate with beauty? María did not know. But Gervasio had come back.

"Will you not come for a few days to our *rancho?*" urged Don Domingo. Paternally he touched Gervasio's shoulder. "Let the Indians work."

"After my *cabaña* is finished," replied Gervasio, "I will come."
María waited long. Would he never return? In the night she listened for his song, but there was only silence. Life droned on in the
iron-barred, deep-windowed adobe house. Oleanders, pomegranates,
and orange trees bloomed; geraniums flamed in red jars. Humming
birds dipped into honeysuckle. Goldfinches fluttered in the rustic
courtyard fountain.

Then the Governor summoned Don Domingo to Monterey for conference. With the master absent, existence was gayer at *Rancho Félix*.
Even the birds sang through the *siesta*-hour. María sang.

Suddenly the dogs in the courtyard began to bark. In a defens ve
pack they bore down upon the visitor—only to stop short and nuzzle
his hand.

"*Dios de mi vida!* You, Gervasio?" cried María.

"Are you vexed, María? I have come here many nights, but I dared
not sing or play the guitar. Do not send me away!"

"*Adiós,* Gervasio."

"María *mia,* not *adiós!*" She seemed to sink into the ocean of love
as his lips sought hers....

Don Domingo had not gone to Monterey. At midnight he found
the lovers in his room, in his own bed! His rawhide *reata* raised red
and blue welts on the young flesh of María and Gervasio. Agile as a
cougar, Gervasio seized the *reata* and bound Don Domingo hand and
foot. Then, rushing from the house with María, he lifted her to the
saddle of his swift horse, mounted behind her and dug his spurs into
the animal's lean flank.

"Where are we going, my Gervasio?"

"To freedom, *querida.*"

"May all the saints save us!" she cried, crossing herself as the horse
thundered through the valley into the hills.

In the small wing of a canyon they rested under the great branches
of a hospitable oak.

"Our first home," he said.

They did not ask what would come on the morrow. They listened to a love call of quail. "They, too, are happy, Gervasio," said María from her bed of ferns.

Gun in hand, all night Gervasio sat at her side watching for prowling wild animals.

A wood dove woke María. Day fell on the facets of her gold crucifix, and before the crucifix they vowed afresh their love. María intoned:

> *Sinners at dawn*
> *From the heavens above*
> *People all regions.*
> *Gladly, we too, sing—*

"Not so loud, *querida,*" cautioned Gervasio. "Hunters—" But she could not be restrained.

> *Come, oh, sinners,*
> *Come, and we will sing*
> *Tender hymns*
> *To our refuge.*

Gervasio's black and white dog welcomed them at their mountain *cabaña*—a two-room pine log cabin with a veranda of young fir branches and rustic furniture upholstered with rawhide. In a niche where Gervasio had placed the statue of the Madonna, María hung her crucifix.

This was their new world: a small gently sloping valley in a cleft of the mountain side, shut in by rocks and fallen trees. Pinnacles above lifted toward the lapis-lazuli sky. Near the cabin was a spring in which Gervasio placed corn, beans, squashes and watercress. Under a pungent laurel tree were flat stones worn hollow—the acorn mill of vanished Indians—where Gervasio ground his corn. He showed her bees he had tamed. In his *milpa* he had pomegranate trees and grapes. Apples, pears, figs and oranges would come later. On the range were his sheep.

"Herds, fruits, flowers, sunshine, mountains, this black and white dog—Gervasio and no Domingo—how can I help being happy?" breathed María.

At the *Rancho Félix* the courtyard chattered when Don Domingo was found bound with his own *reata*. "Doña María gone with Gervasio Alípas!" *"Cristo!" "Madre de Dios!"* "Where are they?"

"May mountain lions eat them!" The maids shivered and envied the lovers' peril as the kitchen clattered on, "Don Domingo is worse than mountain lions."

A very scarecrow of grief, wrath and shame was Don Domingo! Always he had thought himself the essence of the *rancho*. Now he knew that Doña María was the *Rancho Félix!* Without her the house was only a tomb. He rode his ranges trying to ride away from heartbreak, but grief gnawed like a wolf.

On his horse Don Domingo journeyed to Mission San Gabriel. *"Padre* Esténaga, has my wife been here?" he demanded.

"Bless you, no, Don Domingo. Why do you ask?"

"She has gone away with Gervasio Alípas of San Diego."

Padre Esténaga was ill and shattered from the effects of several months' imprisonment by the Indians. "Impossible! The Indians have captured her!"

"Padrecito, no. A week ago at midnight I found them together. I flogged them."

"Misericordia, Don Domingo! Sin cannot be lashed out of human beings!"

"I know. But I was mad. Help me find my wife."

"If she comes to confession?" asked the *Padre*.

"Do not give her absolution until she comes back."

"Don Domingo, we Christians need Christianity."

For one year María confessed her sins only to the figure on the little gold crucifix in her cabin niche. Then one sweltering September day two hunters strayed into the mountain valley. Fear froze the hearts of María and Gervasio. A fortnight later a gaunt black *caballero* rode out of the clearing near the cabin. Hair bristling, the dog barked.

Unarmed, Gervasio sprang upon the sword of Don Domingo, who accused, "You stole her!"

María flew at the stern Don. *"Madre de Dios! You dare!"* Tenderly she bent over the bleeding Gervasio, assisted him back to the cabin and bound up his wounds.

Then she saw before her a new Don Domingo, sobbing, "Forgive me! Poor child, absent from confession for a year! Your soul—"

"Gervasio is my soul!"

"This can't last. You will starve. You and I will go to Mexico City, to Spain. You'll forget—"

"Jamás!"

Don Domingo appealed to Gervasio, "If you love her, send her back! She is young. What can you do for her? Let me take her home. I can't live long—my heart. In a few years she will be a widow."

Gervasio choked out, "María, if you wish—"

"Of what use would be the *Rancho Félix,* without you?"

Reason, threats, bribes—all failed! In the Pueblo of the Angels rode Don Domingo to His Most Illustrious Excellency, the *Alcalde,* Don Manuel Requena, for aid.

"*Señor* Don *Alcalde,* my wife has been carried off to the San Gabriel Mountains. She and her lover disgrace the City of the Angels. Will you not aid me in bringing her back to decency?"

Only one year before, the Pueblo of Los Angeles had blossomed into a city. *El Señor* Don *Alcalde* Requena was eager to assert authority. So he sent soldiers carrying his *baton de justicia,* the black silk-tasseled cane with a gold cross. His order was, "Arrest and bring back Doña María del Rosario Villa de Félix."

María forced down aching sobs and swallowed stinging tears when she said *Adiós* to Gervasio. As the *Alcalde's* soldiers dragged her down the mountainside she called back, *"Siempre."*

How would the *Alcalde* punish her? Would he put her in stocks? Would he compel her to sweep the streets like other wantons? Would he place her with hair shorn outside the church near the Plaza, a warning to wayward women?

Los Angeles stared from gray one-story adobe houses bordering the Plaza when Doña María del Rosario Villa de Félix rode through the narrow streets with the *Alcalde's* soldiers.

The Most Illustrious *Alcalde* and Don Domingo displayed their distinguished wisdom for María. They were realists! She must either pass the rest of her life in the *cuartel* with Indians and common criminals, or return to Don Domingo. *Padre* Esténaga of Mission Gabriel came several leagues to give her the alternatives; hell with Gervasio or heaven with Don Domingo.

The earth alone greatly concerned María. There was no hope of seeing Gervasio again at the iron-barred *cuartel*. At the *rancho*, perhaps! So meekly she consented, "Most Illustrious *Señor* Don *Alcalde*, I will go with Don Domingo."

Padre Esténaga thought it a triumph for faith. The Illustrious *Alcalde* thought it a triumph for law and order. Don Domingo thought it a triumph for himself as his steel hand held her in the saddle. But he asked himself, "Is this the bride that I brought on this same silver-mounted saddle from San Gabriel to the Pueblo of the Angels?"

At the entrance to a narrow canyon they passed a row of poplar trees, ghosts of summer. Suddenly a long black serpent squirmed through the air, flung as only Gervasio Alípas could toss a *reata*. Don Domingo struggled—strangled on the ground like one of his own steers at the rodeo! A quick figure darted out of the ravine. Steel flashed! A guttural moan! The knife was buried in the heart of Félix the fortunate!

María crossed herself. *"Ay de mi!* Gervasio, what have vou done?"

"For love of you, María."

"Pray for Domingo. You sent his soul to heaven."

"You are heaven."

Gervasio swiftly dragged the body from her sight, covered the guilt-red ground with dry leaves, hid under the brush all that remained of the proud *caballero*. "There was no other way, beloved."

All that night when the winds swayed the trees in their mountain refuge, or a coyote screeched, or the dog barked, María thought the *Alcalde's* soldiers had come to take them away.

After forty-eight hours the dog gave warning of the approaching *Alcalde's* men. "*Caramba,* María!" cried Gervasio. "Come!"

Into the thicket toward the mountaintop rode Gervasio with María clinging to him, and at their heels raced the *Alcalde's* soldiers, shouting, "Don Domingo's body has been found. Surrender!"

A *reata* swung out over Gervasio's horse—there was a sudden stop! Another *reata* dragged María and Gervasio to the ground. "In the name of His Excellency, the *Alcalde.*"

Gervasio fought. He gave the armed soldiers fierce blows. But he could not beat them off, five to one. He and María were torn apart. Bound with a *reata,* he rode between four guards; she was strapped to the saddle. At a distance followed Gervasio's black and white dog.

From *casa* to *casa* in the City of the Angels sped the tidings. They were coming, Doña María and her monstrous lover! Muttering *Los Angeleños* gathered in the streets threatening to tear them from the horses. Gervasio was put in irons and chained to a log in the old *cuartel.* María was locked in an empty house.

During that stormy night Don Domingo's friends prayed at his side, awed by his tragic entrance into eternity. "Poor Don Domingo!" The next day in the storm Félix the fortunate was carried to his grave.

From the great Don's tomb, women in black mantillas, men in somber serapes and Indians in bright raiment crowded the street and shook the prison doors, roaring, "Death to the murderers! Hang them as the Yankees do!" All night the blood beast raged, rattling the barred windows, flinging itself against the *Alcalde's* dwelling. "Death to the assassins!"

The black and white dog crouched at the door of the old *cuartel,* while *Alcalde* Requena pleaded, "Do not stain Holy Week with blood." But the sacrifice of that other Holy Week was no deterrent. The lovers heard the roar, "Death!"

At Don Juan Temple's residence half a hundred determined men conferred by flickering tallow light—the first Vigilantes of California! "The *Alcalde* will let the guilty lovers escape. Law is dead; no home is safe! Those assassins, Gervasio Alípas and María del Rosario de Félix—that abominable creature who murdered her unfortunate husband to give herself up to her passions!" And at the door of the *Alcalde* the Vigilantes shouted, "Give them to us!"

"*Señores,* it is Holy Week," appealed the *Alcalde.* "Seven days without bloodshed!"

For seven days the Vigilantes played with their victims. Seven days the black and white dog crouched at the door of the *cuartel.*

María sat on the dirt floor of her darkened room with her hands clasped, her head bent and her hair sweeping the earth. She refused food, she prayed to the Mother of men.

Easter, day of hope! But there was no hope for María and Gervasio. The blood beast roared louder! No matter that María and Gervasio were unshriven. The *Alcalde* threatened the Vigilantes. The *Ayuntamiento* pleaded in vain. "Don Domingo must be avenged," shouted the Vigilantes. "Surrender the assassins!"

The *Alcalde* made a last demand, "Law!"

But all was in vain. Men hammered down the doors, and dragged forth Gervasio. He might have escaped—another hour, and he would have filed off his irons! Side by side against a high wall he and María were pinioned. "*Adiós, amore!*" cried Gervasio.

The crowd roared. "Assassins! Fiends! Adulterers!"

"My Gervasio," whispered María, "*gracias a Dios,* I shall not live after you."

Gervasio had not thought that María was to die. He believed she had been brought to the execution for his torture. Tears strangled him as he spoke, "*Señores,* by the blood of Jesus, Doña María is innocent."

"Adulterers!" came the jeers.

"I alone am guilty, *señores.* Doña María—"

They pulled the handkerchief down over Gervasio's eyes. The firing squad crumpled him into a heap. María slumped to the ground with him, crying, "Take me—"

They lifted her up, bound her hands, pinioned her again to the wall, her blood-red jade lips now white. Guitars, serapes, *fandangos,* poppies, lapis-lazuli sky, lion-colored plushy hills, Gervasio—all blurred through her mind as the guns trained on her. Unshriven she died, her hands like crushed lilies on her gold crucifix.

For two hours Gervasio and María lay where they had fallen. Citizens of the City of Los Angeles filed by, but the blood beast no longer growled. Sheep shears in hand, an old woman approached María. "The wicked shall be shorn," she said.

Gervasio's black and white dog sprang forward in protest. The aged *señora* thought that María del Rosario Villa de Félix and Gervasio Alípas were dead, but the dog crouched again by his master and mistress. He knew that they lived!

XII

CALIFORNIA'S WORST GOVERNOR

1836

AFTER Governor Echeandía issued his premature proclamation to the effect that the government had assumed control of California's twenty-one Missions, their bells sounded mournfully. Neophytes refused to work, but the padres *were still maintaining many Indians at the Mission when the order came to banish from California all Spaniards under sixty.*

The Franciscans knew they must go. Padre *Antonio Peyri, who had spent thirty-one years building San Luis Rey, the richest and most prosperous Mission in either North or South America, decided to retire to Spain. When he set sail from San Diego for Mexico on his way to Europe, several hundred Indians from his Mission followed him—swimming toward the* Pocahontas *to receive his blessing.*

Governor Figueroa brought in ten Mexican Franciscans to replace the Spaniards, and he secularized sixteen Missions. No immediate change was made at San Buenaventura, Santa Inés, San Miguel, Santa Clara or San José; but the padres *knew that soon all Missions would be taken out of their hands.*

After the removal of the Franciscans from authority the Missions were directed by unsympathetic and unintelligent politicians. They gave land to the Indians who refused to work it, preferring drink and thievery. The soul of California seemed no more.

Governor Gutiérrez, Figueroa's successor for four months, discovered that California needed more than cold law. Repercussions followed the execution of María del Rosario Villa de Félix and Gervasio Alipas. Rumors came of a San Diego revolution led by the executed man's brother. With relief Gutiérrez received news that Colonel

Mariano Chico, the new governor, was on his way to Monterey. At last, California would have law and peace.

And tranquil security might have come, had not the Governor himself brought the enchanting Señora Cruz from Mexico to California.

DON MARIANO CHICO, "California's worst Governor," a *diputado* from Guanajuago, was a poet-*caballero*, his heart filled with romance and flowers. They inspired not only his lyrics but his life. When named Governor of California to succeed the able Figueroa, he recalled travelers' tales of northern mountain sides covered with poppies gleaming like beaten gold and visible to ships miles out at sea, and of forests of lilies in mighty redwoods existing before the birth of Christ. Thousands of unclassified flowers also allured Don Mariano, each a new treasure to this devotee of botany and beauty.

Although His Excellency's black hair was beginning to gray, and although he had pored so long over poetry that he was bespectacled and pallid, his worshipful soul adored *señoras,* collectively and singly. After decades of marriage his own charming popular wife, Doña Ignacia Alegre, stirred his poetic spirit no more than did a humble wild zinnia in the mountains of Mexico.

When sudden access of power came to Don Mariano his first thought was freedom! At Monterey, on the bay blue as a lupine field in the northern spring, he determined to live for a few years spaciously, rapturously, unrestrained by Doña Ignacia and the unfaltering inspection of political foes.

With casual audacity and suave phrases, Don Mariano prepared his wife for his departure. "Beloved, how much I shall miss you and the children. The adored ones! They must be spared the northern journey and the rude Monterey existence. It is best for you to remain with them at the family estate in Guanajuago." With maternal devotion and wifely amiability Doña Ignacia opened for her husband the door to belated third youth.

And so it happened that on an April day a century ago His Excellency Don Mariano Chico, California's new Governor, impressive in his gorgeous uniform of state, stood on the good ship *Leonor,* receiving Santa Barbara citizens. At his side was *Señora* Cruz. Subtle, but with eyes too bright, skirts too wide and shawl too gay, she glittered like a rope of opals; she gleamed until the *señoras* of the gay Mission Pueblo seemed to crumble into dust before her. Precisely who she was, history fails to record, but that connoisseur of pulchritude, General Mariano Vallejo, wrote that her grace and charm well-nigh caused him to forget his own lovely Doña Francisca at faraway Sonoma in the north. *Señora* Cruz was presented by Governor Chico to Santa Barbara as "my niece."

Bells of the ivory-towered Queen of Missions chimed welcome as the carriage of His Excellency and his niece was drawn by loyal citizens under arches of Santa Barbara's incomparable spring flowers. Both pueblo and Mission were at their most festive. The de la Guerras, Ortegas and Carrillos, *sombrero*-ed and mantilla-ed in red, black and gold were hosts. Flags fluttered—the green, white, and red of Mexico —and at night rockets lighted up the Mission towers. The long low dwelling of Don Carlos Carrillo was occupied by His Excellency and *Señora* Cruz, and so became California's temporary Capitol.

During the festivities came appalling news of recent happenings in Los Angeles—Vigilantes in the City of the Angels had stood those violent lovers Doña María del Rosario Villa de Félix and Gervasio Alípas against a wall and filled them with bullets. To His Excellency Governor Mariano Chico, a California which barbarously executed lovers was no more a land of romance. What sort of province was Alta California where citizens took prisoners from jail and shot them without trial! What were laws for, if they were to be flouted! Where was the chivalry of Mexico and Spain!—where the *caballeros* of California! In his proclamation His Excellency brandished his sword for all lovers from Adam and Eve to María del Rosario Villa de Félix and Gervasio Alípas.

Burdened with misgivings, Don Mariano went northward with *Señora* Cruz, escorted by eighteen soldiers. At the Missions and *ranchos* where they were entertained he fulminated against the Los Angeles Vigilantes. But he never forgot to record in his scholarly notebook the medicinal properties of each California plant and a description of its blossom; for he hoped to find in the north an herb which would be a remedy for all ills.

While the Governor was making his record of plants on the journey, *Señora* Cruz was coquetting with young officers of the company. Until May Day, when the great world of Monterey, led by the temporary Governor Gutiérrez, rode leagues southward to meet His Excellency and his niece!

The Governor gave a poetic address extolling the beauty of the setting, the flowers, the *señoras*. Surrounded by the mighty of the province, in the royal residence, with wine made at Carmel Mission he drank to the glory and prosperity of California. Soon he and his *señora* rode toward Santa Cruz and had a day of love under the great redwood trees. He garlanded her with azaleas.

When *fiestas* and *bailes* were over Don Mariano proved that although he had come from *mañana*-land he was no *mañana* Governor. An early-rising dynamo, he began issuing orders with alarming energy and earnestness. The City of the Angels was his target. Don Abel Stearns, "the rascal," was commanded to appear and explain how he came to be one of the Vigilantes who martyred the lovers, María del Rosario Villa de Félix and Gervasio Alípas. His Excellency even dispatched the former Acting-Governor Gutiérrez with one hundred men southward to suppress "crime" at Los Angeles. But to his indignation Gutiérrez wrote from the City of the Angels that rightthinking, substantial citizens sustained the Vigilantes' acts.

"*Caramba!*"—was that law and order? So southward Governor Chico himself went to Los Angeles.

With Jovian attitude he confronted the Vigilantes and ordered many arrests. Who had ever heard of execution for the sin of passion? Who had ever heard of sending the unshriven into the Unknown? The *señora* might have been innocent! Did the Vigilantes never think of their mothers and sisters? Many of the Vigilantes were foreigners—he would deport them, would hang every Vigilante to a flagstaff, would restore order if he had to execute half of Los Angeles! Humble *Angeleños* thrilled to the Governor's strong words, but articulate *Angeleños* supported the Vigilantes. The Governor was compelled to recede from his position and, for sake of fortifying his own political security, to begin issuing pardons. For while he was fulminating against the Los Angeles Vigilantes, news crashed into California from the remote province of Guanajuago—*Señora* Cruz was not Governor Chico's niece!

His Excellency soon found himself endowed with all the vices and minus all virtues. No wonder he had defended the evil María and Gervasio! What was his own private life? On his journey northward Mission Santa Barbara's hospitable bells were ominously silent.

As he proceeded toward Mission Santa Inés His Excellency's reception was even more wintry. No Indian runners greeted the Governor with welcoming messages. When his carriage appeared at the Mission the brothers, *Padres* Jimeno, were dining, and they casually continued their repast, asking His Excellency to be seated in the ante-kitchen where he was finally offered food. Indignantly he drove on with *Señora* Cruz to the half-deserted Mission Purísima, where he rejoiced in the wildflowers.

As yet Mission Santa Inés had not been secularized, but within a week after Governor Chico's return to Monterey his obedient legislature voted to seize the Mission. To President Durán, His Excellency complained of the treatment accorded him at Santa Inés. With Franciscan austerity the *Padre* President asked what His Excellency meant by leaving his wife in Mexico and bringing *Señora* Cruz to California! How dared he convert the Governor's palace at Monterey into a seraglio! No wonder he had defended the Los Angeles criminals!

"Banish *Padre* Narciso Durán from California," commanded the Governor.

Now the *Padre* President was Santa Barbara's most beloved citizen, and when he was about to take leave of the Queen of the Missions, the *Barbareños* rose in wrathful revolt. Women refused to permit him to go aboard the ship. So he remained at Santa Barbara, and the pueblo seethed against the Governor.

Back at Monterey His Excellency found himself bedeviled by a whirlwind passion that was in the end to pick him up and sweep him out of California. *Señora* Cruz became a friend of scandalous Doña Ildefonsa Herrera, whose lover, Don José Maria Castanares, was suddenly accused by his wife, Doña Ana Castanares, of trying to poison her. Upon this charge, Herrera had his wife Doña Ildefonsa and Castanares arrested for adultery. Castanares was placed in jail and Doña Ildefonsa was restrained in a private house.

Here then, at the capital, the Governor found a situation similar to that of the lovers of Los Angeles, and once again became the poet-caballero. On his birthday he took a step to save the Monterey lovers.

It was a gala occasion. Montereyans were celebrating His Excellency's natal day. In order to accommodate both mighty and lowly, the largest hall in the Presidio buildings had been decorated for the entertainment, and traveling players and acrobats from Mexico engaged. Boxes had been arranged for government and city dignitaries, and the Governor's box had the place of honor. Would His Excellency have the good taste to request *Señora* Cruz not to appear?

The *sala* was crowded—it was the first entertainment since the Governor's return, and the first since Monterey's scandal had broken. China silk dresses, embroidered Manila shawls, Spanish mantillas, bright *rebozos,* and high shell combs were on display. Fans fluttered, and there was gay chatter as gowns and shawls were inspected. All awaited the Governor. He did not arrive and guitars and violins were played to fill the pause.

At last in glittering uniform His Excellency came. At his side was smiling, lithe *Señora* Cruz in black, an orange Manila shawl over her shoulders, and a high carved comb from Madrid in her hair. Accompanying her, with unconquerable insolence, was Doña Ildefonsa, accused with Castanares of trying to poison his wife.

This *señora* in red was supposedly under arrest in a private house, but here she suddenly appeared in the Governor's box as his guest! At first Monterey was shocked to silence, then murmurs arose. Propriety demanded that the Governor show sufficient respect for California not to appear in public with *Señora* Cruz, but he had come not only with her but also with Doña Ildefonsa—a woman accused of murder! It was his arrival with these two ogresses that gave Don Mariano Chico the title of "California's worst Governor."

Deeply affronted, *Señora* Estrada, wife of *Alcalde* Ramón Estrada, sniffed, picked up her skirts, left the *Alcalde's* box across the aisle from the Governor's, and led other equally indignant *señoras* from the hall.

Alcalde Estrada himself escorted his family to their dwelling, but he brought back from his jail cell the other principal in the adultery case. Castanares, seated in the *Alcalde's* box, carried on a smiling pantomime conversation with Doña Ildefonsa only a few feet away.

Furiously Governor Chico demanded of the *Alcalde,* "Señor, why did you bring this prisoner here?"

More furiously the *Alcalde* replied, "Why did you bring Doña Ildefonsa and *Señora* Cruz here?"

Upon this the Governor's birthday celebration was transformed into an armed fray. The players gave no performance. A few loyalists supported His Excellency, but most of the guests declared for the *Alcalde.* After giving his final order to the *Alcalde,* "Return that prisoner to jail—at once," the Governor sought refuge at the *palacio.*

But the *Alcalde* defied him; he took Castanares to his own dwelling and gave him sanctuary.

Then the Governor sent an aide to Estrada, with the word, "*Señor Alcalde,* apologize."

"Never, *Señor* Governor!" was the *Alcalde's* reply.

This defiance transformed the Governor into a frowning, formidable man of action. That night with Captain Agustin Zamorano, the garrison commander, and a squad of armed men, he surged into the Estrada dwelling, where the *Alcalde* and his friends were seated with Castanares, writing a protest against His Excellency.

"Surrender the prisoner, *Señor Alcalde!*" commanded the Governor with an exaggerated, sweeping gesture.

"I regret, Your Excellency. I decline."

No longer was Chico the *caballero*-poet and lover of flowers. With his own hands he dragged Castanares out of the house and turned him over to a soldier. "Lock him up!"

At the *palacio* the Governor found *Señora* Cruz in tears. "Why did we ever come to California? Why did we think we could be free at Monterey? Are lovers ever free?" she wept.

"These barbarous *vaqueros* shall not send us away," declared the Governor.

His Excellency felt as if he were Napoleon putting down revolt. With Captain Zamorano and his soldiers he rode to the *Alcalde's* residence and unceremoniously surrounded it. Within was assembled a group of prominent Montereyans including Don Juan Bautista Alvarado, a future Governor of California.

"You are suspended, *Señor Alcalde*," decreed the Governor.

Alcalde Estrada was the voice of Monterey. "Your Excellency, our citizens will no longer submit to your rule."

Governor Chico remembered that several of his predecessors had been expelled from California, but he was not to be intimidated by an insignificant Monterey official. "Your duties are ended, *Señor Alcalde*," was his final word.

Furious horsemen clanked through Monterey and to neighboring ranches. *Señora* Cruz felt the storm of revolt.

"Mariano, beloved, these people frighten me." In tears she pleaded, "Give up!"

"Never, *carita*. I am Governor of California."

Suddenly there was loud rapping at the *palacio* door. The Governor heard roaring, angry voices. He boldly opened to a sinister group of a hundred men.

"California is for Californians," said their spokesman. "We demand that you leave."

"*Señores,* you are in rebellion. I am California. My troops are arriving from San Diego. You shall suffer the fate of traitors."

Boldly he closed the door, and forthwith, northward to General Mariano Vallejo at Sonoma, rode the Governor's swiftest horsemen, with the message: "Send troops immediately to protect Governor Chico at Monterey!"

But Vallejo had his own perils—Indian uprisings. Besides, his nephew Don Juan Bautista Alvarado wished to be Governor! He replied that he could not send aid.

Then messengers pounded down the Royal Road to San Diego— "Send troops to guard His Excellency at Monterey!" But no soldiers appeared, and only eight men were left to guard Chico.

It was rumored that *rancheros* were to take him prisoner, that *Señora* Cruz was to be seized! Anything might happen in barbarous California where lovers like Maria del Rosario Villa de Félix and Gervasio Alípas were shot unshriven! Shivering with fear, *Señora* Cruz rushed across the courtyard and flung herself upon her knees before the Virgin in the Royal Chapel. So long as she claimed that sanctuary, traitorous Montereyans would not dare touch her.

Only His Excellency could prevail upon her to return to the *palacio*. The *Clementine* was leaving that afternoon for Mexico. "I have no personal fear, *carita,*" said he, "but it is not fair to keep you in this anxious state. We will return to civilization."

So it came that, after only three months' rule, "California's worst Governor" calmly entered his carriage with *Señora* Cruz and drove to the beach with their portmanteaus. Agape, the people of Monterey watched His Excellency and *Señora* Cruz enter the small boat to be rowed to the *Clementine*. The Governor's sole gesture of farewell to Monterey was his embrace of an aged Indian woman on the beach with the words, "Of all the men in this country thou art the best!"

Governor Chico carried with him from California a large collection of wildflowers and herbs. He thought he had found a panacea for all human ills—save unhappiness.

When the *Clementine,* on its southward voyage, touched at Santa Barbara, the Governor made an effort to land at this port where lately he had been so sumptuously entertained. But he was prevented by the inhabitants. Even the Indians shouted, "Rascal!"

"I will come back," declared the Governor, "and subdue California if it takes five thousand men."

"Insolent Nero!" jeered *Barbareños.*

"But California's worst Governor" never returned. His third youth was ended. He resumed his stable domestic life with Doña Ignacia Alegre and their children. Later he became Governor of the State of Aguas Calientes. "Traitors!" he called the inhabitants of Alta California when he made speeches in Mexico.

But he wrote much poetry about the California wildflowers!

The Governor even left behind him a dictionary of the language of flowers: "*Yerba buena,* I wish to be useful; white Indian cress [nasturtium], I wish to be a nun; red Indian cress, my heart is dripping blood; tuberose, I wait for thee; red rose, thou art the queen of thy sex; white rose, thou art the queen of purity; passion flower, hatred and rancor; hundred leaves, I am dying for thee; turnsol, I cannot bear the sight of thee; dahlia, I love only thee in this world; jasmine, thou art a coquette; red pink, I am justified in feeling jealous; hortensia, I wish to marry thee; violet, modesty; geranium, I will always love thee; the winter gillyflower, I sigh for thee; evergreen, my love will be eternal."

XIII

CALIFORNIA'S FIRST PRINCESS

1840

"CALIFORNIA for Californians!" became at this time the battle-cry of twenty-seven-year-old Don Juan Bautista Alvarado, a son of the soil. Charming, dissolute, a singer, he read all the books banned by the padres *at Monterey, and he spoke English so well that he was popular with foreigners, ever increasing in number.*

Alvarado drove out Governor Nicolás Gutiérrez and proclaimed himself California's ruler. Historians declare that he had more executive ability and intelligence than any three of his contemporaries. At any rate, Alvarado could not be suppressed, and so, in 1836, he was appointed Governor of California.

For six years he ruled. During this time the Mission bells were muted, the Mission ranchos were distributed among private owners, and most of the padres *departed—Padre Sarria died of starvation while saying Mass at Mission Soledad. Alvarado had been charged with looting the Mission for his personal aggrandizement.*

When he was thirty the Governor announced he would marry Señorita Martina Castro, the Star of the North, daughter of Don Francisco Castro of the Rancho San Pablo on San Francisco Bay. Already he had several natural children, and there was little surprise when he did not present himself for his marriage ceremony at Mission Santa Clara. Some said that he was detained by his Monterey inamorata. Others declared that he was kept away by drink to which he had succumbed. But he maintained that he had been engaged in important conference with La Place, the French traveler. He sent his brother-in-law as his substitute at the wedding, with rings to be used during the ceremony made of California gold—ten years before the great gold discovery! Strangely enough the Governor's marriage was happy, and rose petals were strewn all the way from his dwelling to the Presidio chapel at Monterey when his first legitimate child was baptized.

Alvarado's right arm was his uncle, General Mariano Vallejo, military commander at Sonoma, the last and most northern California Mission, Solano. Here Vallejo lived with his wife, Francisca Benicia Carrillo, another granddaughter of that bewitching widow, Mariá Arballo de Gutiérrez of the Anza expedition. Vallejo dwelt in state— he had forty servants for his family. He maintained a small army which he drilled daily as warning to the Russians at Fort Ross, distant one day's ride, to approach no nearer San Francisco Bay. He kept thousands of Indians in subjection, among them Chief Solano, who ruled the Suisunes, Totaytos, Yolos and Chuructas between Sonoma and San Francisco.

But even the armed force of General Vallejo could not control the savage love of Chief Solano when he beheld California's first princess, the fabulous Princess Helena.

BEFORE Princess Helena Gagarin came to Fort Ross a long century ago, California had been her magic dream. Its realization began on her wedding day when she became the wife of Baron Alexander Rotchef, poet and traveler, in the little chapel on the Gagarin estate in Russia. Czar Nicholas I, the blunt, bearded soldier-Emperor of all the Russias, distinguished his godchild's wedding by his presence. With true Romanoff munificence, His Majesty had spread out diamonds, emeralds and rubies on a table in the dark ancient hall of Prince Paul Pavlovich Gagarin's dwelling.

"My dear," said the Czar to the hoydenish bride, "will you decide which jewels you prefer? Rubies, perhaps?—the wine of life?"

For a moment intent on the jewels flashing in the candlelight, Princess Helena suddenly lifted her rumpled blonde head and smiled into the experienced worldly face of the august Czar, majestic in his flashing uniform.

"Your Majesty, they are magnificent! A thousand thanks! But they are too splendid. May I have what I most desire?"

"Choose, Helena," replied the imperial ruler whose Empress bore the same name, Helena.

"Instead of giving me jewels," ventured the bride, "will Your Majesty send my husband to govern Fort Ross in California?"

"California!" echoed the Czar, astounded. "Our little colony among the savages of North America?"

"If Your Majesty will be so gracious."

Concern darkened the Emperor's eyes. "On your wedding day you would send your husband to the world's end? You make yourself a widow?"

Involuntarily her fingers contracted over the heavy white satin of her trailing gown. "No, Your Majesty, I also wish to go."

Just like Peter the Great, Empress Anne, Catherine II, Czar Paul, and Czar Alexander, Emperor Nicholas envisioned the Russian Bear rumbling down the Pacific Coast to Mexico, but to Princess Helena he exclaimed, "California! It is fantastic, child! Only naked Indians, a few Franciscan missionaries, and a company of our seal hunters live there."

A fitful beauty, suddenly Helena's hair became as alive as her smiling lips. "Kotzebue, Chamisso, Langsdorff—they write of the flowers, the great trees, the eternal sunshine! It must be idyllic."

The Czar placed his right hand gently on Helena's wrist; with his left hand he touched the shoulder of the slim red-bearded bridegroom. "Rotchef, can you not persuade Helena that California is no place for a civilized woman?"

But Rotchef, the dreamer, supported his wife. "Your Majesty, both Helena and I wish to go to California on our wedding journey."

"Dear, daring young friends, even Franciscan missionaries have been killed in California. Thousands of savages—"

"Langsdorff wrote that the Indians were handsome, wonderful creatures."

The Czar's voice overrode her words. "Indians are Indians."

"There must be some civilized white people, Your Majesty," insisted the daring young Princess, throwing him a posy of smiles. "Poor Rezanov found a lovely *señorita* in California. May not Alexander and I go, Your Majesty?" Rotchef's eyes followed those of his wife in entreaty.

"My friends, not one of my commandants has risked his wife in California. Russians at Fort Ross are convicts or half-breeds—lawless seal hunters. No Russian lady has entered the territory."

"Perhaps a Russian lady would improve them," ventured Helena.

"Are you really serious?"

"We have spoken of little else for months, Your Majesty," she replied.

The Czar was pensive. "Youth! Fatuous! So it seems to me."

But Rotchef returned, "Is not California's Fort Ross protected by Russian guns? Mexico is only a young republic. Helena and I wish to serve. If Your Majesty will graciously permit us to make the effort, perhaps before we return our eagle will fly over California."

Pleasure lighted the Czar's eyes. "I realize, Rotchef, that courage like yours has made Russia's greatness. If you will accept the responsibility of risking Helena—"

The intrepid young daughter of Prince Paul Pavlovich Gagarin spoke quickly, "Your Majesty, whatever happens Alexander and I will be together."

"My valiant friends, the blessings of Russia go with you," said the Czar warmly. In delight Princess Helena and her husband knelt before their Emperor and kissed his hand.

Helena Gagarin's request for the gift of a wedding journey from Russia to California had been inspired by Court Chamberlain Rezanov's venture. In 1806, to save starving Sitka, he had defied Spanish guns and entered the port of San Francisco. There he became betrothed to Concepción Argüello, and on his return journey to Russia he died in Siberia. Following Rezanov's last suggestion, Ivan Kuskov had boldly landed colonists at Bodega Bay, California, and for a few tools and baubles he bought of the Indians a tract of land that established Russia's claim to Northern California. Here he erected a formidable fortress and raised the Imperial standard.

So at Fort Ross near Bodega Bay Princess Helena and Baron Alexander Rotchef arrived on the completion of their months-long wedding journey. Over Siberia, braving wild seas to Sitka, they had come. Thence they ventured to California in the crazy tub *Constantine* which finally anchored not far from the high tableland crowned by Fort Ross.

Chapel bells chimed, sea gulls screamed and sea lions on the rocks barked in salute. Proud tears misted Helena Gagarin's eyes as she beheld the royal double-eagled flag flying from the log fortress. Looking up at the stockade on the stark, sienna-hued cliff, she said, "It is all just as picturesque as Kotzebue and Langsdorff wrote—only more beautiful."

Aleuts rowed the new Commandant and his wife to the landing. There they were greeted by their nearest neighbor in California, Don Gorgy Tschernikh, and a group of his friends. Indian children presented Princess Helena with fern-festooned baskets of azaleas and rhododendrons. From these blossoms Helena drew the breath of the forest on the mountain rampart encircling the fort. Their fragrance was as incense that made her dizzy. She laughed her pleasure. "I knew I should love California!"

Swiftly she clambered up the precipice. Soldiers stood at attention as the Commandant and his wife passed through the iron-gated entrance of the high redwood stockade and disappeared with their friends into the spacious red-carpeted dwelling.

Tall candles in *torchères* lighted up portraits of the Czar, the Great Catherine, the First Peter. Wide hospitable chairs and settees, a piano heaped with music, a long dining table, dogs, cats, California goldfinches trilling in gay cages, and a friendly group of serving people constituted the Rotchefs' welcome home. Again and again Don Gorgy drank their health in Mission brandy and wine; until at last, expanding under the glow of spirits, the Californian Russians disclosed news that so far had been withheld.

"Toward San Francisco Bay, only a few leagues away, Solano, chief of the Suisunes, has risen. General Vallejo of Sonoma Mission has gone to meet him. Solano fights with flint daggers, lances, and arrows, all poisoned."

Rotchef tried to silence Don Gorgy. "Of course Vallejo will defeat the Indians."

"He has only a small force."

"He needs but a small force; he is a white man. He fights with the white man's weapons."

"And what will happen," asked Helena anxiously, "if General Vallejo loses?"

"Solano ties his conquered enemies to trees and shoots arrows through them. He is chief of the Suisunes, Topaytos, Yolos and Chuructas. He stole one of his wives, Isidora, from the Chuructas and made her give up worshiping the white-feathered god Puís. He made himself chief of the Topaytos. Indians and white men tremble at his approach—all except General Vallejo of Sonoma. He declares he will conquer Solano."

"But if he can't?" insisted Helena.

"Then Solano will lead his four tribes north. He says it is time for the white man to leave California."

The great drama of peril thrilled Helena. "I adore my new home. Nothing like this happens in Russia—dull, stupid life."

"Helena, my empress!" said Rotchef, taking his bride's hand. "Now you know how the Romanoffs feel when the peasants rise."

That night the crouching fog foamed in from the sea and enveloped the bluff. Coyote yaps and cougar cries silenced the muttering surf. "Those sounds—are they Indians?" asked Helena, nestling in her husband's arms.

Courage came with the morning sun. In the log chapel with its high beamed ceiling and redwood walls, Russians, Kadiak Indians, Aleuts—many of them convicts from Siberia—knelt while the black-bearded, white-robed priests intoned the thanksgiving liturgy for the safe arrival of the travelers. In prayer they entreated the Almighty to bring peace to California and all shivered at thought of Solano. The gloom in the chapel was not dispersed by the sunshine streaming through the stained glass windows, the first in California.

Watchful sentries paced the ramparts of the fort while their Commandant and his bride inspected their kingdom. Fort Ross was two hundred feet square with two towers in opposite corners, each mounted with six artillery pieces. Other guns were inside the large turreted barracks and the Commandant's house was also protected with artillery. Portholes were everywhere, in the stockade, the bastions, and even the chapel.

"The walls are only a foot thick," said Rotchef, "but let the Indians attack! Even the Mexicans! We have forty-one cannon and a barracks filled with rifles."

"I have no fear of either Mexicans or Indians," said Helena. "We are eight hundred Russians!"

Outside the stockade they watched men catching seals and otter. In the shops Indian women were making waterproof clothing from sea-lion skins and bladders. Small Indian boys were smearing whale oil in the seams and chinks of *bidarkas*. These light skin boats were being placed on a schooner departing for the Farallones—desolate rocky islands thirty miles from the Golden Gate.

Rotchef explained to Helena: "Each Farallone hunter has his sea-lion jacket lashed to a ring around a small opening of his skin boat so that not a drop of water enters, even when waves dash over him. These rocks supply each year thousands of coarse black sealskin and sea-gull eggs for China."

Helena was all excitement. "Let's go to the Farallones!"

"Only if Solano comes!"

The Rotchefs visited warehouses, blacksmith shops, tanneries, flour mills, shipyards where brigs and launches were being constructed by slant-eyed serfs and convicts, to sell to California Missions. On horseback they mounted the forest rampart encircling the fort and from that jagged peak beheld the profile of Mount St. Helena, twenty miles eastward, the highest visible elevation.

"Your own mountain, Helena!" said Rotchef. "A Spanish *padre* named it for your saint. She is also patron saint of the Empress." The spirit of the mountain summoned her. She could hardly turn away. "We must climb St. Helena some day."

Swiftly they descended through the redwood forest singing *The Spirit of the Russian Hunters,* a song they had learned on the *Constantine.*

In her absorbing new life, Helena forgot the alarms of Indian warfare. She gathered peaches from trees brought from San Francisco's Mission Dolores, and plucked grapes from Peruvian vines. She was delighted to learn that gardening could be carried on any time of the year in California. With her own hands she pulverized the soil and sowed the seeds she had brought from Russia. In the evening she entered the house, her arms filled with roses from bushes propagated in the Sandwich Islands. After decorating the table, skin aglow from a day in the open and hair rippled by wind, she gratefully seated herself before venison, sour cream soup and pickled cabbage. Reared in the outdoor life on the great Gagarin estate in Russia, she rejoiced. "This new land with its virgin soil seems free. At heart I am a peasant-pioneer!"

Besides gardening there were household duties and the sick to be visited. Helena was godmother to half the children born at the wilderness fort. The Rotchefs took long rides along the cliff to the Russian ranches southward, and from their nearest neighbor, Don Gorgy Tschernikh, they had ominous news. Solano, Chief Mighty-Arm, was threatening to drive out the Russians. From the land of the Suisunes came his angry roar—"The Russians must go!"

"He blames us for bringing smallpox to California," said Don Gorgy. "He has buried thousands of his followers in trenches in the marshes. Once the Indians burned Sonoma. Near San Diego natives kidnaped two white women and jealous Indian women at the *rancheria* stoned them to death. Solano steals his wives. It has caused many an Indian war. He knows nothing of civilized fighting."

"Is there such a thing?" asked Helena.

"There is fighting more civilized than Solano's warfare."

But Helena was unshaken. "Fear is another kind of death. I'll not die that way." And, determined to banish the memory of Don Gorgy's horrifying recital, she smilingly added, "Let's look at your lovely collection of California insects. What a beautiful butterfly! Won't the museums at home be delighted!"

Before the Rotchefs left Don Gorgy's ranch a messenger rode in from Sonoma with news. "General Vallejo has defeated Solano, has taken him prisoner! With great ceremony at Sonoma he dressed him in Mexican clothes and made him an ally. Solano is now at Sonoma protected by Vallejo. The *padres* compelled him to give up all his wives save one, the Princess Isidora. She is the civilizing influence on Solano. She made him promise that he will never again bind an enemy to a tree and kill him with poisoned arrows."

After their return from this trip to Don Gorgy's ranch, Helena said to Rotchef:

"Wouldn't it be friendly to ride to Mission Sonoma and call on the family of General Vallejo?"

"Perhaps, Helena. But dearest, the situation is delicate. Repeatedly Mexico has ordered Russia out of California. We feign deafness. Let us not disturb the *status quo!*"

Fresh alarm arrived on the wind. Mexican troops were rumored to be on their way from San Francisco to expel the Russians and take over *El Fuerte de los Rusos*. It seemed credible. After Russia had built Fort Ross in California, Spain retaliated by erecting Mission San Rafael. Then the vigorous new republic of Mexico not only established Mission Sonoma but sent General Mariano Guadalupe Vallejo to Pueblo Sonoma with a force of soldiers—a warning to Russia to venture no farther south.

General Vallejo matched Fort Ross's Commandant in energy. When not making Fourth of July addresses to please Yankees at Yerba Buena [San Francisco] on San Francisco Bay, he was laying out Pueblo Sonoma and erecting adobe barracks on Mexico's most northern outpost in California. He fought a hundred Indian battles, and now at last he had made an ally of Solano, Chief Mighty-Arm, ruler of the Suisunes, Topaytos, Yolos, and Chuructas.

One day this same young General Vallejo came riding along the cliff from Sonoma, a California *caballero* in blue and scarlet on his Palomino horse. He led a cavalcade headed by Solano, the great Mighty-Arm before whom all men trembled, and half a hundred Suisun and Napajo Indians—Vallejo's guard. The natives were gaudily uniformed in cape, short jacket, linen cloak, and silver-trimmed boots. In such state Vallejo occasionally appeared at Monterey with Solano's tattooed followers—to remind arrogant Governors that in the north there was a personage to be considered. Ostensibly to pay a visit of hospitality, Vallejo dismounted at Russia's iron gate, and for the first time his penetrating eyes surveyed *El Fuerte de los Rusos*.

At the entrance he was greeted by Commandant Rotchef, no longer the pioneer shipbuilder, rancher, superintendent of eight hundred serfs! His voice, salutation, and clicking heels were stamped with the Romanoff manner. Of the University of Moscow, Rotchef addressed the frontier General in alternate French and Spanish, but conversation continued in the tongue of California. Would it be too much for the *Señor* General to request his native guard not to enter the walls of the fort?

"*Perdón*," replied the General. His smile was disarming. "I had no thought of bringing in my Indians. I permit only thirty to enter Pueblo Sonoma at one time—one hundred women are allowed."

After an inspection tour of fort and shops Vallejo congratulated Rotchef. "Boats, mills, clothing, all in so short a time! I did not think it possible! No *mañana* at Fort Ross! Congratulations! Your work mirrors our own shortcomings, *Señor Comandante*."

Rotchef tried to surpass Vallejo in amiability. "I hear you have made Sonoma most formidable in the short time you have been there, *Señor* General. Will you not come to be presented to my wife?"

"The *Señora Princesa* honors California by her presence," bowed the General. "May I also bring my friend and new ally Solano, Chief Mighty-Arm? He has a feather mantle for the *Señora Princesa*."

"The Princess will be most pleased to have Californian handicraft, *Señor* General."

Vallejo turned to Solano, who towered above them both, as a redwood tree above the oak, and the Indian chief, splendid with bright Spanish serape and silver-trimmed riding boots, obediently followed Vallejo, who conversed with him in the Suisun idiom.

In the Rotchefs' reception room Solano gazed speechless at the radiant Princess from the north, the fairest woman he had ever beheld! In reverential silence he bestowed upon her the long mantle of blue feathers that had taken years to fashion. An enchanted child, the Princess tossed the garment over her shoulders.

"Never have I seen anything so lovely!" she cried. The blue feathers caught and deepened the blue in her eyes. "I will take it back to Russia and give it to the Empress."

"No!" thundered Solano. During the entire conversation between the Rotchefs and Vallejo he sat silent, his dumb admiration beating upon Helena like flame. He scarcely saw the proffered refreshments of cake and the tea she served from the tall shining brass samovar.

"You find Indians trustworthy do you not, *Señor* General?" asked Helena.

"I understand Indians, *Princesa*. I was born in Monterey. I have fought all over California. Solano and I are allies. When the Indians attacked my Suscol ranch we were obliged to kill thirty-five. I'm sorry. Occasionally I've had to discipline Solano—once for kidnaping children and selling them. But since our treaty he has compelled his followers to keep peace with me. He goes to Mass, is named for a saint, and is becoming civilized."

"California travel is not dangerous?" asked Rotchef.

Suddenly Solano gravely decided to accept tea and cake from Helena's hands.

"Danger is relative," answered Vallejo. "I have a guard of thirty or forty Indians." Smilingly he drank another cup of tea. "Solano makes travel in Northern California safe." He turned to Helena. "Sonoma is having a *fiesta* on the feast day of San Francisco Solano—bear and bullfights, *fandangos,* games and races. Will you not honor us by coming?"

Eagerly Helena replied, "Delightful. Without fail we shall appear." But Rotchef was less definite. "We shall try. Our thanks, *Señor* General."

"We shall look forward to the pleasure," said Vallejo. "Don't be nervous about Indians; Solano will send out the command. When you go through the forest, fire guns, and the wild animals will flee."

Several mules laden with furs, Manila shawls, cotton shirts, glass beads, wine, tobacco, Russian embroidery, and other gifts for Mexicans and Indians, composed the Rotchef pack train which set out for Princess Helena's first visit to the California of Spain and Mexico— General Vallejo's Pueblo Sonoma. Helena looked as if she were going to a Russian fair with her muslin smock and gypsy skirt of blue and scarlet. Over her shoulders was blithely slung Solano's blue feather mantle to ward off the chilly fog as they rode merrily along the rust-colored cliff. The men wore wide *sombreros* and a festive blend of Russian and Spanish costumes.

After a night at Don Gorgy's ranch, where they feasted on sweet wild grapes, they set out at dawn to complete the forty-mile ride southeastward. Midday summer sun silenced banter and song. Wearily Helena wondered whether they would ever reach Sonoma. Had they lost their way? Where was the Pueblo? Where the Mission? Gratefully they came upon the grazing Vallejo herds.

And then approached a half-score of horsemen. Exuberantly Helena cried, "Sonoma!" General Vallejo raised his hat in salutation. His stocky brother Salvador, Chief Solano, and some attendants rode forward, and Rotchef and Vallejo embraced. Solano lifted his hand in salutation when Helena offered hers in greeting. There was a blaze in the Indian's black stormy eyes.

Vallejo escorted his Fort Ross guests into the large Pueblo Plaza, where a fifteen-gun salute was fired in honor of the visitors. The important families of the country looked down from the balconied adobe dwellings and barracks festooned with Mexican colors. At the large Vallejo *palacio* lovely Doña Francisca received the Russians with Californian hospitality. After a dinner heavy with spices, Doña Francisca, seated at one of the three pianos in California, sang *La noche está serena* and other songs of the country.

That evening there was a *tertulia* at the Vallejo *palacio,* and for the first time Helena saw the *jota* danced. She learned the *bamba* and *fandango* and sang with the dancers. Like Doña Francisca, Helena wore her long red-gold hair unconfined. The General was so enchanted to see his wife with her sable tresses falling to her knees that he burst forth with Spanish verses he had composed for her when on their honeymoon, Governor Echeandía had ordered him from his bride to war. During the *tertulia* there was a sharp earthquake shock, but dancing went on.

Next day Indian troops paraded in the Plaza. Women soldiers were as numerous as men. "They will go to battle if necessary," proudly boasted the General.

Seated on the cool balcony of the Vallejo dwelling the Russians viewed Indian dances. Suisunes and Cainameros ran foot races. A bear and bullfight followed. And always following Helena was her silent, intent guard Solano, Chief Mighty-Arm.

When the Rotchefs were about to leave for Fort Ross Solano appeared gravely with farewell gifts for Helena—a bead necklace and belt made from shells; a feather crown for her hair, and earrings fashioned from duck beaks, the bone thinned by rubbing with flint and ornamented with feathers.

"My wife, Princess Isidora, wedding dress," explained Solano. "Princess Helena take."

All of them realized that, with royal disregard for both Princess Isidora and Rotchef, Solano was offering himself in marriage to Helena. She found it difficult to restrain laughter, but her gravity matched Solano's when she said,

"Thank you much, Chief Mighty-Arm. It is too beautiful. I will not take Princess Isidora's wedding dress."

When the Rotchefs set out across the hills for Fort Ross, at Vallejo's

behest Solano accompanied them a few leagues, but he offered no
more gifts. When he turned Pueblo-ward he saluted, and there was
a look in his profile of the eagle soaring skyward.

"Wasn't that a glorious *fiesta?*" sang out Helena to Rotchef.

"Fiesta!—that is what Vallejo called it! In reality, it was a military
display, a threat, his own manner of advising Russians to leave
California."

No more did the Rotchefs assist at Sonoma *fiestas.* There was too
much to be done at Fort Ross. Russian farming, however, was a farce,
performed as it was with California Indians and with the worst of
incompetent laborers—natives from Alaska, where tilling the soil was
unknown. Shipbuilding was a failure. Fewer sea-gull eggs, seals and
otter were obtained from the rocky Farallones. Fort Ross was becoming a costly burden to Russia, and Rotchef conceded the possibility of
selling the fort.

Helena, however, felt she could not leave California until she had
climbed the mountain bearing her name. Its summit was a mighty
magnet, ever charming and drawing her. Often she rode to the peak
of the jagged redwood forest and looked off to the east on St. Helena,
aquiver with the brightness of day. It seemed to weave vapors, wisp
after wisp, floating into the blue.

"We must climb Mount St. Helena, Alexander," declared the Princess. But Rotchef was occupied with harvesting, launching ships, super-
vising factories and shops.

At the close of one dusty summer, some visiting Russian scientists
rowed up from San Francisco to Fort Ross, with the intention of
ascending Mount St. Helena on a collectors' excursion. With the
Rotchefs and their neighbor Don Gorgy, the travelers rode over the
trail. They splashed across bright lowland streams, traversed thickets
of redwood, maple, buckeye, madrono and manzanita. Merrily they
fired guns to frighten away bear, panther, antelope, and elk large as
horses. Up the gigantic cairn of quartz and cinnabar they scrambled.

Halfway in the ascent live rock was left behind. Mount St. Helena,
they saw, consisted of six mighty, domed ash heaps. Its upper half

was a compound of gray-brown dead fragments of pumice, tufa, lava and obsidian. Centuries before it had showered its valleys with ashes and rocks, petrifying forests. The horses' feet slipped in the ashy earth, and the animals panted with their riders. After achieving one elevation another loomed. Would the climb never end? But they dared the northern-most peak and, after another stupendous effort, they reached the summit—the first white people to scale Mount St. Helena!

Despite fatigue Helena gave a shout of joy. "What a struggle! But this outlook is worth it. New life, another world."

They gazed off on the Pacific. North and south mountain peaks loomed. In the east their neighbor was the Sierra. From a tufa bluff they beheld a precipice sheer for half a mile.

Rotchef said, "Do not look down. Look up!" He had raised the Russian flag. "Long live the Emperor of all the Russias!" they shouted. To a mass of tufa rock was affixed a copper plate inscribed with their names, the date, and ST. HELENA. After luncheon Helena slept in the sunshine, her face fanned by breezes from the distant Pacific.

All the way down the mountainside the scientists like gleeful boys caught new specimens of butterflies and beetles, exclaiming as if they had found Queen Califía's golden treasure. On the forested lesser heights Helena dismounted to admire blossoming lilies. Half in reproach to the avid scientists she said, "I'll not gather them. Leave the blossoms in their own home. Don't shorten their lives."

She removed her shoes and romped across creeks; she swam her horse over the swirling Russian River. Where the trail turned toward Don Gorgy's ranch the travelers built a campfire and supped on dried venison, brown bread and onions. The men were singing lustily under the trees when suddenly they heard sounds in the forest. Immediately they fired guns. The sounds neared. More guns were discharged. It was not elk, antelope or panther. Gaudily appareled horsemen rode forward—General Vallejo's guard led by Solano, Chief Mighty-Arm! Doubtless Vallejo was approaching, and waving welcome, the Rotchefs hastened to greet the Chief.

But what a different Solano! Swiftly *reatas* whirred. Rotchef and the scientists were bound, and fastened, white and trembling, against tree trunks. A strange jest it seemed at first. Only Helena was unmanacled and Solano's red-brown hands seized her.

"Where is General Vallejo?" she stammered in Spanish. Teeth chattering she repeated, "The General—where?"

"General white chief—Sonoma," explained Solano. "Russian white chief too many. Solano want Russian wife."

Helena recalled that Solano had kidnaped Indian children as well as his own wife, and the Emperor's warning on her wedding day echoed in her ears. It was her own willful fault!

"Poor Alexander," she moaned. "Beloved, forgive me. Why did I come? This awful California!"

Rotchef, resigned, looked at his wife in pity. "Be brave, Helena! Our deaths will be avenged. Russia will take California from Mexico."

"Why did Kotzebue and other liars write such books?" She sank upon her knees in prayer. "Alexander, beloved, forgive!" Desperately she appealed to Solano, "I'll give you anything, if you save my husband."

"Two white chiefs too many," replied Solano stonily, making ready to twang his arrows.

Just then new sounds came through the forest. Bear, panther, cougar—any wild animal would have been welcome to Helena! She hoped she would be devoured before being possessed by this murderous chieftain Solano. But instead of forest animals, General Vallejo rode forward, escorted by soldiers in blue and red.

"Traitor!" screamed Helena.

"Your pardon a thousand times, *Señora Princesa*," cried Vallejo, "I don't blame you for calling it a trap." He took her hand and freed her from the Indian chieftain. Then he turned sternly to Solano. "Unbind those *señores*, my friends. Solano, you shall be flogged."

"*Perdón, Señor* General. Solano like white wife—" Contritely he freed the Russians.

"*Señora Princesa*, forgive this poor barbarian Solano! When he heard you had gone to climb Mount St. Helena his wife Isidora came to me sobbing. She said he was going to put her away and make you his wife. Thank the Mother of God I arrived in time." Helena wept hysterically as she clasped her husband's neck. "*Señora*, you have a fatal name! I thought I could trust Solano, but no man can be trusted with a woman."

Solano interrupted, "*Señor* General, heart sorry. Like white wife, red hair."

"Silence!" shouted the General. "You shall go to the guardhouse."

"You are our saviour, *Señor* General," said Rotchef. "Will you not accompany us to Fort Ross?"

"I beg," added Helena.

"*Amigos*, I'd gladly escort you," replied Vallejo, "but I must return to Sonoma. Those horse-eating Moquelumne Indians are threatening an outbreak. I'll appear at Fort Ross as soon as possible."

"Bless you. Come soon," entreated Helena. "I shall never feel safe there again."

"You're as safe as my life," assured Vallejo. "If you don't trust me, trust God."

Soon General Vallejo appeared at Fort Ross. His Indian guard had been displaced by his brother Don Salvador and Mexican soldiers. They presented the Rotchefs with Sonoma's most richly ornamented saddles and baskets. The Commandant informed Vallejo that he was planning to sell Fort Ross.

"We shall deeply regret your departure," replied the General. "I will confer with the Governor. Perhaps California will buy the fort."

After the visitors departed Rotchef said to his wife, "I will burn Fort Ross before I sell to Mexico."

Later on, the Swiss pioneer, Colonel John A. Sutter, bought the Russian establishment. With the new owner Rotchef drank to the health of the Emperor of all the Russias. Then Princess Helena and her husband departed from Fort Ross, taking with them only the chapel chimes and the sacred pictures. After twenty-nine years, Russian occupation of California was abandoned. In mid-winter of 1841 the Rotchefs sailed on the leaky old *Constantine* through the Golden Gate for ungenial, rainy Sitka. As the mainland disappeared from view Helena sighed, "California was a great adventure, but Russia is home." California has not forgotten Princess Helena. Her name is still a legend. It is generally believed that Mount St. Helena was named for her. And the Vallejo family cherish a case of silver she sent to the General in memory of her rescue.

Solano also is remembered. One of California's counties bears his name. At Fairfield where he is supposed to have died he stands, twelve feet high in bronze, looking out on the land of the Suisunes, still Mighty-Arm, Sum-Yet-Ho.

Not far from him rests the tall Princess Isidora buried in her bridal dress of a belt and necklace of beads made from shells, a feather crown on her head, in her ears rings wrought from duck beaks and decorated with feathers—all precious to the woman of the Chuructas because they were the gifts of Chief Mighty-Arm when he carried her off from her tribe, declared war against them, and made her his Princess Solano.

XIV

REED OF '46

1846

WHEN Jedediah Smith and his troopers made the pioneer way over the Sierra in 1826, Californians realized that the mountains were no longer a barrier against the East. In 1830 Kit Carson followed Smith, to dally with romance at Mission San José. The Tennessean, Captain Joe Walker, came with his trappers in 1833 and gave his name to Walker Pass. In 1842 arrived John C. Frémont, the Pathfinder, with his buckskin-clad crew, and gave the Golden Gate its name. His important geographical observations and descriptions of California's flowers, climate and beauty aroused the interest of the East. At that time a Spanish rancho could be purchased for a pittance and a promise.

Adventurous Easterners eagerly read of the alluring Pacific Coast, and in 1841 the Captain Bartleson party of thirty-two persons lumbered across the plains. In 1844 the intrepid Murphy caravan came overland, led by Captain Elisha Stevens.

With so many Americans arriving, and with competition for possession of California keen between England, France and the United States, it was not strange that Captain Thomas Ap Catesby Jones, commanding the Pacific squadron, from mistaken information should have raised the Stars and Stripes over Monterey for a day in 1842. The flag was promptly lowered, with apologies to Mexico.

Governor Alvarado was so friendly to newcomers that in 1842 he was displaced by Governor Manuel Micheltorena, who was sent from Mexico with a force of four hundred cholos [criminals] to rid California by force of foreigners who were increasing over-rapidly. The cholos, however, held a fiesta of crime, and they as well as the Gov-

169

ernor were driven out by rebels led by Pio Pico and José Castro.
Pico then became Governor, with Castro commanding the troops.
Monterey was restored to Mexico, but many Americans crowding
into California envisioned their flag always flying. More of them
came each year.

Among them was James Frazier Reed of Springfield, Illinois, who
had read what Frémont and other explorers had written. When he
was banished from the starving Donner party, California-bound, he re-
vealed to what heroic heights a man can rise for those he loves.

ON the California trail James Frazier Reed found himself with a hunting knife dripping crimson in his hand. At his feet was his fellow argonaut John Snyder. "Murderer!" snarled Reed's companions. Can they mean me? he thought. Have I done this thing? Why am I here at Gravelly Ford surrounded by friends suddenly turned into a threatening mob?

Reed was a Methodist leader, an important business man from Springfield, Illinois. Only a few months before he and Abraham Lincoln, his friend and messmate of the Black Hawk War, had prepared to leave for California together. In Springfield Lawyer Lincoln lived only a few blocks from the Reeds. Often he would drop into their house, stand by the sideboard drinking cider, munching apples, eating Mrs. Reed's cookies. Lincoln was excited by reports written of the Pacific Coast. "California and Oregon are wonderful. Spanish grants are only eight cents an acre in California. Their trees make ours look like weeds. And Oregon—"

"Too much rain in Oregon, Abe," replied Reed. "California is the place for Margaret's health—flowers and sunshine all the year."

"A man could be a man out there."

Lincoln became more and more immersed in Illinois politics, but he was enthralled by Reed's preparations for travel. His lanky frame thrilled to adventure as, over a period of two years, he saw Reed assembling cloth-covered wagons—prairie schooners. There was no better equipped caravan; furniture, farming implements, seeds, dried fruit, silks, flannels and furs. Even beads, necklaces, toys, rings and mirrors were brought to propitiate the Indians. Eight cows would supply milk and butter.

When the caravan set out for California business in Springfield paused. At the head was Reed, stalwart and soldierly, on Glaucus, his proud saddle horse, followed by fifty-two hounds. Margaret Reed, his wife, in Shaker bonnet, linsey dress and heelless laced shoes, sat in the comfortable schooner holding her baby Tommy. At her side was chubby four-year-old Jimmy. Looking up at her adoringly was her little black and white dog, Cash. Brown-eyed Martha, nine, occupied much space on the next seat with her dolls—parting gifts from her friends. Virginia, twelve, waved to her envious friends from her pony Billy. The procession was lengthened by the schooners and stock of George and Jacob Donner and their friends and other well-to-do neighbors.

Friends on horseback and in wagons joined the caravan. Farewells took so long that the party did not get out of town until late. Abraham Lincoln gave Reed the last handshake. "If California is what they say, I'll be with you soon. Good luck, Jim."

That night the Reeds camped on the site of the present Illinois State House. Supper was a picnic around a huge bonfire. The Reeds' Springfield friends spent the last evening with the emigrants. They brought fiddles and danced. At dawn Reed's bugle sounded its "Rat-ta-ta," calling the hounds together. After breakfast came the command, "Chain up!"

At last they were off for California. Women in the canvas-covered wagons sewed, mended, knit or pieced quilts while they chattered. Children played with their new toys. When the excitement came of halting and cooking meals, the children waded or swam in rivers or creeks. They were gypsying with every comfort.

After a merry month they reached Independence, Missouri. This was the meeting-place of overland caravans. It was like a fair, with tents and wagons, horses and cattle. Merchants and emigrants bartered in the streets with Indian and Spanish traders from New Mexico.

After one day at Independence the Reed party joined the overland caravan, a moving village of two thousand emigrants with hundreds of mules, oxen and horses. Happy with hope they went toward the unknown West.

Before the caravan set out the American Tract Society had sent them pamphlets to distribute among Indians. Huge, brown, naked Kansas braves, feathers in ears and noses, met the travelers. They were of magnificent stature, lords of the plains. In return for tracts they gave the pioneers their choicest food—cakes made of grasshoppers and berries. At night the emigrants moved their wagons together in a circle for safety.

With dawn the captain's bugle summoned the wagons to fall into position, and again the caravan was under way. Only the bellowing cattle seemed to question why they were going and to protest against always being driven westward. Over the prairies they went, through black buffalo herds following the Kansas Indian trail. Their fuel was "buffalo chips."

On log rafts they crossed the Big Blue River. Often storms turned the sky black, lashing the travelers with terrific blasts—thunder made the dogs skulk under wagons. Safely the caravan came through the prairie country to Fort Laramie for the Fourth of July celebration. Indians were feasting with whites whose Sioux wives were gorgeous in creamy doeskin costumes gaudily trimmed with beads. The Indians, smeared with war paint, armed with hunting knives, bows and arrows, were moving about excitedly. They were preparing for war with the Crows and Snakes, but the emigrants made an early morning start and escaped hostilities.

Mid-July saw the caravan broken into factions. At Little Sandy River a messenger on horseback delivered a letter from Lansford W. Hastings, explorer and author of a book of travel on the Pacific Coast. His message to the California emigrants was: "Take the Hastings Cutoff. Save four hundred miles of travel by following the new road. I will meet you at Fort Bridger and be your guide." The route Hastings suggested is now that of the Southern Pacific Railroad.

The Reeds and Donners, with a group of eager travelers, numbering in all eighty-seven persons, voted to take the Hastings Cutoff, the southwest trail to California; the others followed the old route toward Fort Hall. George Donner was elected captain of the new caravan, and in high spirits the party went forward.

At Fort Bridger, disappointment! Hastings had promised to guide them through the cutoff, but he had gone ahead. His message to the emigrants, left with an agent, was, "Follow directly after me."

The caravan headed for Great Salt Lake. The trail was level and open; water, wood, game and pasture were plentiful. The Reeds and Donners congratulated themselves on their foresight in taking the new route.

At Weber River they found another message from Hastings fastened to a stick driven into the ground. "Change your course." The directions were so vague that Reed said,

"We need a guide, or we'll get into fearful difficulties. I'll ride after Hastings. He must return and lead us or give clearer instructions."

At Great Salt Lake Reed overtook Hastings, who was now conducting another party. The explorer offered little satisfaction. "My first duty is to this caravan, but I will show you the way." And from a high peak Hastings indicated the route, Reed carefully setting down his directions.

Back at camp after an eight days' absence, Reed turned the caravan over the new trail. For three weeks they struggled down a narrow ravine, building roads, chopping through thickets of timber, only to find themselves blocked by a steep mountain. Eight yoke of cattle were required to drag each wagon to the summit. After wasting twenty days they reached Great Salt Lake. Twenty days—the difference between life and death!

They set out across eighty miles of white-hot alkaline plain. Two days and nights they struggled. One by one even the hounds limped farther and farther back into the thirsty desert. Reed would not leave them to be eaten by buzzards; he stopped and buried them where they died. Only seven survived the crossing. Sadly Reed left his favorite horse Glaucus under a mound of sand.

Alone he rode over the desert seeking water. Caravan oxen staggered trying to pull the wagons. Tortured with thirst some horses and cattle lay down in the sand to die; others fled madly over the white waves of salt and sand. In the heat the desert seemed to quiver in agony, taunting the emigrants with mirages of palm-bordered lakes. The drivers unhitched the oxen and removed their yokes, hoping instinct would lead them to water. Suddenly smelling the distant water, the animals fled. Now Reed had only one cow.

That night he and his wife walked till dawn carrying their youngest children to a water hole. Virginia and Martha dragged along. Finally all sank exhausted to the ground. For a week they camped at the water hole, but they could find no oxen. The animals were never heard of again.

After Reed and his men abandoned hope of finding the cattle they buried in the sand one of the wagon beds filled with their most precious possessions. Little Martha begged, "Ma, let me take my dolly to California."

"All you can carry is your little self," replied Margaret Reed, "we must walk."

Weeping, Martha said good-by to her largest doll and buried it in the grave with the other family treasures. But in the ashes she found a wooden jointed doll no larger than a clothespin, with painted face and a knob of wooden hair at the back of its head. A scrap of white muslin with a girdle of pink tape dressed the dolly. This treasure Martha hid in the lining of her dress.

Before the caravan went forward Reed divided several hundred pounds of dried beef among the company. A few of the most necessary things were carried in one wagon. Members of the company lent Reed an ox which he harnessed with a cow to his wagon.

Early snow fell—the first of the winter. Delay meant starvation. Again the Reeds set out for California, all on foot but the baby. In

MR. AND MRS. JAMES FRAZIER REED.

MARTHA JANE REED.

MARTHA JANE REED'S DOLL.

THE DONNER MONUMENT AT DONNER LAKE.

Margaret Reed's carpetbag was the Black Hawk War muster-roll bearing the names of Abraham Lincoln and James Reed, a silk shawl, a silver soup ladle, and Reed's Masonic emblems. Martha's secret, her doll, was hidden in her dress. Little black and white Cash trotted after them worriedly.

Again snow fell. Without food they could not cross the mountains. Charles Stanton and William McCutcheon volunteered to fetch supplies from Sutter's Fort in California. Would it be too late?

Loss of cattle, food scarcity, anxiety concerning Indian attacks and delays, had set the nerves of the company on edge. At night each family kept its separate campfire. On the fifth day of October, 1846, the Reeds reached Gravelly Ford, and Reed left the caravan to hunt game.

At the base of a steep hill the wagons halted. They changed position daily so that each might lead. On this steep, rough, sandy hill each had to pull up the other's wagon. Milton Elliot was driving the Reed wagon, fourth in line. John Snyder believed his oxen could make the grade unaided.

"John, yoke the teams together for the upward pull," Milton Elliot said.

"My oxen can pull the wagon alone," declared Snyder, beating the animals. They strained and tugged. When they paused for breath the heavy wagon dragged them back.

"They can't make it on a slippery trail," said Milton.

Snyder rapped, "Don't interfere!" With the lead-loaded end of his whip he struck the oxen over their heads and, half insane with fury, drove them to their knees.

At this moment Reed came riding back from his hunt. He saw the sides of the oxen throbbing over their pounding hearts.

"Hold, John!" he called. "The oxen can't pull the wagon alone! Let Milton double up our team with yours!"

"Damn you—keep out! Mind your own business!" Furiously he beat the heads of the fallen oxen.

"Don't!" commanded Reed, "you're killing them!"

Little Martha clutched her father's hand. Reed seized Snyder's hand as it was descending with a heavy goad.

"Stop!" Snyder snarled at Reed.

"Wait till we get to the top of the hill," said Reed. "We'll settle the matter then."

Snyder brought the heavy whipstock crashing down upon Reed's head. "We'll settle it now!"

"Hold, John, hold!" commanded Reed, staggering under the heavy blow. He crumpled to his knees.

Martha flung her arms about her father. "Pa, Pa!" she cried. Margaret Reed sprang to the aid of her husband and Snyder struck her over the head as he had struck the oxen.

On the instant, Reed drove his hunting knife into Snyder's heart. "Forgive me, John," he moaned in agonizing regret.

Faint with death, Snyder replied, "Forgive me, Jim! I was to blame."

Reed offered his wagon boards for Snyder's coffin but the glowering caravan declined the gift. They forgot that Reed had divided his dried meat among them, that he had risked his life seeking water for them in the desert. They remembered only that John Snyder was murdered!

Quickly a caravan council was held from which the Reeds were barred. Margaret Reed and the children alone gathered around the husband and father to await the council's decision. They saw a wagon tongue hoisted into the air in sinister silence, and Reed recognized his own gallows! Mounting a stump he drew his pistol. "Come and take me!"

Muttering threats the council began to disperse, and Milton Elliot entered Reed's tent. "I'm sorry, Mr. Reed. Leave quickly! Save your own life!"

"I'll not go," replied Reed. "My wife and children shall not be unprotected."

Milton Elliot went back to the council and returned with their final decision. "It's too bad, Mr. Reed. They say you must leave the company alone."

Reed insisted, "My family will not be safe in the hands of such people."

"Go," begged Margaret Reed. "Go, husband, they will kill you if you stay! Bring us help from California."

"Wife, how can you get along—alone?" asked Reed.

"I'll take care of Mrs. Reed," promised Milton Elliot, the driver. Reed and Milton shook hands in silent compact. Then the driver brought another verdict from the camp judges. "Mr. Reed, they say you must leave without food or even a gun."

After a silent farewell to his family Reed rode westward unarmed, on Virginia's pony Billy. But in the night Milton Elliot and Virginia stole after the exile, gave him a gun and a few crackers and once more said good-by.

Choking down tears Margaret Reed and her children tramped behind the caravan, anxiously watching for traces of the outcast. Sometimes they found a message left in a cleft stick or other trail fashion. They came upon ashes of campfires where game had been cooked; these camping places of the dear outcast were hallowed ground. At least, he was still alive! Margaret Reed tried to walk in his footsteps, and continued the struggle. She carried her heavy pack of blankets forward on the trail, left them and returned to carry Baby Tommy to the blankets. So they dragged along making six miles a day. Sheltered Margaret Reed had become a pioneer!

But a day came when she saw no more ashes, found no cheering messages. The children continued to question, "Where is Pa?" Her courage was nearly spent, but she said, "God will lead us to Pa."

"I don't see God," protested Jimmy. "When can we say, 'Now I lay me down to sleep'?" And as they trudged over the harsh trail, Margaret Reed and the children murmured, "Our Father who art in Heaven, lead us to Pa."

Finally all had to walk. Some carried packages. They lived on starvation rations. The cattle could not find fodder. Many animals died of hunger; an Indian shot others at night. The oxen could hardly draw the wagons.

Two weeks after Reed's banishment the caravan was at the present site of Wadsworth, Nevada, starving. They could go no farther. But suddenly a message came from welcoming California. Stanton returned with mules laden with flour and dried beef—a gift from Captain Sutter of Sutter's Fort. The travelers were heartened, and Margaret Reed said, "Children, we'll get over the mountain before the winter storms." Already dark clouds hung over the high crest.

Stanton and his Indians took Mrs. Reed and her children behind them on their horses. There were eighty-one in the party—including thirty children and seven nursing babies. Steadily the emigrants climbed. Darker, deeper, more ominous were the clouds on the Sierra peak.

Margaret Reed and her children had dreamed of California as a paradise. At Prosser Lake, three miles below Truckee, they woke in their blankets to find themselves caged in snow five feet deep—snow that shut out all hope! Fear-maddened, the travelers were already divided by difficulties. But at what is now called Donner Lake, then known as Truckee, they united in one effort—to cross the mountains.

Ravines were filled with snow and the road could not be found. Animals could not climb the snow-covered rocks. Wagons were abandoned and sank in the snow. Mules and oxen tried to carry packs, but they floundered about seeking the trail, and evening drove the emigrants back to the lake.

They decided then to kill mules and oxen, and to store what meat they could not carry. The mountain must be traversed on foot. Before more snow fell they must reach the summit.

In one hour that night three feet of white death drifted down from the sky and the emigrants were trapped at the lake. Mrs. Reed spread a blanket on the snow under a tree—the bed of the four Reed children. The mother covered them with another blanket and stood beside them shaking snow from the upper covering. She had no cattle to kill for food—all seemed doomed.

Help must come from the outside world. To struggle over the mountain or to die—this was the resolve of the group called the

Forlorn Hope. They took enough food to last six days and on the sixteenth of December they set out on snowshoes with an Indian guide. On the fifth day the leader, Stanton, died. The Forlorn Hope was without food. They drew lots to see which should be killed and eaten so that the others might go on to save themselves and those remaining at Donner Lake.

The most popular man of the party was the unlucky loser! Kill him they could not!

The Indian guide saw them again casting lots. Silently he departed. He was followed, shot and eaten. Then despairing cannabalism began. Human flesh was eaten as the "bread of life," and the survivors staggered onward.

At the lake, Mrs. Reed found shelter for her children in a cabin with the Breens. It had been built in 1844 by some emigrants of the Murphy-Schallenberger party. The Breens had a little dried meat and Patrick Breen said, "Mrs. Reed, you may sleep here on condition that you never watch us eat."

She was fortunate to find this shelter. Most of the party lived in snow houses—the Breen cabin had a rawhide roof. After she and her children had devoured a rawhide rug, they toasted and ate a piece of the roof. Always their thoughts were with the banished husband and father. "Is he starving?" "Is he alive?" "Has he been killed by Indians?"

The Breens were Catholics, the Reeds Methodists. Night after night Catholics and Methodists knelt together and prayed for rescue. Patrick Breen began reading the Thirty Days' Prayer. At night Patty Reed held the pine torch for him.

Even under sixty feet of snow Mrs. Reed did not forget Santa Claus. On Christmas Day she brought forth hidden treasures—tripe from the last ox, a handful of dried apples, a small piece of bacon, a teacup of white beans! Turkey in Springfield had never been so good. It was their last appetizing meal.

They ate their shoelaces. Only one small piece of rawhide was left. One day Margaret Reed announced, "Children, I have a rabbit for you," and each child had a paw. They tried to persuade their mother to eat of the rabbit, but she clung to rawhide. Soon little Cash was missed. "Cash is lost," moaned Tommy. "Ma, where do you suppose he has gone?"

The mother was silent. She knew Cash had lived only for them, and that, had he understood, the faithful dog would have gone happily to death. Cash kept the Reed children alive for five days. Then they went back to rawhide.

With the new year was born the courage of desperation. Margaret Reed and twelve-year-old Virginia determined to cross the mountains with Milton Elliot and a young woman—the Second Forlorn Hope. "Babies," Mrs. Reed explained to the children, "it's the only way to save us all. Mrs. Breen will take care of you." In agony she left her children.

For a week the Second Forlorn Hope struggled over the white steeps while timber wolves shrieked through the pines. The travelers seemed to be hunting down Death in his kingdom, instead of awaiting his approach. Margaret Reed was torn between thought of her children in the cabin and her exiled husband. Virginia's feet were frozen and she could not walk—the travelers were compelled to return to the lake.

The starving babies wept to see their mother. Little Martha had mothered Tommy and Jimmy. Death soon took Milton Elliot, their protector.

Then began the winter's most violent storm. Some went mad; others dying bequeathed themselves to survivors, and begged that their bodies might serve as food. Little flesh remained on the skeleton dead, but their hearts were toasted over fires. Only one ox hide remained as food.

On the nineteenth of February, 1847, a strange distant voice called over the snow, "Mrs. Breen! Oh, Mrs. Reed!" Seven men had struggled over the bloody trail of the Forlorn Hope. The First Relief had come, led by Aquila Glover.

Out of the frozen holes staggered the starving and dying. Food from Sutter's Fort! Bony hands of those who had cursed their Maker for their suffering were now clasped in gratitude. Sunshine had burst through from the smiling valleys below.

But the starving were not permitted to eat all they desired—it would have been fatal. Besides, the rescuers had been able to carry only a small supply of food.

"Hurry, hurry! The strongest must leave," said Glover, the leader.

Margaret Reed and her four children went singing up the trail with eighteen of the strongest. "God will take us to Pa," promised the mother.

"God is slow," complained Martha.

"I guess He is tired," commented weary Jimmy.

"If you keep up, son," promised his mother, "I will give you a pony when we get to California."

"I don't care, Ma. Bury me in the snow," said Jimmy.

At the end of two miles the younger children could walk no farther.

"I'm going back to the cabin," said Margaret Reed.

"No," commanded the leader, "everyone who can walk must leave. Those who go help the others behind. If you go back with the children, what you eat will starve them."

So Martha, Jimmy and Tommy were torn from their mother and carried back to the cabin, while the rescuers and the rescued went swiftly forward on snowshoes, only to be confronted by new catastrophe. Glover looked at the trees where he had hidden his food supply. "Gone! Catamounts have eaten it!"

Margaret Reed thought that God had failed them, but in a few hours her faith returned. Voices were heard below. More men were coming with food. One was James Frazier Reed, leader of the Second Relief, and, after months of separation, starvation and suffering, husband and wife were once again in each other's arms.

"Tell me what happened," she pleaded.

"What I suffered was nothing—but you and the children!"

"Tell me."

"I had no food for three days. I arrived at Sutter's Fort, my horse half dead. All the men had gone to war with Mexico, but Captain Sutter promised to send you aid. He said no *gringo* was safe at Yerba Buena [San Francisco], so I went to San José, where I was conscripted and fought as a lieutenant in the battle of Santa Clara. After the war was over, I raised a thousand dollars at a Yerba Buena mass meeting to bring you and the others over the mountains. Until I reached Sutter's Fort I didn't know what had happened to you. Thank God, you're alive and we're together! There's real life for us in the California valleys."

But Reed's face went white for thinking of Martha, Jimmy and Tommy, who were still at the lake. Hastily he divided supplies with the First Relief and, leaving his wife behind him, went striding over the snow with the Second Relief to rescue his children and his former companions of the trail.

Little Martha fluttered to him over the snow like a thin bird and fell sobbing into his arms. "Daddy, you and Ma and Virginia, Tommy and Jimmy! We'll all be together, won't we?"

In silence Reed pressed to him the nine-year-old child whom starvation had so stunted that her tiny stature was never to increase by a single inch.

"Murderer! Cain!" had been hissed at Reed when he had been driven away from Gravelly Ford. Now he rescued those who had banished him, bathed and nourished some of those who had denounced him. "Forgive us!" they wept.

When he brought his children safely over the mountains to the Sinclair ranch near Sutter's Fort, where their mother had waited, she reproached herself, "Why did I ever doubt God?"

"If I had not been driven away at Gravelly Ford," said Reed, "we might all have died."

In the peace of the olive orchards and vineyards at ancient Mission San José, under the protection of hospitable *Padre* José Maria Real, the Methodist Reeds found their first California home.

"California has made us happy at last," said Reed to his wife and

children. "Let us never mention anything that happened on the trail."
"I'll never cry again," promised Martha.

For many years the tragedy was not spoken of by the Reeds. Fortune and honor came to them at San José. Streets bear their name. They left their grief behind—to melt with the mountain snows that ran down to redden the roses of the Santa Clara Valley, where they lived.

When she was in her late eighties little Martha Reed Lewis showed me her wooden doll and said, "I've never parted from it. It is all of me." Her children, Martha and Frazier Lewis, still treasure it at Santa Cruz, California.

Winter and summer, Donner Lake is a popular resort. Airplanes look down upon its waters—a silver dimple folded into the mountains. Travelers forget that once human beings lay there dying in brushwood tents under sixty feet of snow. On a tall shaft at the lakeside are engraved the names of these pioneers of 1846, and the words of the late Benjamin Ide Wheeler:

> *Virile to risk and find,*
> *Kindly withal and a ready help*
> *Facing the brunt of fate:*
> *Indomitable—unafraid!*

XV

TAMSEN DONNER
OF THE BISON TRAIL
1846

THOSE who died at Donner Lake in that winter of 1846 and 1847 never knew that while the party was crossing the parched alkali plains and suffering in the Sierras, history was moving forward rapidly in California.

Fighting still went on south of the Rio Grande and overzealous Americans in buckskin, led by Ezekiel Merritt on June 15, 1846, captured the old Mission town of Sonoma, and made General Mariano Vallejo and his friends prisoners. Then from rags and paint they fashioned the Bear Flag bearing the words "California Republic." It was raised upon the Mexican flagstaff and is the state flag of today.

This was before Commodore John D. Sloat, *in command of the* Savannah, Cyane, *and* Levant, *beating up from Mazatlán, Mexico, ran up the flag over the Monterey Custom House on July 7, 1846, while a man-of-war fired a salute of twenty-one guns.*

Consul Thomas Oliver Larkin greeted his countryman Sloat who, upon taking possession of California's capital, announced, "I declare to the inhabitants ...I do not come among them as an enemy....I come as their best friend ...and its peaceful citizens will enjoy the same rights and privileges as those of other territories."

Captain Montgomery landed fifty marines and raised the American flag over the Custom House at Yerba Buena, the chief settlement in California—later to be San Francisco. Flags were sent to Sonoma and Sutter's Fort. Now the thirty-starred flag of the United States

waved over the mountains and plains from the Atlantic to the Pacific.
A new territory rich in gold, fruits and flowers was added to the United
States. None of these happenings affected those who suffered at Don-
ner Lake. One of the Donner party, Tamsen, wife of Captain George
Donner, had her choice—to go down into sunshine and live in the
beauty of California, or to remain in the snow with the man she
loved.

TAMSEN DONNER—of all women who came over the bison trail
in 1846 to California, her name shines starriest! She was New England's flower, born Tamsen Eustis of Newburyport, Massachusetts.
Not beautiful or majestic, only five feet tall, slender, with the face
of an artist, she had gray-blue eyes full of sympathy, understanding,
character. Especially her voice enchanted, her self-giving in conversation, her nice perception of beauty in drawings, in water colors,
and lyrical verse. During an era when higher education was rare, Tamsen studied philosophy, botany and geometry, as well as French. She
dressed with Quaker simplicity, but she betrayed coquetry in her
black silk stockings and gloves.

Tamsen came from New England to Springfield, Illinois, when
it was a village, to teach her brother's children, and she became the
local schoolmistress. Young as she was and weighing less than a hundred pounds, she delighted Springfield by vanquishing the big school
bully with her ferule—it was the winter's sensation.

George Donner, six feet tall, with black eyes and dark hair, fell
under the charm of the little brown-haired teacher with the musical
voice. He was a community leader—was consulted by neighbors about
farm and herd problems. Tamsen was in the mid-twenties and he was
thirty years older, a widower with two daughters; but the sensitive
New England girl was drawn to the man of the Great West. She
became his wife, mother of his half-orphaned daughters with her
own—Frances, Georgia and Eliza Donner.

Springfield neighbors smiled because Tamsen Eustis Donner wrote
poetry and painted pictures instead of immersing herself in farm

and dairy work, but the Donners' spacious dwelling on the knoll became the village social center.

John C. Frémont's books about his travels in Oregon and California woke the interest of the East in the unknown West. Like neighbors, Abraham Lincoln and James Frazier Reed, George Donner and his brother Jacob were allured by fruitful semi-tropical California where Spanish grants might be had for baubles and brocades, and where youth went on forever. When the Donners and the Reeds decided to make the new land their own, Springfield felt real regret. But it chiefly lamented Tamsen's going; she was the town's poet, naturalist, artist—to Springfield she had brought something of Boston, of Emerson, Thoreau and Hawthorne.

Tamsen shared her husband's enthusiasm for the far Pacific country—California. The war with Mexico was imminent and, like other Americans, the Donners believed that soon the United States flag would fly over the new wonderland. Tamsen planned a girls' school in California, and she bought supplies for the seminary she intended to found—books, oil paints and water colors.

As guaranty for his new home George Donner had ten thousand dollars in cash stitched in a quilt, and when the day of departure came he had neglected nothing—there were horses, cows, watch dogs, clothing for Spaniards, trinkets for Indians, and Tamsen's school supplies. Everything seemed propitious for the journey as the three covered wagons moved away from the secure, quaint old house on the hill with its orchards, meadows and corn lands. Now the Donners were to be wanderers on wheels over trackless prairies. Tears stood in Tamsen's eyes, and the little mother held her children's hands tight.

The first night out of Springfield Tamsen's reading society held a farewell meeting around the Donner campfire. The guests remained till midnight and Tamsen promised to relate her experiences in letters to the *Springfield Journal*.

Adventure was life to her—that night she could scarcely sleep. Early next morning they were off for Independence, Missouri, where the Pacific Coast caravan would assemble. On May Day the Donner and Reed children waded in brooks, made mud pies, played Indian and gathered posies. Weary from the jolting of the prairie schooner, Tamsen at last slept in spite of yelping wolves and hooting owls.

When the four hundred and twenty wagons left Independence for California and Oregon, the Donners, along with the other adults, each had a Bible. The children had New Testaments—missionary gifts. Over a trackless valley waving with grass they went toward the Big Blue River, following the Kansas Indian trail made long before by bison.

Tamsen found congenial travelers in the caravan, among them Andrew Grayson, the Audubon of the West. Together they sought geological specimens and collected an herbarium—wild tulips, lark-spur, creeping hollyhocks—and Tamsen made pencil and water-color sketches for a book. Another interesting acquaintance was Edwin Bryant, later the author of *What I Saw in California*. Like Tamsen he was from Massachusetts. Both wrote letters for newspapers and left them along the trail. Their postoffices were the bleaching skulls of animals, or tree trunks. Tamsen's interest expanded to the tribal chiefs they encountered—she entertained them in her tent. George Donner bartered "tobac" with the Indians for "jerked" meat and dried buffalo tongue. The Donners feasted on antelope, deer and buffalo with wild honey from bee trees.

In spite of her Quaker-like clothing, the artist in Tamsen compared her own woolsey dress and sunbonnet with the gaily trimmed raiment of Indian women at Fort Laramie. She wished that New England women were not so greatly restrained in color.

At Fort Bridger Tamsen lost her friends, Grayson and Bryant, who went with the larger part of the caravan on the longer trail. George Donner, leading forty wagons, took the new Hastings Cutoff. At Little Sandy River on July 20, 1846, he was elected Captain.

Already on the trail the afflicted turned to Tamsen. Luke Hal-loran, dying of tuberculosis, was driving in a buggy to California in a desperate effort to save his life. But he grew weaker and weaker, and his illness was intensified by anxieties and by the obstacles on the new trail which delayed the travelers three weeks. Finally he could go no further. He asked Captain Donner if he might ride in their wagon, and there, his head resting on Tamsen's lap and his gold bequeathed to George Donner, he breathed his last. Shrouded in a buffalo robe, he was buried in a grave of salt on the Great Salt Lake shore where they encamped September third. Autumn frosts were already tinting the Wasatch Mountains crimson and gold and their tops were white with snow a month earlier than usual. Ice was in the air.

Again delay came; as they crossed the Great Salt Lake Desert, the Donner party lost many cattle. Swift disaster followed. Captain George Donner, and his brother Jacob, wagons close together, were leading the caravan. They were not present when Reed was driven out to starve in the wilderness because he had killed John Snyder in the quarrel at Gravelly Ford. The man who had offered his wagon tongue as a scaffold for hanging Reed before it was decided to banish him, was Lewis Keseberg, a cultured Prussian, master of four languages, tall, soldier-like with fierce blue eyes, bushy beard, and arrogant manner.

Keseberg seemed to blight all that he touched. His infant son was the first child to succumb to the bitter cold. When the company was obliged to walk in order to quicken the speed of the forty wagons, Keseberg's traveling companion, the aged Hardcoop, a Belgian cutler, could not keep up with the caravan and Keseberg, making no effort to save him, left him behind. Winter threatened from the mountain-top, and he said that the entire forty wagons could not be risked to save one weak aged man.

Up, up, they mounted to the castellated Sierra crest. There at the foot of Fremont Pass, in a grassy meadow valley, lay Truckee Lake [now called Donner Lake], three miles long and half as wide, and here they camped. It was November, and winter suddenly clamped upon them its trap of snow and ice. The Donner party decided to slay all cattle and mules, store the meat for emergency, leave wagons and their contents at the lake, and cross the summit on foot.

More snow came that night, pitiless snow! Purple-black clouds silently dropped snow in long lines, filled ravines and gulches, covered pines and larches with thin feathery plumes, choked the forest, deadened sound and shrouded the Sierra. The Donner party slept on a white beautiful bed of death. For days snow fell in large heavy masses, and they struggled not to be buried alive. Continuously they shoveled snow off their tent; they cut steps through drifts sixty feet high. Nothing but rising coils of smoke showed that there was life in the tent. The Donner party went about in the snow, looking for buried cattle. Gold and silver they had in plenty, but after their meat was exhausted they were obliged to live on beef hides, bark and pine twigs. The children filled tea cups with fallen snow and ate, pretending it was custard.

Babies succumbed first. Jacob Donner died sitting at a table. The George Donners were living on Alder Creek. George injured his hand and it would not heal. Tamsen was without antiseptics, but she bathed the wound many times daily with frayed linen. Even in disaster she held her spirit high. She wrote in her journal; she knitted and sewed. There were no lights in the cabin and the pine-tree tops, rising above the snow, stirred with a homesick murmur; but in the darkness, holding Eliza the youngest in her arms and with Frances and Georgia on either side, she told them tales of Joseph in Egypt, Daniel in the lions' den, Elijah healing the widow's son. Gently she taught them how to meet the world, how to gain friends, and how to be a friend. In later years the Donner girls realized that their mother knew they were living through their final days together.

When the First Relief came Tamsen's stepdaughters went out over the mountains to California. Although the dying bequeathed their bodies to survivors for food, Tamsen would not eat human flesh. Finally the children were too weak to play and the last nourishment that the mother had to offer Frances, Eliza and Georgia was a thin mold of tallow. Each nibbled a little square daily until it became toc small to hold.

Only ten men were in the Second Relief; one of them was their banished companion, James Frazier Reed. He urged Tamsen to save her life and leave with them.

Her husband agreed. "Tamsen, you are young. I've lived sixty-three years. You can do little for me. My life is almost spent. All I could do if I lived, would be to care for you and the children a few more years. You must look after the girls. You'll be carrying on my work. Take them and go!"

Wistfully Tamsen gazed westward where sky and mountain seemed to meet. Beyond lay California's garden with food, safety, and a new life with her children. But she turned her back on it all and said to her husband, "Let the girls go. I'll stay here with you."

"It's suicide," he urged. "Tamsen, it is useless. Go, go!"

But there was no other way for Tamsen Donner as she saw life. "I'll stay here till we are rescued."

"We may never be rescued, Tamsen."

"Then till death parts us."

Tamsen feared that her children could not survive another storm in the tent, and she begged the members of the Second Relief, "Take my little girls to their half-sisters at Sutter's Fort! Here is five hundred dollars in coin!"

"All right, Mrs. Donner," answered the men.

Tamsen gave them the money, combed the children's hair, dressed them in linsey frocks with quilted petticoats, woolen stockings, heavy shoes, knitted hoods and warm cloaks. Frances Donner was seven; Georgia, five; Eliza, four. Tamsen led them to their father's bedside to take leave of him.

"Please come with us," the children begged of their mother.

"I can't, my pets. Your father is lonely and ill and can't travel. I must take care of him. Be brave! We will both follow. God will take care of us all."

Tamsen collected a few keepsakes for the children, held the little girls in her arms, then gave them over with her trust and prayers to the Second Relief, and returned to her husband.

For the first time deprived of her children, Tamsen had no rest.

All that night she looked into the eyes of her babies, pressed them to her heart in final embrace. She was up early, resolved to see the little girls once more, soften their fears and reassure them as to their future. On snowshoes she hastened seven miles to the first camp on the lake. There she found the three girls in a cabin, abandoned by the men she had paid.

Tamsen offered another man, William Eddy, fifteen hundred dollars in silver to save her children's lives. "I'll take them out," promised Eddy, "but I can't carry so much money."

"Swear that you will save them," pleaded Tamsen.

"With my life I swear to take them to safety," answered Eddy. "But save yourself, Mrs. Donner. Your husband has only a few days to live. Come with us."

"I can't leave him to meet death alone."

For the last time she held her clinging children to her heart, and then gave them into Eddy's keeping with her love and prayers. After she saw them depart she went back alone on her snowshoes seven miles to the vigil of starvation at George Donner's side.

Eddy kept faith. He nourished the children on sugar, and he and broad-shouldered John Stark carried them over the trail, up and down, around snowy peaks that seemed ready to give way and crush them. Heroic Stark of the rescue party would stride ahead, two children on his back, deposit them on the trail and return for others too weak to keep up. Over the summit they went, and at Sutter's Fort the little Donner girls reached their half-sisters.

For two weeks Tamsen sat alone in the cabin on Alder Creek at George Donner's side. But always she saw the children struggling over the trail! Were they hungry? Were they cold? Were they again abandoned? No, of that she was certain—they would live! Her prayers would guide their feet to safety. And then she would take up again the task of ministering to her husband's dying needs.

One twilight she performed for him the last service. She shrouded him in a sheet and prepared him for burial. Then, penniless—for after the long death watch she was too weak to carry gold or silver—

she set out alone in the darkness on the desperate trail to go to her children. Divine Power could not fail her! But she wandered from the trail; she fell into a water hole and, wet and icy, went on. At last after seven miles she saw a light, a cabin—Lewis Keseberg's.

The fierce Prussian was happy to hear a human voice.

"Let me rest," she pleaded, "just a minute, Mr. Keseberg. I'm on my way to my children." She sank on the floor, exhausted from hunger and cold.

Keseberg had survived only by eating human flesh. This he offered her but life at such loathsome cost would have been death to Tamsen Eustis of Newburyport, Massachusetts. She declined food; it concerned her little. She hardly touched the coffee Keseberg made to warm her. Frances, Georgia, and especially four-year-old Eliza were in her thoughts.

"Take all the gold in my tent, Mr. Keseberg!" she said. "There is plenty. You may have everything I have. Only help me over the trail —tonight!"

"I can't go in the darkness," replied Keseberg. "We'd be lost. Wait till morning."

"I'll go alone. I can't wait."

"You must, Mrs. Donner. I'll go with you in the morning." He covered her with a feather bed.

Morning for Tamsen Donner was not on this earth—Keseberg found her as cold as the ice in the creek.

In after days, three little barefoot girls walked hither and yon in California saying, "We are children of Mr. and Mrs. George Donner." So enhaloed were they by the heroism of Tamsen Donner that even Indians who did not understand their tongue shared food with them and at all California tables they were welcome.

Keseberg, the fierce Prussian, the so-called evil spirit of the Donner party, remained in his cabin till the Fourth Relief party came, fighting off wolves howling for human flesh. Over the mountains the wolf cries continued. Tamsen Donner's body was never found, and Keseberg was accused of killing and eating her. He was charged with six murders, denounced as a cannibal and threatened with lynching. Wherever he went children threw stones at him. Women shunned him. Houses were closed to him. He acquired several fortunes but they were all swept away. The tragedy of the trail blighted his entire life in California.

In Keseberg's final years little Eliza Donner, by this time wife of Congressman S. O. Houghton, interviewed Keseberg to learn of her mother's last moments. On his knees he swore to the description of Tamsen Donner's death given above. "I tried to help your mother. I don't know what became of her bones. I ate the flesh of those who starved to death because I wanted to live. If it was wrong, I hope God will forgive me. Perhaps it would have been better if I had died. If I did wrong, forgive me, Mrs. Houghton."

And Tamsen Donner's daughter forgave. In the end little Eliza came to believe, as did all the survivors of that winter of '46, that the sufferers on the trail did what they could to save themselves and each other; and that no one was to blame for the misfortunes that overtook the Donner party at Donner Lake.

XVI

DOÑA RAMONA CONQUERS
THE CONQUEROR

1846

JOHN CHARLES FRÉMONT, the Pathfinder, came swash-buckling through California at this time. Fiery, half-French engineer from Savannah, Georgia, and son-in-law of the brilliant Thomas Benton of Missouri, he was the husband of the famous Jessie Benton and a child of fortune.

He had a wide knowledge of botany, and urged on by eagerness for fame and adventure, he set out for the Pacific Coast in 1842 with Kit Carson as guide. He returned to California in 1843-44, and again in 1845, when he played a part in California's history. Many felt that he presented California to the United States.

When he arrived at Monterey in 1846, he had with him sixty followers, including twelve Delaware Indians, all dead shots and armed with pistols and tomahawks. Prefect Manuel Castro considered it a menace to bring sixty strangers into the territory, but Frémont explained that he was sent by his government to discover a practicable route to the Pacific. Nevertheless, General José Castro ordered Frémont and his men out of California.

Defiantly the Pathfinder led his followers to the summit of Gavilan Peak near Mission San Juan Bautista, erected fortifications and raised the flag of the United States. This was in March, before the flag flew over Monterey. Castro began drilling over two hundred men on the plains below Gavilan and Frémont marched to Oregon.

A few days after the Stars and Stripes were raised at Monterey, Frémont and his company appeared there. They were at Mission San

Juan Bautista when information came from the south of the revolt led by José Maria Flores, former secretary of Governor Micheltorena, who was leader of Southern California, which would not remain conquered.

Flores and many other Spanish-Californians had broken parole; one of the most important men among them was Governor Pio Pico's cousin, Don José de Jesus Pico of the Rancho Piedra Blanca *to the north of Mission San Luis Obispo. Frémont, who was longing for conflict, set out to put down the insurrection in the south and to punish the violators of parole. But at San Luis Obispo he met Doña Ramona, she who loved California more than life.*

WHO was Doña Ramona? One of the five Carrillo beauties of San Diego, daughter of Don Joaquin, and true granddaughter of that charming disturber, Doña María Feliciana Arballo de Gutiérrez of the Anza expedition that founded San Francisco in 1776. Her sister Josefa had maddened His Excellency Governor José Echeandía and had excited all California, but she had eloped to South America with Captain Henry Delano Fitch.

What was Doña Ramona like? Her very presence made the air vibrate with romance—the romance of Moorish Spain, Cortés' Mexico, and the California. For her, *caballeros* sang serenades, thinking of magnolias, pomegranates and poppies agleam on the warm red earth. That was Doña Ramona! And the Governor's secretary, knightly young Romualdo Pacheco, immediately fell under her spell.

Their wedding was followed by days of feasting and dancing at San Diego. Then came the long ride to Monterey, half the length of California, with a military escort and a cavalcade of *señores* and *señoritas*.

Such perfection of happiness was not to endure. While Doña Ramona's first child was in her arms, Don Romualdo rode out with his lance at Cahuenga Pass, in the revolution against Victoria, to meet that daredevil horseman Avila of Los Angeles. He never returned to his bride.

California mourned with Doña Ramona, but in a few years the picturesque widow married Captain Juan Wilson, a Scotsman, the greatest landowner in the San Luis Obispo district. Doña Ramona held regal sway at the *Rancho la Cañada de los Osos,* Portolá's old campground near San Luis Obispo, and her *hacienda* became the center of life in Central California.

Four months after the Stars and Stripes floated over Monterey, couriers brought tidings to Doña Ramona that revolt was roaring through the south. Flores, the rebel commander near Los Angeles, appealed to Californians, *"Amigos,* shall we be slaves to *gringos?* No! Die first!"

Like all the Carrillos, Doña Ramona throve in revolution and counter-revolution. *"Viva* Flores!"

"Hush, lass! Treason!" warned Don Juan Wilson. "The American flag is flying over California."

They were at supper in the candlelit *sala.* Doña Ramona took a carving knife from the table, and with an imaginary line slit the air. "That *diablo* Frémont! My knife is in his heart."

Don Juan seized her hand. "Lassie Ramona, you will get us into trouble! Reckless!" She was subdued—for a moment.

But Don José de Jesus Pico, cousin of the former Governor Pico, rode in from his own *Rancho la Piedra Blanca,* as it was called by Cabrillo in 1542—the oldest ranch name in California, now the site of William Randolph Hearst's fabulous San Simeon. Pico gloried in having broken his parole. From ranch to ranch he spurred his dark horse, a California *caballero* in silver-bedecked saddle, stirring sons of California with "Rise against the Americans! They have stolen California!"

"There speaks the Californian!" said Doña Ramona, exuberantly embracing the rebel Pico. "Drive out the *Yanquis!"*

When the Yankee Lieutenant-Colonel John C. Frémont heard of the revolt, he was less than fifty leagues away at Mission San Juan Bautista. The wiry energetic half-Frenchman, with bearded sun-bronzed face, burning eyes and flowing hair—the greatest adventurer of the West—felt that his three expeditions over the Sierras had predestined him as the future Governor of California.

But Pico's revolt at Mission San Luis Obispo threatened Frémont's future, and he determined to crush the rebellion. The Stars and Stripes never retreated! As day broke on the grim thirtieth of November, Frémont and his battalion of four hundred and twenty-eight men were on the march southward from Mission San Juan Bautista. The commander led, wearing buckskin, blue shirt thrown open at the neck and a cotton handkerchief knotted around his brow. Five swarthy Delaware Indians with feathered headdress formed his bodyguard.

Among the motley marchers were Missourians, Kentuckians, Walla Walla Indians, California Indians under Chief Antonio, and Edwin Bryant, future *Alcalde* of San Francisco and author-to-be of *What I Saw in California*. No peacock plumage, no gaudy trappings were theirs; officers and men alike were clad in buckskin, woolen shirts, slouch hats or coonskin caps; at their waists were leather girdles with Bowie knives and pistols; and long heavy rifles were flung across their saddles. Pack mules lengthened the procession, and beeves for slaughter were driven along. There was little gaiety on that march— one battered bugle supplied music.

It was no time for music, but the men went singing *Yankee Doodle* up the San Benito, over the hills to the Salinas and up that valley past Mission San Miguel. The soldiers' blazing campfires at night spread terror. After the marchers plundered the Soberanes' *Rancho Ojitos* and burned the buildings because two of the sons were with the rebels, Doña Ramona again stormed and stamped her foot in fury when the fleeing Soberanes arrived at her home.

South of Mission San Miguel Frémont's battalion came upon Don José de Jesus Pico's servant, Santa Maria, who had been sent to watch for Americans. A spy!—he should be shot! Some officers opposed but the men insisted. The Indian was bound to a tree, and from a near-by *rancho* natives were summoned to witness the execution. The soldiers fired. Santa Maria fell to his knees, so remained several minutes, then silently sank upon the earth. When Indian runners brought news to Doña Ramona of Santa Maria's death she sent a *vaquero* to the Pico ranch urging the family to hasten to her *hacienda* and go southward: for Frémont was coming! At Don Mariano Bonilla's quiet ranch, not far from the Cuesta de Santa Lucia, all the family were taken prisoners—they might warn the countryside of the approaching Americans.

On blistered bare feet Frémont's men struggled through bushy gorges. Thirteen beeves were slaughtered daily. How the men ate! Ten pounds of beef each at the three meals! For nearly a fortnight they had been on the march—no wonder beeves gave out! Frémont commandeered the *rancheros'* cattle until no more were obtainable. But now the Americans were in bear land—they killed twenty-six grizzlies and devoured the meat.

Snow was on the mountaintops, but rains began and no campfire could live in the storm. Frémont's men were in darkness. Horses were mercifully shot. Soldiers waded swollen creeks, then dragged artillery up the Cuesta de Santa Lucia—the grade approaching San Luis Obispo. At last the battalion camped on the mountain overlooking the Mission of Saint Louis. It was December 14, 1846.

The boisterous storm was drenching them, but Frémont gave the command, "Saddle up, men! Surround and take San Luis Obispo! Capture Pico!" and down they rumbled into the old pueblo. In pitchy darkness they saw a distant light, the enemy! They rushed forward. Frémont assembled three hundred men and called, "Charge!"

With Indian war whoops they fell upon the pueblo and dashed through the streets expecting to terrorize the enemy.

Pueblo San Luis Obispo was asleep—even the *Alcalde! Padre* José Miguel Gómez was asleep in his room off the corridor of the missionaries' residence. The few neophytes remaining at the Mission were asleep. Drowsy pueblo inhabitants were startled to find themselves prisoners. All were placed under guard in the adobe buildings surrounding the Mission Plaza.

Pico, where was he? demanded Frémont. The *pueblaños* did not know. Scouts reported that Pico was not at the *Rancho Piedra Blanca.* Some said he had gone southward.

"Ride after Pico!" Frémont commanded. "Capture him! Bring him back!" Fifty of Frémont's best horsemen galloped southward to seize the rebel leader.

In confusion Frémont's battalion quartered themselves in the San Luis Obispo Church—a sad day in the history of the establishment. Not only was a new flag flying over the pueblo but the church, the pride of the community, with its hallowed memories became the conqueror's barracks. Frémont, however, ordered, "Protect the chancel. See that no vestments or sacred images are profaned."

For the first time in nearly a month Frémont's men had shelter. Half-starved, they seized whatever food they could find and gorged themselves sick on meat, *frijoles,* pumpkins and juicy fruits of the *tuna* from the prickly pear that hedged high the Mission garden wall. While rain beat in cataracts upon the old tile roof—the first in California—soldiers played airs on the hand organ they found in the church. Gratefully they stretched out on the hard floor paved with *ladrillos*—large square brick.

Frémont himself did not sleep. Anxiously he paced the corridor, awaiting the return of the soldiers. Don José de Jesus had gone to Los Angeles, they reported. Scouts were hurried there through the rain.

Reluctantly an imprisoned Californian supplied the desired information. Pico was at the *Rancho la Cañada de los Osos,* where intrepid Doña Ramona was giving the Pico family a farewell *tertulia* before they left for Los Angeles. Doña Ramona was a Californian; she could die dancing. On this stormy evening she was dancing defiance to Frémont.

The *hacienda* was festive with toyon berries, candles in tall *torchères,* music of violin and flute. The *señoras* and *señores* were facing each other in the *jota*—the favorite California dance. Doña Ramona's joy-

ous dark presence warmed the room, made the dancers forget the
enshadowing fear of approaching *gringos*. Gaily she led the singers:

> *Que yo soy el necio;*
> *Como si quererte*
> *Fuera necedad.*
> *Pero anda, ingratota,*
> *Que algun dia entre sueño*
> *Tú te acordarás*
> *Que yo fui tu dueño.*

> *I am a fool,*
> *If to love thee*
> *Be folly.*
> *Never mind, ingrate,*
> *Someday, in thy dreams,*
> *Thou wilt remember*
> *That I was thy master.*

All were rollicking through the dance when Frémont's armed horsemen poured through the deep doorways of the *hacienda*—the fifty
men seemed five hundred. *Gringos* had come with grim guns, demanding of white-faced Don José de Jesus Pico, "Come with us to
Lieutenant-Colonel Frémont."

"Frémont—*el diablo!*" moaned *Señora* Pico and fainted.

Doña Ramona exulted in tumult and drama. English she had
learned from her Scotsman husband, and she defied the invaders.
"*Señores*, if you please, leave my house!"

Don Juan Wilson discreetly intervened. "Lass, it is useless. These
men are part of an army. Do not resist."

Don José de Jesus took tragic leave of his wife; then he turned to
Doña Ramona. "You are too kind, my friend," he said. "I must not
embroil you in trouble with the Americans."

"They will kill you, *querido*," wailed *Señora* Pico.

"Gladly I die for California," replied Don José de Jesus. "Be brave, *carita.*" Once more he held his wife to him; then he embraced his weeping children, flung a heavy gay serape over his shoulder, and departed with the soldiers.

Gray of countenance, as Bryant afterwards reported, the prisoner arrived at the Mission. Don José de Jesus had no doubt that he would be shot as his Indian servant had been a few days before while the soldiers were marching into San Luis Obispo. Pico was incarcerated in a room and placed under guard. Food, even water, he refused.

Next day at the council of war the prisoner offered no defense. It was all true! He had violated his parole! He had incited California against foreigners! His apology? He loved California.

"Guilty!" was the council's verdict and solemnly the Judge gave the sentence, "Death!"

Frémont approved, and the prisoner was brought from his room to hear his doom. Doña Ramona learned that, on the following day, as the sun's shadow showed eleven on the dial in the Plaza, he was to be placed against the whipping post and shot in front of the Mission Church.

A pall of gloom glowered over the pueblo. It filled the church of Saint Louis, who had renounced royal honors to become a humble follower of Saint Francis. That evening the bell ringer was about to toll the *campana* at vespers, when a soldier roughly forbade it. The man was so frightened that he dropped dead.

One person alone was not cast down—Doña Ramona! Sleep she scorned. She comforted *Señora* Pico. The children sobbed in her arms. At intervals she knelt before the altar in the *sala*. She sent *vaqueros* in all directions. San Luis Obispo's men were prisoners of Frémont, but she summoned the women.

Quickly they assembled in Doña Ramona's *sala—Señora* Pico and her kinswomen the Villas, the Estradas of the Santa Rosa *Rancho,* the Canets of Morro Bay, the Narvaez and the Avilas. With ghostly faces they came shivering through the storm. It was life or death, they knew; otherwise Doña Ramona would not have sent the messengers. When morning came they sang the hymn to the dawn, and on their knees solemnly invoked the aid of the Highest.

"Now we must all go to the Mission!" declared Doña Ramona.

Señora Pico, arrayed in black, crossed herself as if to fend off evil spirits. "Frémont, *el diablo!* I cannot see my husband shot, Ramona."

"We will save him, *carita!*" replied the unconquerable Doña Ramona.

"Those terrible *gringos!* Ramona, they will kill us! Do you not remember their knives, their guns?"

"Women are stronger than their silly weapons."

"*Dios de mi vida!* It is too much, Ramona."

Placing her hand on the head of her tall, dark young son Romualdo who too often brought back the memory of his gallant father, Doña Ramona said, "Frémont dares not kill women and children."

The storm had quieted, but dark clouds still threatened in the southeast as the women and children rode in the sharp December air over the rough muddy trail from the Ranch of the Bears. Doña Ramona took two of the small Picos on the *anquera* of the saddle; other women rode holding three children. The older boys and girls sat their saddles alone.

Already a company of men in buckskin was drawn up on the Plaza —Pico's executioners. The shadow on the *Padre's* sundial in the Plaza neared the fatal hour of eleven. From his window in the Mission, Frémont was to witness the execution. *Padre* José Miguel Gómez was in the small dark prison room praying for the doomed man. Two sentinels guarded the door.

Suddenly they came—Doña Ramona leading *Señora* Pico, who carried a baby in her arms; the Pico children, and the women of San Luis Obispo! Edwin Bryant described them in *What I Saw in California,* as they charged down the pillared corridor before the missionaries' residence. All were in black, saying their beads; their faces covered with somber *rebozos* to protect them from curious eyes of foreigners—all save Doña Ramona. She walked with uplifted head, exalted as if in prayer! Bryant said that her proud face was too beautiful to be covered. Unannounced and to the amazement of all they swept into the presence of Frémont.

The overwrought commander's glance fell upon Doña Ramona. Something in her air of authority and in the quality of her countenance made him think of his own Jessie Benton Frémont in faraway Missouri. Sobbing *Señora* Pico, the tear-stained children, the women with clicking rosaries, stirred him. Calmly Doña Ramona began:

"*Perdón, Señor Comandante,* of what service can the death of Don José de Jesus be to your great country?"

"*Señora,* Pico has stirred up revolt."

"*Señor Comandante,*" replied Doña Ramona, "Don José de Jesus loves our California as you love your United States. If we had gone over the mountains to conquer your country, a brave man like you would be first to risk life for your native land, just as our friend risked his life for California."

"But I should know, *Señora,* that stirring up revolt would mean death."

Tenderly Doña Ramona held *Señora* Pico's shuddering form. She took the mother's baby in her arms and went on:

"Don José de Jesus did not realize it. He loves this beautiful land. It was in his heart, his blood, to urge the *hijos del país* to make one effort for California."

Frémont tried to remain unshaken. "The court has decided, *Señora.*"

"*Señor Comandante,* you're greater than the court."

"Pico—he is a leader. His example—others will imitate him. The court—"

"There is a higher court, *Señor Comandante.* From the sky He looks down upon us. If you permit our friend to die, you will never be happy."

Frémont opened the door to terminate the interview. "I'm sorry, *Señora;* it is too late."

"Kill Don José de Jesus, *Señor Comandante,* and you kill his wife, all of his little children! Spare their lives!" And *Señora* Pico fell like one dead at Frémont's feet.

The Commander's boast was that he had conquered California without bloodshed, and such was his intention. His dread of drenching the ground with blood, his gallantry, the beautiful Doña Ramona, the sobbing *Señora* Pico, and the sight of the grief-stricken children who recalled his own little girl—all this caused him to turn suddenly to a young officer in the room and say, "Fetch the prisoner here."

Don José de Jesus emerged from his dark small prison, believing that he was saying farewell to Mission San Luis Obispo and to life. He thought he was being summoned to death but, unshaken, he walked with his guard along the corridor, into the presence of the Commander. Amazed, he beheld his own wife and children, Doña Ramona and the other *señoras* of San Luis Obispo.

Frémont gestured toward the window, indicating the troops in the Plaza. Pico had not known they were there and, recognizing his executioners, he bowed his head. Soon he would be in another world.

Then Frémont spoke. "Pico, you were about to die. Thank these *señoras* for saving you."

On his fingers Pico made the sign of the Cross and knelt before the American. "I was about to lose the life God gave me. You have given me another. My new life I devote to you."

Then for the first time, Doña Ramona shed tears; joy brought them, and Frémont rejoiced with her over Pico's reunion with his family.

Most of the officers also were pleased with the mercy shown Pico, though a few were dissatisfied. Why should Don José de Jesus be saved when his Indian servant had been shot! But temporary discontent was subdued by Frémont's order, "Saddle up!"

Don José de Jesus marched away to the south with the Americans and became Frémont's valued, faithful friend. In a fortnight the battalion was occupying the buildings at Mission San Fernando with its beautiful mid-winter roses, its oranges, lemons and olives. Mission wine dispelled the mid-winter chill.

The rebellious California troops were under the leadership of Don Andrés Pico, a cousin of Don José de Jesus. The released prisoner accompanied Frémont to Don Andrés' camp, to dissuade him from futile semi-guerrilla warfare against the United States, and through his efforts revolt in California was ended. Frémont negotiated the treaty of peace in a deserted ranch house near Cahuenga Pass, January 13, 1847. His generous terms to California made him popular in the conquered land, and the people hoped he would be the territory's first Governor.

To this position he was appointed by Captain Robert F. Stockton, but the mirage of power soon vanished. General Stephen W. Kearny arrived at Monterey from Washington—California's duly accredited Governor.

Frémont wished to determine his real status and perhaps placate Kearny. With his usual impetuosity he decided to ride to Monterey. Who would go with him? His newfound friend Don José de Jesus Pico volunteered.

Off they galloped from Los Angeles at daybreak, March 22, 1847. With them rode Frémont's black servant Dodson. Each had three horses with loose mounts driven ahead—when fresh steeds were wanted they were lassoed and saddled. Forward the riders swept— one hundred and twenty miles the first day, one hundred and thirty-five miles the second. Near El Rincon, for fifteen miles they plunged through the surf which mounted almost to the horses' necks—and so on to San Luis Obispo!

Here they were briefly entertained at a *fiesta* arranged by Pico's friends for Frémont. "Now, we are all *Americans, hermanos, amigos,*" said the people of San Luis Obispo. "*Viva los Americanos!*"

With two of Pico's finest horses as gifts Frémont pounded forward. The riders made seventy miles the third day; that night they slept in a canyon on the Salinas, but they were stampeded by prowling bears. Mid-afternoon brought them back to Kearny's headquarters at Monterey. Then, at their highest speed, they dashed back to Los Angeles. In seventy-six riding hours they had covered eight hundred and forty miles, almost the distance between New York and Chicago—one of the famous rides of history! Burnaby's ride to Khiva had been surpassed.

Frémont's visit to Monterey resulted in more conflict. Arrogant officers would concede nothing to the explorer who had played so gallant and notable a part in acquiring California for the United States. Kearny made it clear that he intended to remain Governor. In hot argument Frémont challenged Colonel Richard B. Mason to a duel.

California's conqueror returned to Washington virtually a prisoner. After a long bitter court-martial Frémont was dismissed from the army for insubordination. Immediately President Polk reinstated him, but the hot-headed explorer declined to re-enter the army.

California, however, with its abundance, did not forget Frémont. It tossed into his lap the office of United States Senator. Later he was candidate for President and in 1856 was nearly elected.

Throughout their long interesting lives the Frémonts and Picos remained friends. Whenever General Frémont arrived, San Luis Obispo was always in *fiesta*. Doña Ramona reigned at the *Rancho la Cañada de los Osos*. Knightly Romualdo Pacheco, who rode out to meet Avila with a lance and died in a duel, often returned to her with vivid quality. Her greatest happiness was when she beheld their son, young Romualdo Pacheco, become California's first and only Spanish Governor after the American occupation.

XVII

THE SHERMAN ROSE

1850

ABOUT this time, General William Tecumseh Sherman, who was to march to the sea during the Civil War, marched as a young lieutenant into the romantic story at Monterey, California. He came in 1847 with General Stephen Watts Kearny, California's first resident military-governor. Young Sherman was appointed adjutant general with quarters in the little adobe at the rear of the Thomas O. Larkin house. He held this office all through his stay at Monterey. In 1850 he left for the East with dispatches.

Resigning from the army, he came back in 1853 as partner in the banking business of Lucas, Turner and Company. Later he became superintendent of the Louisiana Military Academy, and president of the St. Louis Street Railway Company. In 1861 he re-entered the military service as Colonel. He is best known for his triumphant and terrible march to the sea and for his aid in winning the Civil War, but he summed it all up with his oft-quoted remark: "War is hell."

Sherman's headquarters in the garden of the Larkin house are of unceasing interest to travelers, and his portrait in the living room of the Sherman Rose house, restored by Mr. Percy Gray, but now owned by Colonel and Mrs. H. A. Schwabe, gives authenticity to one of the unforgettable romances in California's love saga—that of Señorita María Ignacia Bonifacio and the young American officer.

ABOVE Monterey, California's old capital, at the base of the pine-spiked hills, the starry flag flaunted its red, white and blue—colors of the fair conquerors from across the Sierra. The frigates *Savannah, Cyane* and *Levant*, riding at anchor on the larkspur-blue bay, boomed a triumphant salute of twenty-one guns. Even whale spouted spume like geysers in the July sunshine. Rear Admiral Sloat and his officers in fresh blue and gold uniforms waved their caps and cheered. At last, the United States had an unbroken boundary line on the Pacific Ocean from Canada to Mexico!

At sight of the new colors that had been run up on the flag pole over the Custom House, one *señorita*, eyes strong with her own fire and fury, blazed out: "Flag of the barbarians, flag of the Sonoma Bears! *Madre de Dios*—curse it!"

Trembling with rage and grief she gathered up the faded green, white and red flag of Mexico that had drooped sadly to the ground. Amazed American officers saw her clasp the fallen banner as if it were her own flesh and blood. Swiftly she sped down the plank sidewalk of narrow Alvarado Street. Through the arched entrance to a flowering garden behind the high, adobe, tile-topped wall she hurried and burst open the heavy door.

"I've saved our flag, *Mamacita!*" she cried. "One day we'll raise it again over Monterey."

Since dawn Doña Carmen Pinto de Bonifacio and her smaller children had been on their knees in the *sala* of the cool adobe house invoking the Deity and saints against the foe who had raised the American flag over Mexican California.

"The *gringos* have conquered!" moaned the widow, clasping her gnarled brown hands over her withered bosom. "*Ay, triste de mi!* California is lost!"

"*Mamacita,* California will never be conquered."

"*Si, si!* We are aliens in our native land. The *gringos* are strong, without heart. They've driven out Governor Pico and General Castro! They've imprisoned General Vallejo! They will take our land. We shall be peons."

"Those *gringos!*" María Ignacia's eyes darkened. "Their blue uniforms make me hate our lupine, and their gold braid makes me want never to see our poppies, our blessed *dormidera*. I cannot sleep under the *gringo* flag. Always I will sleep under the flag of Mexico."

That very night the girl kept her vow. Her high mahogany bed was overspread with the vanquished flag. Against her tear-stained cheeks she held the faded colors. Others might yield to the conqueror, but her own white room with its shrine to Our Lady still belonged to María Ignacia and to Mexico.

American bands played in the streets. Pleasure-loving Montereyans hummed *Yankee Doodle,* the *Star-Spangled Banner,* and *Home, Sweet Home.* Even cows in the streets stared, and geese babbled excitedly in the gutters.

Nachita was self-exiled in the Bonifacio garden. There she strummed her guitar, touched the strings of her harp and sang ancient songs of Mexico. Head erect, draped with her *rebozo,* she went daily to Mass at the Presidio Chapel where she said her beads and prayed for the destruction of *gringos.*

Others shared her spirit of resistance. Every evening a s. 'eet tenor voice sang under her window, *El corazón del amor palpita....*

In response Nachita lit a candle. She knew what Doña Carmen, her widowed mother, only half suspected—that the singer was Don Pedro Estrada, half-brother of Governor Alvarado.

But evenings came when there was no serenade. Like many other Spanish-Californians, Don Pedro had followed the lodestone of the fabulous mountains where the blue-eyed conquerors had unlocked the great treasure awaiting them. By thousands they were sweeping up California. Even from Mexico surged gold seekers. Save for General Halleck and his officers, the *señoras* and their children, Monterey was deserted.

Magic mounted. Overnight California was admitted to the Union, and Monterey was to dance at a great *tertulia* in celebration. Colton Hall was transformed into a bower of pine branches and flowers. Sixty *señoras* and *señoritas* accepted the inevitable. In fluttering brocade gowns, hair twisted coquettishly to the top of the head with tortoise-shell combs, wearing their most precious necklaces and pearl earrings, from behind waving fans, brown-eyed *señoritas* smiled up at tall, erect American officers, who guided them through the dreamy waltz. Dire mutterings came from throats of *caballeros*.

"Americans," apologized some worldly-wise Montereyans, "come as friends not enemies."

"I will not be dazzled by the very gold the *gringos* stole from us only three years ago," declared María Ignacia Bonifacio. In her garden she still defiantly strummed her guitar and sang California's songs. Another Fourth of July! Flags and quick music! Rockets flared from the Custom House and guns boomed from the new Presidio on the hill. Defiantly Nachita's voice still came from the walled-in Bonifacio garden, not far from the house of Thomas O. Larkin, the headquarters of the military governor.

In secret Montereyans thrilled at Doña María Ignacia's prolonged rebellion, but experienced *Padre* José Maria Real came from the Presidio Chapel to counsel:

"Child, it is useless. Give up. Farsighted Californians have yielded. In the south Don Juan Bandini has given Colonel Frémont his favorite horse. General Vallejo of Sonoma has made peace with the conquerors and has a position with the new government. Who are you, one *señorita,* to resist the great American nation? *Gringos* have come to remain."

"All the more reason why one should be brave, *Padre mio.* Poor California!"

When rockets shot skyward from frigates at anchor, and the American band paraded up and down Alvarado Street playing the national air, Nachita's Mexican flag was flung over the high adobe wall in front of the Bonifacio dwelling, the last defiant gesture of California unconquered! Musicians of the American band paused, conferred, then marched on.

Nachita did not deign even to lift her head to peer over the wall or through the gateway at the men in blue and gold celebrating their national holiday. On this Fourth of July she was busy in her garden setting out a rosebush that she had cherished in an earthen pot.

Already it was putting forth shoots. Although it was summer she determined to plant it. With a trowel she hollowed out a space not far from the fragile pergola leading from the garden entrance to the doorway of the two-story adobe. She was on her knees in a bright-flowered gown, a bandana over her head, and was about to take the rosebush from the pot when there appeared at the garden wall one of the hated blue-eyed conquerors in uniform. She looked up and saw him, tall, straight as the bayonet sheathed at his side, his hand on the flag of Mexico—her beloved, vanquished green, white and red.

"*Señor!*" she commanded. "Do not touch that flag!"

The *Señor* Lieutenant was trying to express himself in a strange tongue. "*Señorita, perdón.*" He removed his cap. "Perhaps you do not understand. Today the United States celebrates independence. Only the red, white and blue should fly."

"So, *Señor*, so!" defied Nachita. At him she hurled the brown jar containing the Castilian rose! With a laugh and the agility of an acrobat he caught the pottery vessel.

"*Gracias, Señorita,*" smiled the young officer. "It is reported that for three years you have flown this flag on your garden wall. The General requested me to say he does not need to remind you that at least it is discourteous for you to raise the Mexican flag on the Fourth of July. The United States is a powerful nation. We do not like to fight women, but—"

"*Señor!*" Nachita's lithe body nearly reached his shoulder as she defied him. "We California women do not shrink from battle."

"Americans admire courage, but the General requests that you cease displaying the Mexican flag on the Fourth of July."

"That flag, *Señor*, is my country. It covers me at night. It will cover me when I die. If you touch that flag, *Señor*, you will think you have laid hands on a cougar's whelp."

The American, who had intelligent, deep eyes, saw that argument with the overwrought girl was unavailing. He glanced at her and then at the Castilian rosebush in his hand.

"I'm afraid you're trying to do a man's work," he said coolly. "We

Americans do not like our women to do that. Won't you let me plant the rosebush?"

"*Gracias,* no, *Señor,*" she replied, attempting to take the shrub.

"Please, *Señorita,*" begged the officer, "with your permission!"

He swept aside her protests as his countrymen had swept aside the small California army. Smilingly he took the trowel from her, in spite of her unwillingness.

"I have planted everything in this garden," she said, "geraniums, fuchsias, rosebushes. I make them grow. I want no one to touch my plants."

On his knees the officer was enlarging the hole in the ground. "And they grow very well. You have the green hand." He pulverized the earth, filled the bottom of the opening with the blackest loam.

"No, no, *Señor* Lieutenant!" protested María Ignacia.

"And now let us water the bush," he insisted.

"That I myself will do," she declared, fetching a gourdful of water from a small low pool.

In spite of Doña María Ignacia's objections, something in the planting of the rosebush had brought them closer together, and the officer went on:

"*Señorita,* will you not reconsider? May I ask you not to affront the Government of the United States by flying the flag of Mexico on our Fourth of July?"

"No one asked you to look at the flag of Mexico, *Señor.* If you do not like our green, white and red, stay on the far side of the mountains. Our countrymen were here long before you came."

"*Señorita,* if all Monterey behaved as you do—"

"California would be free! Take me to prison, *Señor,* if you will. Lock me up with thieves and murderers, but María Ignacia Bonifacio will fly the flag of Mexico!"

The young Lieutenant saluted. "*Señorita,* I am merely delivering my superior's orders. I didn't make this war with Mexico. War is—" As he disappeared through the arched entrance he added, "—hell!"

That night a strange American voice sang in faulty Spanish under

ORIGINAL SHERMAN ROSE HOME AT MONTEREY.

RECONSTRUCTED SHERMAN ROSE ADOBE HOUSE (REAR VIEW).

HEADQUARTERS ADJUTANT-GENERAL (LATER GENERAL) W. T. SHERMAN, 1847-1849, IN THE THOMAS O. LARKIN GARDEN, MONTEREY, CALIFORNIA.

her window. In the darkness Doña María Ignacia thought she saw an erect soldiery figure on a prancing black horse, but she did not light the candle—the customary response to the serenade.

Next day Nachita again brought forth the colors of Mexico and placed them over the arched opening in the adobe wall. No sooner had she finished festooning the entrance with her green, white and red flag than again the American Lieutenant entered. Doña María Ignacia bristled, she thought he had come again to command her to lower the flag.

But military orders were no part of the Lieutenant's visit. "I came to see the rosebush. May I water it?"

She was disarmed. "*Gracias. Muchas gracias, Señor,* but—" Already the determined officer was bringing a gourdful of water from the low fountain and pouring it upon the bush.

"A freshly planted rosebush cannot be watered too often," he casually explained.

Doña María Ignacia was coldly civil. "*Gracias, Señor,* I will be my own gardener."

Daily the Lieutenant returned to water the rosebush. Daily he was compelled to pass under the Mexican flag. Finally, amused, he began saluting the colors over the entrance to the Bonifacio dwelling. One day he said with a smile to Doña María Ignacia,

"What an obstinate little rebel you are, Nachita."

Her glance and her voice warmed as she replied, "How did you know my name?"

"How could I help know it, Doña María Ignacia—defender of Monterey—"

"You never told me your own name, *Señor.*"

"It is only an ugly English-and-Indian name, William Tecumseh Sherman."

That night again came the sound under her window. She recognized the American intonation and foreign construction. But she lighted no candle.

Next day the Lieutenant came twice—to see the rosebush, he said.

In the afternoon for the first time he found no flag over the gateway. His eyes glowed.

"The rosebush is sprouting," he exclaimed. "We are good gardeners, you and I." His glance grew grave. "You will not neglect our rosebush?"

A new wistfulness in his voice caused her to ask quickly, "You're not coming again?"

"I've been ordered to Washington." As he spoke the rosebush seemed to wither, the bright fuchsias and geraniums to fade, and fragrance departed from the garden. "When I come back our bush will be in blossom, I hope. If it is, will you wear the first bloom in your hair?" Heliotrope, jasmine, and orange scented the air as he spoke, "I want you to be my wife."

"*Señor,*" she protested.

Like blue fire the young Lieutenant's eyes burned into her own. "What does it matter, the color of the flag over Monterey, if we both love the same rosebush and the life of which it is the heart?"

"*Señor,* you cannot conquer me."

"You are the conqueror, *Señorita.* I am not ashamed. You made me forget the General's orders to tear down the damn flag of Mexico. I reported to him that if I had to fight a woman because she loved her defeated country, he might have my sword. The General decided that there were some victories the great United States could do without. From the first I've been your prisoner. When I return—"

"*Señor!*"

"Tomorrow I will come—for *Adiós.*"

When Lieutenant Sherman returned he found draped over the arched entrance in the garden wall not the green, white and red of Mexico, but the red, white and blue of the United States. He paused in salute. "Our flag—made of silk. Where did you find it?"

Her reply gave new meaning to their lives. "*Señor,* my William Tecumseh Sherman, my *gringo* with blue eyes, all night I worked making your flag from my silk dresses...."

Nachita saw the Lieutenant's mighty ship sail southward, but the waves lashing its keel had a funereal note; sea gulls cried and pine trees moaned. Her faith was that her Lieutenant would return for the spring blooming of their rosebush, and that when she became his bride at the Presidio Chapel its blossoms would adorn her hair. Spring forgot to bring the Lieutenant with blue eyes back to the Bonifacio adobe, and all the springs that followed also forgot. On prancing horses *caballeros* sang serenades under Nachita's window, but never again did she light the candle. Alone in her room she garlanded her head with roses, waiting for the ship that never arrived.

When she heard that the Lieutenant had taken a wife at Washington, no longer could she endure the color of the flower that she had hoped to wear. Over the rosebush she bent, tempted to cut it down, but such an act seemed butchery. And so, with her own hands, she grafted onto the Castilian bush a branch of the Cloth of Gold.

High and higher mounted the new bush, smothering the Bonifacio adobe with its bloom. Sherman marched to the sea and to glory in the Civil War. Doña María Ignacia's life was closed to all but memory, more beautiful than any substitution of tawdry reality. She still fingered her harp and made filmy drawnwork. In her bed chamber was a camphor wood chest filled with wasp-waisted, full-skirted dresses, with crimson velvets, embroidered Chinese slippers, pearls and filigree from Baja California. Doña María Ignacia's story became the Sherman Rose romance, a part of the life of the old Spanish capital of California.

And so, she still lived when I saw her in the 'nineties, a little birdlike, brown-skinned woman with eyes of fire and glamour under her *rebozo*. She stood in the deep doorway under the rosebush that gilded her house with its garment of bloom—the spirit of romance of Spanish-California about to take flight.

After Doña María Ignacia Bonifacio was no more, Monterey cherished even her silken garments, mantilla, and dainty painted Chinese fan. Today they are in the Custom House Museum. No one questions the truth of the oft-recited romance save some dreary workaday historian with a prosaic passion for facts! The love of Doña María Ignacia and Lieutenant William Tecumseh Sherman, whether truth or legend, is as much a part of the story of California's royal city as is the life of *Padre* Junípero Serra.

Only a few years since a financier bought Doña María Ignacia's adobe house to replace it with a bank. Protesting voices rose not only at Monterey but through Northern California. The banker might as well have purchased Serra's tomb at Carmel for a counting house! What mattered it where a bank stood! The Sherman Rose was romance watered with tears of love, substance of the spirit whereby Monterey lives! Down with the materialist who dared raze the Bonifacio adobe and erect a money changer's mart!

It was a crisis that called for an artist. And he came—Mr. Percy Gray. On Monterey's mesa he built a reproduction of Doña María Ignacia's dwelling. Therein he installed windows, doors, stairway, woodwork, and railing from the Bonifacio adobe. Around his garden he reared a high adobe wall mounted with the same tile that had protected Doña María Ignacia's adobe wall. He transplanted her shrubbery and plants to the mesa garden. The shrine of the lovers was saved and indignant, scandalized Monterey was calmed and consoled.

Already the fragile pergola leading from the garden entrance to the doorway is covered with the Sherman rosebush. In transplanting, the grafted Cloth of Gold died, but the original Castilian root said to have been set out by Doña María Ignacia Bonifacio and William Tecumseh Sherman survived. Each spring it puts forth warm rose Damascene blossoms, a symbol of love imperishable.

XVIII

JUANITA OF DOWNIEVILLE

1851

The cry of gold,
Around the world
It rolled,
And legions of men
All young and bold
Rushed to the Golden State.

SO Joaquin Miller would sing of this discovery of gold in the new territory, California, for which the United States had paid eighteen million dollars to Mexico. Strangely enough, only nine days before the treaty at Guadalupe Hidalgo was signed on February 2, 1848, at the close of the Mexican War, the great gold discovery was made. On January 24, 1848, James W. Marshall, an unlearned wheelwright, found something glittering in the sand of the millrace being made for Captain John A. Sutter in a fork of the American River. "Boys, I believe I've discovered a gold mine," said Marshall to his friends.

At first the San Francisco merchants refused to accept the gleaming metal as gold, even when the Mormon editor, Samuel Brannan, holding a bottle of dust in one hand and swinging his hat with the other, passed along the street shouting, "Gold! Gold! Gold from the American River!"

But when the metal was brought to them by the ton the greatest gold rush of all time was on. Merchants nailed up their doors and set out for Coloma, where gold had been discovered. Towns throughout the territory were depopulated. Only women, and the men in jail, remained at home.

*The world thrilled and the cry became "On to California!" From
Peru, Australia, Manila, China, Japan, Europe, New England, adven-
turers rushed to catch some of the flood from the rivers of gold. The
song of the day was:*

> *"I'll soon be in 'Frisco,*
> *And then I'll look around,*
> *And when I see the gold lumps there*
> *I'll pick 'em off the ground.*
> *I'll scrape the mountains clean, my boys,*
> *I'll drain the rivers dry,*
> *A pocket full of rocks bring home,*
> *Susannah, don't you cry."*

*A man mining with a butcher knife, shovel or shallow pan could
wash out a thousand dollars a day. Indians laughed at the greedy
white men. Twenty-five cents' worth of beautiful beads was in their
opinion ample pay for one hundred dollars in nuggets.*

*Within a few months California's population had increased to one
hundred thousand. Camps were at Jamestown, Sonora, Columbia,
Murphy's Camp, Chinese Camp, Big Oak Flat, Mariposa, Snellings,
Placerville, Marysville, and Downieville on the Yuba River.*

*In this population of men any kind of woman was desirable. At a
miner's ball each woman had twenty partners. Enterprising Mrs.
Eliza Farnham was not only the first woman to drive alone in a
wagon over the Sierra, but she brought to California a number of
respectable women all under twenty-five years of age, each of whom
had contributed two hundred and fifty dollars for her fare. Mrs.
Farnham found them all husbands.*

*Husbands, however, were not for all women. Indian girls were sold
at camps. Kidnaped women were brought from the Marquesas
Islands. From Peru girls came to dance. French women presided at
gambling tables. Señoras and señoritas came from Mexico; but one
of these was to learn the bitter cost of fidelity.*

AT Downieville among the pines and cedars of the towering Sierras, there was Juanita. What was her last name? *Quien sabe?* No one in that boisterous camp knew or cared.

Downieville, more often called The Forks, was then in all its glory. To be sure it was only a camp of tents, log huts and shanties, but it was the county seat of Sierra County. In that winter of 1851, gold was $16 an ounce, and the mines had yielded three millions.

Juanita, just turned twenty, lived with her husband José in a cabin on the edge of the town. He was one of the unremembered many who came from Mexico to seek fortune in the streams of Mexico's alluring daughter, California. American miners were dead set against Mexicans staking off claims and, as many of his country did, José turned to gambling. Juanita kept the place in order.

Miners swarmed about her. Such a smile—gray eyes and dancing teeth that lighted up the camp with enchantment! Miners followed her small feet as she went down the rough main street in her black silk dress widened with crinoline. From camps on the swift-running Yuba they came. Even Mexican women were rare as angels' visits. There were not more than eight on the river.

American women were mostly "Volunteers," girls who had drifted up from San Francisco lured by rich diggings. When they arrived in gaudy raiment, men followed them in swarms from the stage to the Gem or Magnolia saloons. The Volunteers swaggered into the gambling houses, played chuck-a-luck and, drinking and smoking like men, watched fortunes on leather tables vanish, to be rewon and lost again. It was nothing to venture fifty thousand dollars on the flip of a card.

Most decent women kept away from Downieville and other camps. Men were too hungry for the sight of a girl's face. Some walked forty miles to look at a woman. Rough miners held dances around an old bonnet stuck on a May pole, or around a rusty hoop skirt. One man charged a five-dollar admission for his wedding to a plain pioneer girl, and the handsome sum resulting was spent in roistering jollification.

It was not strange that Juanita's rustling skirt vibrated through the great tangled melée at Downieville. For all at the gambling tables she had a smile and a coquettish word—nothing more. She seemed not to belong in the rough shanties with sawdust floors and rawhide chairs, smelling sourly of cheap whisky, *tequila,* and tobacco smoke, or among the long leather tables laden with cards and nuggets.

Juanita was always at José's side, and her love gave dignity to her bearing. At times she was almost afraid of being a woman as she looked at the red- and blue-shirted, bearded miners with broad hats, speaking a strange language. Each day she nestled closer to José, her beloved *hombre.*

In the sparkling morning air Juanita baked bread in the outdoor oven built by José. Her blithe fingers spun out flat *tortillas* for him. Afternoons she made fine embroidery and Mexican drawn work, or sang to her guitar.

Among miners Juanita had only one friend, a physician just out of college, blue-eyed young Charles Aiken with high head, fair hair and sturdy shoulders. He did not work in the camps; he built himself a cabin and hung out his shingle. He knew Latin and Greek. Sometimes he went to Juanita's cabin to speak Spanish with her, aided by a dictionary. Patiently she tried to talk with him in her own tongue, and she did not often smile at his errors. Aiken was different from the others. He did not call her "greaser." A man of books, he planned to study at the University of Mexico.

And so Juanita's life ran on untroubled, with José her husband and her cabin to care for, and with her friend the tall blue-eyed American physician to talk to in Spanish.

Fourth of July came—a great Fourth! Downieville celebrated with parades and bands. Only the preceding year, in September, 1850, California had been admitted into the Union, and on this first Fourth of California's proud statehood, claims were deserted and also the creeks. Gold could wait—three thousand men roared in the streets and saloons! Whisky barrels rolled about the camp. Reeling Americans lost at monte. By noon every man in Downieville was at his drunkest, or well on the way.

Downieville's orator of the day was Colonel John B. Weller, later Governor of California. Refreshments were abundant. What could be more appetizing than pork and beans with tangle-foot whisky in tin cups?

From a platform erected on the south side of the lower Plaza, with a shelter of pine boughs as protection against the July sun, Colonel Weller the spell-binder sonorously spoke of liberty and freedom. "The United States is the greatest country in the world and the most free. California, the youngest State, is the greatest in the Union. And who made it? The miners of California!"

With hats in the air Downieville hurrahed itself hoarse. Jack Cannon, a sailor-goldhunter, yelled louder than all the rest. Scotsman as he was, filled with tangle-foot and under the spell of Colonel Weller's eloquence, he imagined that he had fought with Washington.

That night Cannon improvised his own show. He had lived ten years at Shanghai, and he gave a Chinese play, varying his voice so that he was lover, bride, and bride's father. The crowd applauded. Applause stimulated his exuberance, and mounted on a horse he rode into Craycroft's saloon for Juanita to admire his horsemanship. She was not there. "Let's go down to see Juanita!" he said.

To Juanita's little house he rode with Lawson, his partner. Juanita was alone, her door locked against noisy *Americanos* celebrating liberty. Her fear became terror when she heard Cannon's drunken voice outside the barred door. Then came an arrogant knock. "Who is there, *Señor?*"

"Jack Cannon. Let me come in."

"My husband is not here, *Señor.*"

Juanita flung the entire weight of her body against the door, already locked. Cannon kicked on the door. With one staggering blow the flimsy thing fell in and he stumbled forward. His breath reeking with brandy was a stench in her nostrils. Back against the wall she stood before the towering Scotsman, her face like stone. He was trying to bury his face in her heavy hair. When she felt the touch of his coarse hands, she screamed.

"Come out of here, Jack," snapped Lawson to his partner, and he led the drunken man away with the apology, "I'm sorry, *Señora.*"

"Too damn stuck-up for a greaser," stammered Cannon quickly. "Ought to be proud a white man spoke to her."

Juanita stood trembling, gazing at the shattered door, her only protection gone! Would the day celebrating American independence never end? She shivered in fear of Cannon's return. The streets were filled with drunken miners. Knife in hand she went about her tasks. Never had she so realized the cost of being a woman.

When José came back she sobbed out in his arms the story of the day. He quieted her and rebuilt the door.

Early next morning Jack Cannon was beating upon the door. Later his friend declared that Jack had "washed down in the river," and, sobered, had come to pay for damage done. Juanita began trembling. She was baking *tortillas,* but she seized a knife.

José went to meet Cannon and stood, a hand on each door-post, defending his house. Juanita was at his back. Cannon spoke Spanish. In that language passersby heard him say to Juanita, "What's the matter with you—you whore—"

Juanita plunged the knife into Cannon's heart. With José she fled up the street to Craycroft's saloon. After them crashed the news, "Cannon is dead!"

To the farthest camp up and down the Yuba, sped the words, "A greaser woman killed Jack Cannon!"

Leaving picks and pans, miners hurried into Downieville. The bitter feud that had begun with the conquest of 1846 flared up anew between Mexicans and Americans. "Clean out the greasers! Lynch the greasers!"

The Mexicans fled. There was no jail in Downieville and for safety Juanita was lodged in a log cabin.

Handsome Jack Cannon, roistering Jack Cannon, dead, became Downieville's saint. His body was placed in the largest tent in town.

His only garment was a red shirt with neck folded back revealing the ugly wound in his mighty breast. As Downieville beheld the dead hero "laid out," the camp got drunker and drunker—the usual ending of a funeral or murder.

Juanita heard Downieville's wrath roaring like lava from a volcano. José had begged to remain at her side, but he was flung into a solitary cabin under guard.

From the Fourth of July platform, John Rose of Rose's Bar asked, "What shall we do with this woman?"

"Lynch her! Hang her!"

Still befuddled Downieville felt nobly dispassionate when it agreed on the compromise: "We will give the greaser a fair trial before we hang her!"

On the platform erected for Colonel Weller's speech the trial took place. John Rose of Rose's Bar was judge. William Speare elbowed his way through the crowd demanding, "Let me prosecute the hussy!"

A lawyer from Nevada named Fair who had been campaigning for Weller mounted a whisky barrel and said, "I'll defend the girl. Mob rule—"

Barely had he spoken when a dozen miners kicked his barrel from under him. Fair was booted to the outer circle of the crowd. Bleeding, he fled for his life from Downieville. Colonel Weller himself had no chivalrous word for Juanita. Greasers did not vote, and there were several thousand votes in Downieville.

Lawyer Thayer took the place of Fair as defender. With much emotion he appealed from the platform, "In the name of mothers, sisters, wives, and sweethearts we left behind in the East, I beg you not to shed this woman's blood. As Christians—"

"To hell with Christians!"

Thayer was battered from the platform. Downieville would have no soft stuff. The jury took another look at handsome Jack Cannon in his red shirt. With his mighty chest, arms and great sinewy bare thighs, he seemed a fallen Hercules. With another generous supply of whisky the jury retired to a cabin to deliberate dispassionately on justice.

Those were days when wild bulls and bears fighting in the arena delighted the public—the days of dueling and lynch law. California was ruled by a tyrant—violence—born in the mad craze for gold. After the mocking trial it was inevitable that the Downieville jury should return the verdict, "Juanita must be hanged on Jersey Bridge at four."

"What are they saying?" questioned Juanita anxiously. Someone translated for her. *"Si, si, la corda!"* she replied. "I would rather die than beg my life of such men. Give me the rope."

It was one o'clock. Juanita had three hours to live. She asked whether she might spend them with José. Impossible! Her husband had been jostled, bruised and bleeding, into the hills. But Juanita was allowed to return to her cabin.

There was not much for her to do. She sent her few simple garments and personal belongings to some poor Mexican women. She played a little on the guitar, but music had departed from her listless fingers. Everything looked distorted and faraway—even the pine walls of the cabin, the morning glories spiraling in at the windows, the outdoor stove where she baked *tortillas* for José! She had no priest. She said a few prayers to Our Lady in the little porcelain shrine always filled with fresh flowers. Why was she so utterly alone? What had become of her friend, the courtly physician?

Dr. Aiken had not forgotten, even in all the confused fury. He sought out Judge Rose, Speare, and other leaders. "I tell you it is true. I know it. Juanita consulted me—she is going to have a baby."

"We ain't greenhorns, Doc," jeered the miners.

"Men you are mistaken. If this woman dies, you take two lives— I'll prove it."

Dr. Aiken led the miners to Juanita's cabin. He pointed out to the baffled men in medical terms the symptoms of approaching maternity. For a moment Judge Rose, Speare and their friends were nonplused. They assembled opposing medical advisers. Another examination was

MRS. CHARLES AIKEN, OF DOWNIEVILLE.

DOCTOR CHARLES AIKEN, OF DOWNIEVILLE.

FANNY OSBOURNE.

ROBERT LOUIS STEVENSON.

made. "Not a sign of pregnancy!" heatedly pronounced the prosecution experts. "Run Aiken out of town. He is trying to save the greaser."

"Get the hell out of here, Aiken, or we'll hang you!" shouted the mob. Dr. Charles Aiken was jostled into banishment.

Now Juanita had no defender. Downieville gave the unanimous verdict—the rope.

Juanita heard the news. That last hour ran swift as the waters of the tumbling Yuba. They were coming for her, the wrathful *gringos*. Of one of the guards she asked in Spanish, "Will they bury me after, *Señor?*"

"Yes."

"Gracias, gracias."

The death procession began the last solemn march. Three thousand miners, silent and somber, escorted Juanita to Jersey Bridge. Pity— even to speak the word—had become treason in Downieville.

Alone Juanita walked the length of the bridge. There in the middle she beheld her own scaffold, a plank four feet in the air extending from side to side beyond the edge of the bridge, lashed with ropes to each end. On this plank she was to stand. There was a stepladder for her to mount to her death trap.

When she reached the stepladder her friends were frightened— but not Juanita! She took a last look at the great school of fat salmon leaping in the Yuba, at the Sierras, at the banks of the river where thousands of men had gathered, and at that new object dangling high on the bridge—a yellow rope.

"Big" Logan gave her the noose. Gravely Juanita looked at it, and at the two men standing over the rope on planks with sharp axes raised shoulder high. Her blue-black hair bound neatly about her head was sleek as hides of seals in San Francisco Bay. Her deep gray eyes grew black, vivid, bold, and challenged the thousands looking at her in that last moment. There was a blaze of sudden flame in her glance, then contempt froze her face. So the Iberians faced death, so the Aztecs proudly died.

Hank Monk, the stage driver, was in the crowd. He often said, "I never seen a woman show grit like that." But he made no protest; nor did Stephen J. Field, afterwards Chief Justice of the United States Supreme Court; nor Charles N. Felton, later United States Senator from Nevada; nor William M. Stewart, who was to be United States Senator from Nevada; nor that peer of England, Baron Charles Fairfax. All were too farsighted to fight mad men.

Both feet on the plank, Juanita stood. Then she took off her wide straw hat, and recklessness came over her. Far out over the crowd she spun her hat to a friend. *"Adiós, amigo!* It is to remember Juanita by."

When her guards asked for her last words she looked into their eyes one by one and slowly replied, "I would do it again. That man insulted me."

Juanita herself adjusted the hard thing about her young throat as if it were pearls from Loreto. She smoothed down her blue-black tresses over the rope. What was it—only a bit of hemp. Men envied her calm as with unshaken hands she put back the long braids. Juanita's guards tied her small brave hands behind her back and placed a white handkerchief over her eyes.

"Adiós, señores!" spoke Juanita. She dropped the handkerchief she held in her hand to signal that she was ready. Two pistols barked the signal to the executioners.

"Back!" cried the men around the scaffold.

There was no word from Juanita. Axes glistened. One slipped. Another blow and the rope holding the plank was hacked off. The board fell. Like a ghastly top Juanita's body twisted round and round and for half an hour hung in mid-air.

On July 5, 1851, three thousand men stood watching her dangling from a rope.

Some of Juanita's countrywomen laid her body tenderly in a small room facing the main street, and left its doors and windows open wide to the plain view of passersby. They covered the dark red mark on her neck with lace. So calm was her smiling face that she seemed to be asleep. There was a rumor that she had come back to life and all rushed to the building where she rested. But Juanita smiled on in the silent unknown.

Jack Cannon in his red shirt lay in another building. Perhaps it was with a gesture toward democracy that Downieville buried Juanita and Cannon in the same grave. But her house was torn down and Mexicans did not linger at the camp. To them Downieville was an accursed place.

That winter Jersey Bridge was swept away by floods and blood seemed to stain the Yuba. Prosecutor Speare was afterwards scalped and burned by Oregon Indians. Judge D. Houston, one of Juanita's prosecutors, met violent death. Harry Smith, foreman of the jury, was a suicide.

Till the 'seventies Juanita and Cannon lay undisturbed in the old cemetery, but their grave ceased to exist; the ground had to be "mined off." At that time someone stole Juanita's skull. For years it was used in initiation ceremonies by a secret society.

Even today Downieville does not understand why California hangs its golden head in shame for the lynching of Juanita. Its defense of her manner of going is, "She was an immoral woman."

Eighty years after Juanita gallantly went to death I motored into Downieville. With its iron-shuttered windows and doors, it looked like a place that had lived, a lesser Tyre or Nineveh, one of the ghost towns of the Mother Lode. My glance caught a house with a balcony, a muted fountain, a deserted aviary, a dwelling of poetry and imagination among old trees. "Who built it?" was my immediate question.

"Dr. Charles Aiken, the man who tried to save Juanita, the Mexican girl. He died in 1870."

I felt like one of the miners of 1851 who had discovered a great nugget when my informant added, "His widow still lives in the house."

My historical sense emboldened me to venture immediately into Dr. Aiken's garden and dwelling. There his frail, aged widow, who came to Downieville after Juanita's time, recounted her husband's story of his efforts to save the Mexican girl. "Downieville never forgave Dr. Aiken," she concluded.

"Was Juanita really about to become a mother?" I asked.

"No," she said proudly, "my husband lied. He was like that—he would do anything to help a friend."

XIX

LOLA MONTEZ AND PATRICK HULL

1853

EVEN before the golden rivers of California were discovered there had been wandering companies of entertainers and acrobats in the province. In 1847 William T. Sherman saw Adam and Eve *performed at Monterey with Dolores Gomez as the star, and he was amused that Eve wore a spangled skirt. A play was given by the United States garrison at Sonoma in September, 1847, and another by an amateur company of Spanish-Californians at San Francisco. About that time Monterey and Santa Barbara had minstrel entertainments.*

Mission Dolores, like the other establishments, had fallen into decay and was now an amusement center. Here were two arenas for bull-fighting. Soon two more were erected in San Francisco. Cockfighting was another popular form of entertainment.

In 1849 Steven C. Massett gave a series of entertainments and a concert at the Plaza schoolhouse, in San Francisco. In that same year the Bandit Chief *was played at Sacramento.*

The Wife *was produced the following year at San Francisco in that city's first theater,* The National. *In 1850 the* Jenny Lind *was erected on the Plaza. It was proposed to raise five hundred thousand dollars to bring Jenny Lind herself to California, but she never came. Gifted actors, however, arrived—Junius Booth with his brilliant young son, Edwin. Other actors who appeared were Stark, Atwater, Kirby, Bingham and Thorne, Sr. They played not only in San Francisco, but in the mining towns, all of which had entertainment halls.*

When the miners approved of a performance they tossed nuggets at the feet of the players, and gold pieces of ten, twenty and even fifty dollars were rained upon performers, especially women. A woman violinist or piano player could fill any house. When Kate Hayes gave concerts in 1850, the first tickets at San Francisco and Sacramento sold as high as twelve hundred dollars each.

Miners forgot the puritanical Sabbath and Sunday was play-day. Mexican influence was shown in the colors worn, broad-trimmed hats and scarlet sashes, diamond shirt studs, and breastpins of gold specimens.

To this lavish land came Lola Montez, the dancer, who felt that her castle in Spain lay through the Golden Gate and in the valleys of California. She had broken under her disastrous romance with King Ludwig of Bavaria, but as soon as she set foot on the steamer at New Orleans and sailed for San Francisco, she plunged into another romance—this time with a Californian.

LOLA MONTEZ ran up the gangplank of the *Northerner* at New Orleans with light dancing step, in her arms a black poodle—Flora. Maid, pianist and theatrical agent followed, weighted down with Madame la Comtesse's luggage.

In that year of 1853 America was still roaring west to California. Travelers turned to look at the most-talked-of woman in the world, charmer of Bavaria's King Ludwig. Amethyst Irish eyes underneath the black plumed bonnet met their gaze. In envy women stared at royal jewels burning insolently on Lola's fingers. Men's eyes feasted on her hibiscus-red mouth and skin iridescent as a shell. Even her full-skirted black gown could not conceal her provocative body.

Editor Patrick Hull, also San Francisco-bound, had read that Ludwig, King of Bavaria, had made this woman Countess of Landsfeld, Baroness Rosenthal, and Canoness of the Order of Saint Theresa. She had been more than queen—she was king. But revolution dethroned the dancer. Here she was passing so close to Patrick that he could almost touch her bronze hair. He caught the fragrance of her exotic beauty. Involuntarily the tall editor removed his massive beaver hat. "I understand why she caused a revolution."

Lola Montez and Patrick Hull did not speak until the *Northerner* was well on its way. Patrick's approach was journalistic. "Madame, may I tell San Francisco and California, through the *Whig and Commercial Advertiser,* of your experiences in Europe?"

Seated on the deck they looked out on the swelling Gulf. She laid her hand on Flora's head and said, "Let's not talk of me. Flora is my only friend—so much better than men or women."

Hull caressed Flora's back and his voice boomed, "No one is better than a nice dog. You're lucky to have one."

Patrick Hull had the animal touch. Flora nuzzled his fingers and licked his hand. It was the best possible recommendation to the dancer.

Lola rolled her R's in a slightly foreign way. "Tell me of California. Is it so beautiful? I long to see it, especially those great trees. Are there mountains of gold? Perhaps I shall pick up a few handfuls and never again have to think about tiresome money."

Patrick Hull blindly loved California. He spoke of the flowers, the titanic trees, the Yosemite, the Sierras. Lola's manner of listening had charmed even kings.

"I'm so happy to be going to California," she said. "It is Spanish. We were the Spanish Montalvos. Many Spaniards came to Ireland."

"A Montalvo's book gave California its name," exclaimed Patrick.

"I knew destiny was drawing me to California." Lola often spoke in the Byronic and Napoleonic way! She poured out her life to Patrick: "I've been blown about like a lost leaf. I began as Betty Gilbert of Limerick on the Shannon. When I was no more than a child, I married Lieutenant James in India. Love failed me. Or did I fail love? I didn't understand stupid laws. I thought I was free in England, but my second marriage to Cadet Heald in London made me a fugitive. I always hated England, but Paris—ah, there I lived! I had many friends—Dumas *père,* Liszt. Poor Dujarier, he died in a¹ duel. I tried to save him, I couldn't."

"And Munich, Countess?"

"Ah, why did I ever go there? I suppose it was because Ludwig, poet as well as king, drew me. He was not young—a king need not be young to be charming. He was too beautiful—like Byron! I made him desire to meet me—trampled upon the flower beds of the King of Preuss and Ludwig's curiosity was piqued. Of course, life was beautiful for a time. Bavaria was mine. I wished to liberalize the country. So did Ludwig. The politicians feared me. They made the students drive me out. Those flying rocks! Ludwig had to choose between his throne and me. He failed me." She took Flora in her arms and caressed the dog's black hair. "Only Flora is faithful."

Patrick Hull bent over Lola as she touched Flora's face with her own. "Some men are as faithful as dogs."

After the sophisticated intellectuals of Europe she delighted in Pat Hull's simple admiration. His sunburned skin, leonine head, broad shoulders, and primitive strength made him seem like a sheltering mountain.

All the afternoon they talked. Stars rose over Mexico, and they were still speaking of themselves. "Isn't it strange," he asked, "that we should have been hurled together from opposite sides of the planet?"

"As we go westward I feel my life being renewed. Civilization bores me. I want to be a pioneer and lose myself in California."

He gazed at her like an admiring boy. "And they call you a tigress." She laughed at his *naïveté*. "A woman Napoleon."

Through the night until morning neared they talked, each with a hand on Flora. Their fingers touched. Flora woke and kissed her mistress' hand, soft as petals. Hull pressed Lola's fingers. "My California bear," Lola said.

Antony and the lovers of all beautiful women throbbed in his heart. He had a sense of dazzling glory. "I feel as though I were touching Cleopatra. That mystical charm—did I love you in a previous existence?"

"Perhaps." As she spoke she seemed veiled in enchantment.

"Tonight," he pleaded, "give me tonight."

No sooner had Pat possessed Lola than he was jealous of Dumas,

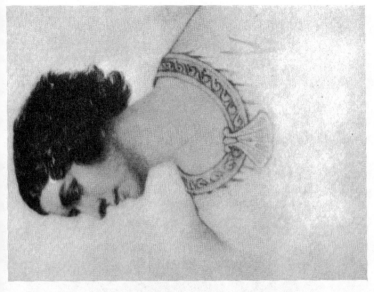

LOLA MONTEZ [Engraved by Rogers from a photograph by Meade].

LOLA MONTEZ [From a daguerreotype taken in Boston].

HOUSE IN GRASS VALLEY WHERE LOLA MONTEZ AND PATRICK HULL LIVED.

Dujarier, Liszt, Heald, James and Ludwig, the King! Could he, Pat Hull, hold her? Especially could he hold her in delirious San Francisco where each hour there was new romance, new drama. Only a few years previously this city had been the little Mexican pueblo Yerba Buena. Twenty men to one woman dwelt in the new San Francisco sprawling over tented hills.

"Lola! Lola! Lola!" chanted bearded lips as the *Northerner* docked. There were red- and blue-shirted miners, gamblers in dignified black, gallant Spanish-Californians.

Patrick Hull began to suffer when half a hundred men unfastened the harness from the horses and drew Lola through the sandy streets of the four-year-old metropolis to the Oriental Hotel. They would not depart till she came to the window. She threw kisses to them through lace curtains, and Pat Hull's torture was intensified. She comforted him by placing her arms around his neck and calling him, "Don Patricio." Laughingly she added, "My adorable bear, you look like a *chic* iceberg."

The pressure of her body against his set his flesh to throbbing. Her voice stirred him like the melody of a lovely chord. Pat was happy—

For only a moment! Sam Brannan, the boisterous editor with white cravat and a ruby ring, came to pay court carrying tuberoses and sweets. Lola fed Flora the sweets.

"Brannan is a Mormon," protested Pat.

"All men are Mormons," retorted Lola.

Daily Brannan dashed up to the Oriental Hotel to take Lola for a drive over the plank road to the Mission Dolores that lay brooding at the foot of Twin Peaks. He had the finest horses in California. One he named for Lola. Again Pat suffered.

Boldly Brannan explained to Lola his reason for coming to California. "I hoped to reach here before the Yankees and raise the Mormon flag."

"At least, you are frank, my friend," smiled Lola. "You have a most entertaining religion. *Merci!* I shouldn't like to be your tenth wife. I have the devil's own temper. I might strangle the other nine wives." But Lola's lace-mittened hands drove Brannan's spanking bays to the races. She loved horses as much as dogs.

Men who were afterwards Governors and Senators sent camellias to Lola. Young Edwin Booth, who was playing *Hamlet* for the first time, brought roses red as blood. Despairing of competition, Pat Hull appeared with wild poppies and lupines.

"Weeds," he apologized.

"I am a weed, Don *Patricio mio.* I like weeds!"

When Lola strolled the plank sidewalks of San Francisco in black, her classic throat revealed by the white Byronic collar fastened with Ludwig's brooch, men thronged the streets. Pat Hull suffered. When she appeared at the American Theater as Lady Teazle in the *School for Scandal,* and two thousand men applauded from seats, some of which had cost sixty-five dollars, tortured silence held Pat. When later she danced the Spider Dance she was music, song, a smiling *señorita* from Spain drifting through a sunlit meadow in a pantomime set to music! The audience was whipped faster and faster to fury until the entire throng stamped to the untamed rhythm of the music. Later at supper Lola's frantic adorers drank her health in champagne from her slipper.

Pat was irritated by this wild pioneer emotion. "You care more for applause than for me."

"Darling *Patricio mio,* smile—you're so handsome when you smile."

In negligée Lola received suitors while she sipped coffee in bed.

"Why aren't you like other women?" demanded Pat. "Why do you let men see you in a nightgown?"

"Pardon, *mignon,*" she corrected, "in a *peignoir*—Worth's!" With stabbing frankness she went on, "I think, act and live like a man, my *Patricio.* I have had many lovers."

Words tumbled from his lips. "I don't want to be one of your many lovers. More than your body I desire your soul." Like a hot-eyed boy he gazed deep into her eyes, then laid his cheek against her throat. "I wish to be your husband."

"And I wish to be free, my *corazón,* to live in songs, sculpture,

careers, the inspiration of great men. Let me not spoil our love
with stupid ceremonies. Marriage shall never destroy me again."

"That damned king! Sometimes I think he is the devil."

"I am the devil, Saint Patrick. Adore me."

More and more Pat Hull drank brandy smashes. He neglected
his work at the editorial rooms. His partner, Louis Lull, said, "That
woman is ruining you."

Flora the poodle was lost. Pat's newspaper was filled with Flora.
He left his office to seek her. Other editors joined in the hunt. The
fire company searched for her. Pat absented himself from his office
to comfort the weeping Lola. He rolled her cigarettes, told her she
was beautiful, implored her to be brave. Flora could not be found
and Lola wept.

"I have lost my best beloved, my only friend," she moaned.

Pat Hull's partner reproached him. "You are making a show of
yourself. Lola Montez has bewitched you."

Again Pat appealed to Lola, "Marry me. We will go away to the
mines together."

Lola was bored. "Marriage—"

"Unless you marry me, my life will end."

Forty guests were bidden to assemble at dawn on the second of
July, 1853, in the little adobe Mission Dolores at the end of the
plank road. Few knew the purpose of the invitation. Only Spanish-
Californians came here for devotion. Most of the guests wondered
why they were bidden to the Mission founded by *Padre* Presidente
Junípero Serra and *Padre* Palóu in 1776 for the glory of Saint Francis.

Patrick Hull and Lola Montez entered the gray-walled Mission, from
which the whitewash peeled. Suddenly it seemed the center of gay
life. For the third time Lola Montez was being married.

Twice before it had been in July. Again July had come. Devoutly
Lola carried two tall vases filled with white roses. After placing them
on the altar of the Virgin she knelt and prayed. In her bonnet trimmed
with pink roses, wearing a pink ruffled gown, an embroidered shawl
falling from her shoulders, she looked twenty-one. Father Flavius

Fontaine married Lola and Hull. He wrote in the book of marriages that she was twenty-seven. In reality, she was thirty-four.

Lola felt that the saints looking down from the walls would understand and bless her union with Patrick Hull. She believed that their vows of eternal love would shield them from unhappiness. The white roses at the feet of the Virgin who had once heard Serra's prayers seemed a little sad as Lola left the Mission Dolores.

Festive San Francisco rollicked all day with Lola Montez and Patrick Hull at their apartment, where they received their friends. Even Sam Brannan brought belated, crestfallen blessings. Pat was happy; Lola belonged to him alone!

Soon spots appeared on the sun shining on Pat. Miska Hauser, a Hungarian violinist, gave a concert in San Francisco. Lola was charmed and sent one hundred and fifty dollars' worth of roses to her "dear friend." Honeymoon happiness did not increase when Lola said, "I will tour the mines with Hauser." Daily Lola sent Hauser flowers. Pat Hull's heart swelled with anguish as Lola merrily sang:

> *I'll soon be in the mining camps*
> *And then I'll look around,*
> *And when I see the gold dust there*
> *I'll pick it off the ground....*
> *Oh, Susannah, don't you cry for me!*
> *I'm off for Sacramento with my washbowl on my knee!*

Pat sold his paper, the *Whig and Commercial Advertiser,* and became the manager of his wife. With Miska Hauser he sailed on the *Comanche* for Sacramento. With all her faults and caprices, Pat accepted Lola. "I must take her on her own terms," he thought. "There is only one Lola Montez."

As the boat idled upstream Lola said to Pat, "I love rivers. The Sacramento makes me think of Ireland's Shannon, India's Ganges, England's Thames, France's Seine, Italy's Tiber, Germany's Rhine. We'll live in the Sierras forever."

Seventeen days after Lola Montez had married Patrick Hull she quarreled with Miska Hauser. When Pat interfered she hurled him down two flights of stairs at Marysville, declaring wildly, "This marriage is already too long. I will succeed without Pat Hull and Miska Hauser."

Pat realized that he had thrown away his world for Lola, but he had doglike fidelity and he went on with her. "No woman should tour the mines alone."

Lola flung both arms around him. "My *corazón*, I didn't know what I said. Words are such liars."

They sat in the embrace of honeymooning lovers as the stagecoach rolled up and down the dusty road over hills soft as chamois, through gorges of sienna-hued earth, down steeps of oaks and manzanita. Men toiling in the Yuba River with water up to their knees waved their hats as Lola passed by. They pressed gold nuggets into her hands. Through virgin pine forests peopled with Indians, bears and cougars, the stage dropped down into the richest mining camp in the world—Grass Valley.

Rough-bearded men wearing belts heavy with gold rushed down pine-covered slopes from river beds only to look at Lola Montez, "The most beautiful creature this side of heaven."

Once more Lola was reborn. She was glad to be far from the Munich palace with its crystal staircase, ermine rugs, gold dinner service, and a diadem with diamonds larger than her thumb. It was relief even to escape cultured conversation. She also rejoiced in being far from San Francisco's red-carpeted hotel rooms. At the Exchange Hotel at Grass Valley a cowbell summoned ungrammatical guests to meals. She enjoyed dazzling the mining camp with her black velvet riding habit, her ostrich-plumed hat and her riding stick with its gold handle engraved with Ludwig's crest.

The mining camps were starved for women. Men living in tents and log houses at Grass Valley and at its rival Nevada City, paid ten dollars to see Lola dance. Her bright-colored skirts, her feet like scarlet songs, her castanets accenting the stirring music—all brought them up cheering, caused them to toss her as tribute their hard-earned nuggets. On a tour of the camps at Rough and Ready she discovered precocious Lotta Crabtree and set the child dancing on an anvil in a blacksmith shop. Lotta continued to dance until she was one of the famous women of her time.

Pat Hull found no nuggets in the Grass Valley streets. He longed for San Francisco, but Lola was fascinated by the contrast between her Munich palace and her four-room cottage in the camp of log houses and tents. "My castle," she called her dwelling with its knotty pine walls. It had been a dance hall owned by Jennie-on-the-Green. She installed French windows, and from San Francisco brought mahogany and rosewood furniture, a gold-frame mirror, costly toilet articles, curious ink stands, embroidered frames, and a guitar. She erected a neat picket fence around her property, transplanted shrubs, ferns, plants, wild flowers, and sent for garden seed.

Finally Pat fell under the spell of the cottage. "Never dance again," he implored.

"Lola Montez, the dancer, is dead in your arms at Grass Valley, my *corazón*. I shall never leave."

She appeared in the streets wearing simple garments, but with long earrings, at her heels two dogs. She spoke French, Spanish and German with the miners. Pets filled her cottage. Her cats respected the birds in their cages on the porch. A miner found a bear's cub lost in the forest and whimpering. He brought it to Lola. Almost overnight it was no longer a cub but a bear and a house was built for the animal. Finally Lola had him chained to a stump.

"Get rid of him," warned Pat, "the bear will turn vicious."

"Get rid of my friend?" she rebuked.

Lola had a comb filed from a section of iron hoop and while the bear ate she scratched his back with the comb. She was delighted when Bruin turned from dinner to caress her.

"Give that bear away!" Pat still warned. They quarreled. She went to San Francisco to buy a piano. "She is leaving Pat," said the gossips. Gladly she came back, survivor of a shipwreck on Benicia Bay.

LOLA MONTEZ AND PATRICK HULL AT GRASS VALLEY, 1854. THE START OF A HUNT-
ING TRIP.

JOAQUIN, THE TERRIBLE [From a painting by Charles C. Nahl].

After the storm Lola had never known such tranquillity since leaving the River Shannon in Ireland. She made brick walks, planted musky red and yellow roses, and roses of Castile. She built a rockery for ferns and had greenhouses made of window frames. From the spring she laid a pipe and created Grass Valley's first fountain. The camp thought it one of the Countess' caprices when she sent to Southern California for cacti. It was the first cactus garden in the West, and later it became the pride of the community.

San Francisco called Pat Hull, but Lola loved the dark pine-scented hills and she refused to leave Grass Valley. Contentedly she dwelt with her bear, her dogs, cats and birds. She dashed about in a sleigh filled with dogs, her horses hung with cowbells. Wading in Deer Creek, she washed pans of gravel. A mine was named for her. She nursed miners' sick children and dressed miners' wounds. She taught the child Lotta to play the guitar. She fed every Indian who came to her door. Her heart was filled with pity for the doomed red race. Standing knee-deep in snow she scratched her bear's back.

Finally the bear bit Lola. Miners said it was her first conqueror. They held a mock trial of the bear. Pat returned to Grass Valley to kill the animal. Lola defended the bear and pushed his food to him with a stick from a safe distance.

Lola and Pat gave a large Christmas party. The house was decorated with candles and wreaths of mountain laurel and fir. Guests feasted on antelope, duck and quail. Lola danced the polka and mazurka and sang *Pop Goes the Weasel*. The bear escaped to wander about the camp, but was captured and brought back.

"Give him up!" warned Pat.

"Never!" shouted Lola. Again they quarreled; all Grass Valley heard. Pat shot the bear—he might as well have shot Lola!

"You're lower than a beast! Go!" She flung his clothes at him. It was their last Christmas together.

Pat never returned to Grass Valley. In San Francisco he established a new paper, *Town Talk*, and tried to reconstruct his life.

Lola invested her last few thousand dollars in the Empire Mine, but the flood of gold fluctuated and for a time almost ceased. She clung to the only home she had ever known. She began reading the Bible. "I've been converted," she said gravely. Grass Valley smiled.

Henry Shipley, a local editor, reprinted an article against her from a New York paper. "Hypocrite!" she was called. Once in Munich she had horsewhipped a man for kicking her dog. Now she seized a riding whip, found Shipley in a saloon and lashed his face.

A Methodist minister criticized Lola for her costume. She put on her Spider Dance dress, went to the minister's house and danced. "I apologize," he said. "Your costume is not offensive. It is pretty!"

The happy hills enchained Lola, but they gave her no gold. Edwin Booth wrote urging her to go to Australia—that he himself was going. But she lingered in Grass Valley to nurse a mining friend. Caroline Chapman, the actress, came to camp and insisted that Lola go to Australia. Reluctantly she began practicing the Spider Dance for her Australian tour. Before she went she held a reception. To all she said, "I'll make a fortune in Australia and return to Grass Valley."

Faithful Pat Hull drove with her to the steamer at San Francisco. She went away wearing a new pink bonnet, holding one of her dogs in her arms. With misty eyes Pat watched Lola waving a green parasol as the steamer sailed for Australia.

Already on the boat with Lola was a young love to whom she clung as the thirsting seek water—Augustus Follin. His love for Lola was like poisoned wine. With her he traveled to Australia, which refilled her hands with gold. Follin set out with her from Australia for San Francisco. Some said he leaped overboard while drinking. Others declared that the dancer's tempestuous hands plunged him into the sea.

Lola returned to San Francisco, thin, ill, nervous, with only the fragrance of her beauty remaining. No white cockatoo on her shoulder, no pink ribbons—she was dressed as simply as a nun. The whispered charge of murder followed her. Pat Hull did not print her name. Did he recall that Dumas had said Lola brought ruin to all men who loved her? In San Francisco the Vigilantes' bells were tolling. Horrified, Lola saw men swinging from gallows in the streets. Some were buried in the cemetery of the ancient Mission Dolores where she and Patrick Hull were married.

She planned a Spider Dance to help Follin's children. Isadora Duncan's father sold Lola's jewels at auction in eighty-nine lots. She even parted with her royal feathered capes from the Sandwich Islands, the birds and white cockatoo. She accepted only four hundred dollars from the sale of her house in Grass Valley—thirty thousand dollars went to Follin's widow and children. She tried to commit suicide by poison after making a will leaving everything to them. "Doctor," she said, "you can't cure a broken heart."

Patrick Hull knew. Soon he died.

In queer black Lola stood on New York City's Broadway distributing religious tracts until her feet became stone. Paralysis seized her. Like a gentle ghost she lived a few months at Astoria. She died in a room curtained with old carpet, without bed or chair, lying on a ragged coverlet and blankets. A clergyman was with her at the last. "Are you happy, madam?" he asked. She smiled.

Forgotten were the titles Countess of Landsfeld, Baroness of Rosenthal, and even the names James, Heald and Hull. In 1932 I went to her grave in Greenwood Cemetery, Brooklyn, and read on a low stone:

MRS. ELIZA GILBERT

DIED JUNE 16, 1861

AGED 42 YEARS

Within the year someone had planted on her grave a rosebush. Even on that cold November morning pink roses still bloomed for Lola Montez.

XX

JOAQUIN, THE TERRIBLE

1853

CALIFORNIA mines produced a thirty-thousand-dollar gold nugget, and this intoxicated the adventurous youth of the world. As one man expressed it, "A frenzy seized my soul; unbidden my legs performed some entirely new movements of polka steps—I took several. Houses were too small for me to stay in. I was soon in the street in search of an outfit. Piles of gold rose up before me; castles of marble; thousands of slaves were bowing to my beck and call. Myriads of fair virgins contended for my love. The Rothschilds, Girards and Astors appeared to me but poor people—in short, I had a very violent attack of gold fever."

Bitter feeling had been bred between Americans and the Spanish-Californians and Mexicans by the conquest and the border war. The Mexicans felt that their country and its gold had been wrested from them unfairly, but the blue-eyed races combined against dark foreigners, contemptuously called "greasers."

The ill-disguised enmity was extended to Chileans, Peruvians and even Frenchmen. At one time foreigners were not allowed to carry arms. All alien miners were taxed twenty dollars a month and thousands abandoned the gold fields. Deer Creek elected an alcalde to expel all foreigners, and Rough and Ready forbade mining by the alien-born in the district. Some liberal-minded Americans, however, permitted foreigners to work their claims, but native Spanish-Californians suffering from land spoliation and other injustices planned to migrate to Mexico.

At one itme as many as ten thousand Mexicans centered at the

Sonora Camp, famous for its "dry diggings." There their bull rings and monte banks continued their community life.

Calaveras County in particular had widespread expulsions. Many miners of Spanish extraction were forcibly ejected from desirable claims which usurpers continued to work. Especially did this happen in the central and northern counties where Mexicans were few in number and unable to resist. Impelled by want and by revenge some became highwaymen.

Joaquin Murietta, generally accepted as California's most famous bandit, was deprived of his claim. He bore that injustice, but for love of Rosita he became the terrible Joaquin.

ONLY in the wild fierce days of the California gold rush could such a man as Joaquin Murietta have flourished. See him at eighteen lying at the feet of Rosita, his first love! Daughter of the great *ranchero* Félix, she sat in her father's shadowy doorway, near Hermosillo, straining Joaquin's boyish head to her breast and half smothering him with the flame of her lips.

For the first and last time—Joaquin pleaded with a woman. "Rosita *mia,* my brother Jesus writes from Monterey, 'Come, be rich—dip your hands into the gold of California. Be Murietta, the great Don.' But Rosita, no matter how much gold I have, if you're not with me, I am a pauper." The girl's deep eyes reflected his own passion but when she hesitated he went on, "I kiss your hand, your feet, Rosita. Come."

Like Joaquin Murietta, Rosita was Castilian, with fair skin and black hair, smooth and deepened in blackness with oil of almonds. How hard for her to resist the pleading bold eyes of young Joaquin, six feet tall, strong-muscled, with sunburned sandaled feet and a bright serape about him.

Who was this Joaquin? His family were the Spanish Basques who came from the Pyrenees to receive a grant of leagues of land near Hermosillo, only to be driven from it by Yaquis and Apaches, who swept down from the north in the eighteenth century and devastated Sonora. Rosita recalled what her father had said that very day of Joaquin, "A nobody! Did I bring you from Spain to be the wife of a *vaquero?*"

It was Rosita's family or Joaquin. She had never been far from the gray Félix adobe sprawling among the cacti. She knew little of the California of the north save that three years previously it had been despoiled by dread white-faced *gringos* who ate pickles and pie and drank tea. Distance frightened the girl, also the great ships at sea, and perhaps a premonition of the future. But her trepidation was all swept away by the stony passion of Joaquin, the breaker of horses who was to terrorize California.

And so, when California's gold was dazzling and summoning the youth of the world, Rosita, blind with love, went to Joaquin in a plain black dress and gold-embroidered shawl. When her lover, a brave red sash about his waist, placed her on the leather *anquera* behind the broad Mexican saddle, her warm smooth arms clung to him piteously as they set out for the land of gold in the north.

That day new history was written in California as Joaquin and Rosita thundered across the cactus-studded desert, entered the little gray church at Hermosillo and knelt before the altar. Probably they were married there. Possibly love could not wait. "Rosita," he said to her, "you're like the Virgin in the church where I first prayed."

Down the Gulf of California they sailed, rounding Lower California; then they turned northward to the coast of gold. They followed the sea paths of Cabrillo, Vizcaíno and Drake. Up the green high coast, through the gate of gold guarded by Fort San Joaquin, to San Francisco they went, holding each other's hands, looking into each other's eyes, believing that they had entered a new and enchanting life.

What a crazy city, this adventure city of 1849 over which the Stars and Stripes had waved only three years! A new world! Rats swam hungrily out to reach the ship. A fortune in merchandise lay on wharves, left by merchants who had hastened to the mines. Men in blue and red flannel shirts with high boots and broad hats were everywhere on the crooked streets and trails. Chinese in gorgeous brocades clicked through muddy pathways. Here were aged Indians who, in the year George Washington won his first battle against England, had helped build the Mission of Saint Francis which was still like a crumbling dream from another century. Mexico also was here—women in black, men in bright colors with cigarettes in black and yellow papers—all old neighbors from Sonora, chattering of the strange arrival of the daughter of the rich Félix with the *vaquero* Joaquin Murietta.

Proud Joaquin did not intend to remain a *vaquero*. "I'll be richer than old Félix," he thought. "Rosita shall have the most beautiful pearls in Loreto."

He was intoxicated by love, by youth, by gold in bags, in tents, in unlocked houses—not a lock in San Francisco! Youth, the best and the worst, was pouring into California, spending itself in gaudy saloons, the El Dorado, the Green Devil, the Rising Sun! Women were singing and drinking, shaking dice, playing cards with men who wore gold belts and loaded guns. Maddened by the sight of gold, Joaquin was off for the mines and fortune. His thought was to return to dazzle Sonora as a Don from California, and to spend the rest of his days with Rosita in the land of hot sunshine where the cacti grew gray and fat.

When Joaquin sailed up the Sacramento River on the steamer *Senator* with Rosita, she was the only woman on board. Like the other miners Joaquin had a gun, an iron pan, a pick and shovel and a grubstake. The enraptured pair sat together listening to wild anthems of gold. They had no time to marvel at this busy town of Sacramento, erupted overnight with ten thousand gamblers and traders. Here were prairie schooners from the plains and ten-horse teams from Oregon.

At an auction Joaquin bought a long-eared mule. With the mule carrying mining tools and a sack of *frijoles* and cornmeal, Joaquin and Rosita set out for Sonora. They were lured by the name Sonora, their native province. With all the faith of youth they believed that Sonora would give them fortune.

At Sonora all land was staked. Joaquin lifted Rosita to the saddle once more, and they were off on their quest for new adventure. They camped on the Calaveras bank of the Stanislaus River where Rosita deftly spun flat gray *tortillas* for supper and baked them on hot stones. Her great eyes rested proudly on Joaquin as he staked out with willow pegs fifteen square feet, their share of California. Those wonderful fifteen square feet! What treasure might they not contain! Rosita's Joaquin could not fail. Already she felt rich, even before he walked out into the Stanislaus.

Swish went the shiny black pan through the gravel. Impetuously Joaquin stirred the pebbles. Only black sand. No matter! Soon they would find gold. Why should they desire precious metal? They had each other. Gold seemed the treasure of the earth. Theirs was the treasure of the spirit—love.

Strangers in Upper California, Joaquin and Rosita slept like children in a serape on the gravelly bed, drinking in warm earth odors. Their roof was the stars. The pines murmured a lullaby.

Soon they had neighbors on the opposite bank of the Stanislaus. Americans had struck color. Their belts were sagging with gold. Their luck gave hope to Joaquin.

Through long wearing days he toiled knee-deep in the Stanislaus. Still only black sand showed itself. On the opposite river bank Americans were shoveling gravel into "long Toms"—stationary mining cradles made of wood, with a froth of water running through to wash the gravel. The sun was high. In the manner of Mexico, Joaquin and Rosita took a *siesta* in each other's arms. The Americans on the opposite bank smiled.

One afternoon Joaquin left the *siesta* with heart singing. He waded into the Stanislaus, took up a panful of black sand and stirred it with his finger.

"Rosita!" he shouted. "Gold!" He was at her side. "Now for Mexico!

We'll buy back the Murietta *rancho*. Rosita, *querida*, why should I be so happy? I have you, and youth and gold!"

Joaquin turned up more color. Nuggets grew larger. These two young gypsies in paradise feasted on *frijoles*, brown beans and jerked beef eaten on *tortillas*. As the gold nuggets clicked in her hands Rosita sang folk songs of Mexico. Too loudly she sang. Her song and chatter brought Americans from the opposite shore, red-shirted miners, bearded, wearing high boots and big slouch hats.

"Struck any color, *hombre?*" asked the leader, looking over their heads at the sand in the pan.

Joaquin wished everyone to rejoice with him. His white teeth glittered in the sun.

"*Si, mucho color.*"

The Yankee understood *mucho color*. He stirred the black sand with his finger and whistled. His was not a generous soul rejoicing in another's good fortune. Enviously he looked at Rosita. This "greaser" had a pretty gal as well as a fortune. At that time there was only one woman to a hundred men in the county.

Joaquin went on digging, panning and laying his treasure at the feet of Rosita. Her voice was ever gayer and gayer. After work at night over their campfire, Rosita and Joaquin planned their garden in Mexico. She wished to take back to the Murietta *rancho* some of the pretty flowers that had been the couch where their love had blossomed.

"I'm nineteen," boasted Joaquin. "I'm rich. I feel as mighty as the mountains of California!"

Mirage of happiness! Eight Americans from the camp across the river stormed into their camp. Joaquin and Rosita could not understand all they said, but they recognized, "Greaser, you've got no right here. Get out. Vamoose!"

"No, no! Mine!" shouted Joaquin in Spanish. "I paid my tax. I paid for my claim."

Who drew the first gun in that fight at the campfire no one knows. It was eight against two, and one of those a woman. Joaquin fought until death seemed to curtain his eyes with black.

But something in him would not die. He awoke clotted from head to foot with blood. "Rosita," he called, "Rosita!"

Her answer was a moan. "Holy Mother, let me die."

There at Joaquin's side was Rosita, trampled upon, strangled, outraged, dying. "Live, *querida,* live for me! Live for our love! I can't go on without you."

Moaning she breathed her last in his arms, her soft cheeks stained with tears of shame. Till morning he held her close. Dawn found her violated body shrouded in her gold-embroidered shawl splashed with red. He laid their silver crucifix on her bruised breast and buried her in the earth rich with gold in the hills of Calaveras, also called the Place of Skulls.

Only Joaquin knew the resting-place of Rosita Félix de Murietta. It was the hidden home of his heart. His last words to her were "Rest, sleep well, Rosita."

Before the sun was red over the Calaveras hills Joaquin was gone. No more tears! Like a madman he rode about the Sierras—"the lone rider with velvety eyes," he was called. With hatred and despair he plunged into the world. Now he had a new goal—to avenge the death of Rosita.

At Sonora he tasted his first sweet vengeance. Within three months after Joaquin's well-beloved lost her life every American in that camp on the Stanislaus was dead. Stealthily he crept upon them one by one. Some were strangled by the lariat; the bullet took others. Some were slashed from ear to ear with a cattle knife. Who cared? Each man for himself. It was the law of Forty-Nine.

The eighth man eluded Joaquin, but Murietta hunted him down. He became a monte dealer at Murphy's. His swift clever fingers dealt cards with hatred, veiled with a subtle smile. Night after night he watched for the coming of the last, the eighth man. Finally the doomed man came with his noisy friends into the tent filled with fumes of tobacco and whisky. When he saw the marked man, Joaquin's breath went through his body like a sword. Life shrank to one thing for Joaquin—a lean, shrewd *gringo* face.

For the first time Joaquin Murietta struck in the open. Between the bar and the flapping doors the miner fell, a red bandana about his throat stained dark by a bright ruby fountain. Knife still in his hand, Joaquin ran from the tent. Back through the night came his challenging cry of outraged love,

"I am Joaquin! Murderer of my Rosita, this is your reward!—say your prayers in hell!"

Now all the world saw him fleeing before a dozen men on panting horses. Food ran wild in California—quail, rabbit, deer and bear. Like an endangered eagle he sought the heights and followed lonely burro trails through the chaparral. As if glued to his saddle he tore down the steepest rockiest hillside.

Forty strong, desperate men now came to Joaquin, all bewitched by the bright eyes of peril, and headlong down the State they roared. "I am not afraid," boasted Joaquin. "I'll not be caught by a lasso like a branded steer. I will never slip into the noose—not Joaquin! I will kill every *gringo* in California. I was not born to be hanged. I am Joaquin—I am California!"

And yet he never forgot to enter the abandoned Missions to go to confession and to prostrate himself in adoration before the Virgin. He also found time to go back to the Stanislaus and fling himself in bitter grief by the side of Rosita's grave.

It was the age of duels—men fought fast at a drop of the hat. Joaquin's duels were not with guns as Americans fought, but in Mexican fashion. Serape wound over his arm like a shield, a knife in his strong hand, and another between his teeth for emergency, he offered his body to anyone who dared strike. Few dared. Fear of Joaquin mounted as he went on.

Music could not be fast enough, stakes high enough, women gay enough when Joaquin played! There were always girls for Joaquin—dark eyes to signal his; lips hot as flame that did not have to be won. Was he not Joaquin? Women worshiped him, followed him, fought over him. Joaquin was magnificent with his cry, *"Venganza! Venganza! Todos Americanos! Murietta vengador!"*

Joaquin Murietta became a name to speak slowly, never to be cursed in public, lest some dark night in the store, saloon, or *fandango* there might be a knife in your back.

Joaquin had left Mexico in leather sandals and faded serape. California had given him broadcloth and scarlet, silver on his saddle, gold in his belt, and now his horsemen numbered seventy. But the shaggy blue peaks of his homeland summoned him. In February when the first poppies gilded the western valleys and hills Joaquin and his seventy men rode down the Shasta slopes through poppyland, adventuring to friends, music and the lazy sunshine of Mexico.

Once more women with tortoise-shell combs, pearls from Loreto, and clicking castanets as in Castile since the days of the Moors! At Montape not far from Hermosillo Joaquin met Mariana Engrada— small, dark, with high cheekbones and insolent, imperious eyes, more Aztec than Spanish. While she rolled for him long black *cigarrillos* she pleaded, "Joaquin, take me to California with you." Family, friends, home did not matter to this wild Mariana as she rode away from Mexico in tight-fitting blue breeches, serape and black *sombrero* into the blue and gold paradise of California with her Joaquin.

Every day of their life was a storm, a furious battle of jealousy. Soon Joaquin the magnificent became Joaquin the terrible! He had learned to kill without a quiver. Around his saddle was a string of human ears torn from the heads of his enemies. Now his company numbered seventy-eight. Said Joaquin, "With forty-eight men I will conquer California."

Into Cantua Canyon, the great yellow valley opening into the plains of San Joaquin, he brought Mariana, his bride beyond the law. Like a slave she had followed and obeyed him, but she fretted under Joaquin's long absences. His neglect was like a steel whip scourging her heart. While Joaquin and his men were smearing the face of California with blood, Mariana's face darkened with brooding. Longer and longer Joaquin was absent.

"I must drive out the Americans like pigs," he said. "The gold mines and the cattle belong to Mexico. I will give California back to the motherland. Gold will be for all."

Rewards offered for the delivery of Joaquin were increased by the State. He laughed. "Kill me if you can. I am Joaquin. I am California!"

Alone in her tent near Stockton Mariana brooded until her eyebrows came together dangerously. Joaquin had ridden away with his men and sent back no word. Always he came back under cover of darkness. Would he ever return? Was he with some other younger Mariana with a fresher allure?

While she was in a moment of fierce Aztec resentment the sheriff at Stockton came to her with gold. "When Joaquin returns," said he, "light a candle in your tent as a signal. I will come."

Mariana took the gold, but it was jealousy that drove her to the betrayal of Joaquin.

That very night he came with his old fierceness, his sullen lips parting as if to drink in all the passion of life. Mariana gave him kiss for kiss. Suddenly she lighted a candle in the tent. Joaquin's eyes flashed devil-black. He knew.

"Because you are a woman I'll let you live. But I'll make this of you!" His knife cut Mariana's cheek to the bone.

Joaquin slashed his way outside of the tent before it went down under the stampeding sheriff's men. Knife in hand, he wriggled out between them and was away with his men to the safer South where there was no Mariana.

Under the heavy tent on what seemed a bed of blood lay Mariana mangled. From that day and from that last night with Joaquin she became known as *Mariana la Loca*—Mariana the Mad.

When Joaquin left Mariana half dead in the tent near Stockton there departed his last interest in human nature. His price of outlawry was loss of all belief.

More and more California bled under the iron fingers of Murietta. Men barred their doors and sat with grim guns cocked. Joaquin feasted upon their terror. When he and his men rode across the desert valley like whirling sand spots, flank to flank with death, Joaquin always took the dangerous position, the center of the road. At times he felt immortal.

"I'm only trying to take back what has been stolen," he apologized to his confessor. "The Americans took everything—my Rosita." In his last days Rosita was his only touchstone for truth.

Now Joaquin had four hundred men. Through all the golden breadth of California his name was spoken in horror. Citizens were warned against stirring abroad save in groups of six. California could have no peace so long as Joaquin should live. Harry Love and his California rangers were hired by the State to ride Joaquin to death.

Twice Joaquin outwitted Harry Love. The third test came. For three months Harry Love and his keen-eyed rangers had vainly hunted Joaquin. Love knew that Joaquin regarded Cantua Canyon as his home. The highwayman would return always to his favorite lair. Love and his men sought him at Cantua. They expected to find him hiding like a rabbit under the cottonwood trees. But no Joaquin!

Love and his rangers were confident that the lure of Cantua would draw Joaquin. They hurried toward Lake Tulare, a shimmering blue expanse in the plains of the Tulares, hiding place of cattle thieves and renegade Indians from the Missions.

On Sunday, July 25, 1853, tragedy blazed. Love and his rangers came upon a *vaquero* camp with seven men playing cards on a gaudy serape spread out on the ground. Love recognized Three-Finger Jack, Joaquin's most bloodthirsty lieutenant. He took after Jack, because as he afterwards related, "Jack was the ugliest of his crowd, and I was the ugliest of mine."

Jack twisted back to shoot, his horse bucking as he fired. He fled on for five miles. Suddenly Three-Finger Jack hurtled from his horse. Even after he was dead Love sent seven bullets into Three-Finger Jack's head.

As for Joaquin, there could be no mistaking the strong-muscled giant who was washing down his horse. Only one man in California looked like Joaquin Murietta. The sun had beaten his body to the color and hardness of brass. At his belt he wore only a Bowie knife. He was as haughty as a frowning *hidalgo*. "I am in command here," he declared quickly.

Joaquin mounted his horse, kicking it swiftly with his spurs. He slept in spurs. He rode low at the right side of his horse, no reins in his hands, no saddle. Ranger Burns and five men followed firing, but Joaquin's horse leaped between bullets. The animal took a twelve-foot spring over a washout. Wounded in mid-air he fell dead. Joaquin landed on his feet, staggered and still ran, leaping from side to side like an Indian escaping arrows.

Suddenly up went his hands. "Enough! You have done your work!" he cried as he sank to the sand, his face turned toward the sun, his eyes staring toward the hills of Calaveras where lay Rosita.

Joaquin was twenty-three. His bronzed body was left to feed the coyotes of the Tulares, but his unholy head was taken to San Francisco, where it remained in the glass case of a museum of horrors until it fed the flames of the great fire of 1906.

Mariana—she could not believe that Joaquin was dead. Joaquin, "my *hombre*," could not die! Others said the same, but his head was identified by his sister Clara, by his confessor Father Dominguez Blaine of Stockton, and by Salome, the courtesan of San Andreas.

After Joaquin died Mariana roamed from house to house, town to town, a pioneer mendicant living on charity, treated with respect by Joaquin's friends. At sixty young men begged to dance with her —was she not the woman who once rode with Joaquin? Proudly she showed the white scar on her dark skin and with savage boastfulness she would say, "My Joaquin gave me that."

Into Cantua Canyon where Joaquin had brought her as a bride from Mexico, at last wandered Mariana. As prophetess of Cantua there she lived by the Three Rocks. She called them the Rocks of Galilee —they were her tabernacle. There she lifted up her arms in strange incantations before throngs of Mexicans. She professed to have divine power to heal. Her life was blotted out by a railway train in the same Tulare country where Joaquin fell before rangers' bullets.

XXI

MOTHER OF MYSTERY

1853

CALIFORNIA'S twenty-one Missions received their mortal wound when Mexico separated from Spain in 1821. Indifferent Mexican padres *displaced the Spaniards who had consecrated their being to the California Indians, and soon ebbed away the blood of faith and fiery enthusiasm which had stirred Serra and Palóu to risk life in founding Missions. Neophytes quickly felt the change and returned to their* rancherias *and the old pagan life, even before the Mexican government completed secularization by placing the Missions in the charge of politicians.*

So the desecration seemed less poignant when Frémont's company clanked through Missions San Rafael, San Juan Bautista, San Luis Obispo and San Fernando; and when American troops after the conquest made barracks of Mission San Luis Rey and San Diego. Carmel's roof had crashed in, and to this ruin came Joaquin Murietta seeking refuge. La Purísima in the vale of flowers was a lair of the bandits Salomon Pico and Jack Powers. Deserted San Miguel contained a saloon and shops, and was haunted by the ghosts of eleven dead bodies found heaped up one night in 1848 in the Mission. At San Francisco, Mission Dolores was an amusement center with several saloons, two race tracks, bull and bear fights and dueling. In the north Santa Clara alone had been able to maintain the life of the spirit. Here, in 1851, the Jesuits established California's first permanent college in the Mission buildings.

But at Mission Santa Barbara in the south, the altar light continued to burn and the Franciscans still carried on the message of Saint Francis. It was the Vicar-General Gonzales Rubio of Mission Santa

Barbara who, shortly after the conquest, was responsible for rescuing Juana María with her strange story of mother-love.

JUANA MARÍA was a woman of mystery. No one knew her race or language. Perhaps she came from the north—one of the Indians brought by Russians who in violation of laws of Spain and Mexico preyed on the California coast, hunting otter. But because she loved greatly she will never be forgotten.

In 1853 *Padres* Tomás Esténaga and Alexis Bachelot of San Gabriel Mission heard that on the sterile sandy Island of San Nicolas, two hundred miles off the coast of Santa Barbara, a few Indians were starving. The *Padres* flamed with zeal to make converts. *Padre* Bachelot himself had experienced starvation when, after being banished from Hawaii by Queen Kaahumanu, he had been put ashore by his ship's Captain at San Pedro, and both *padres* were eager to rescue the Indians. There were only a few ships on the coast, but the *padres* sent Captain Charles Hubbard on the schooner *Peor es Nada* [The Worst is Nothing] to bring the Indians to the mainland from San Nicolas, most distant of all the Santa Barbara Channel Islands.

Captain Hubbard arrived at San Nicolas in a storm. Even the Kanaka sailors found it difficult to reach shore in the wild sea. Owing to the danger of the ship being wrecked on the shoals the sailors quickly herded twenty Indians together and drove them into boats. Among them was a mother, Juana María.

A Kanaka sailor was carrying Juana María's nursing baby, a boy. In the hurly-burly and haste he set the child down, expecting to return for it.

When the small boats reached the schooner, Juana María, a fiery figure in a loose chemise of otter skins, began demanding with wild gesticulations and moans and in a tongue strange to all, but which had unmistakable meaning, "My baby—where is my baby?"

An Indian baby was not much more important to the sailor than a jackrabbit. Juana María was frantic. She dominated the entire ship with her strong, brown body and her hair, faded golden brown by exposure to the sun, tossing wildly over her bare shoulders. She made all understand that already she had lost her husband and other children. Now her baby was gone! She moaned; she flung her arms around the sailor and implored him to go back for the child. The Captain came.

"I must have my baby. Send the boat back for him!" she gesticulated. The Captain pointed to the raging sea. "It isn't safe. The schooner will be wrecked in these shallows. When the weather is calm we'll go back."

But Juana María understood no explanation. Her baby was there alone on the Island of San Nicolas among wild animals. Fore and aft on the steamer she ran crying out. Could they not understand—were they not human—had they no children—had they no heart? To suffering Juana María life had no meaning without her baby.

As the ship set sail she screamed wildly. Captain Hubbard and the Kanaka sailors tried to restrain her, but she burst out of their grasp, leaped overboard and struck out with the strength of a man through the foamy kelpy waters for the island shore.

No man among all those on the *Peor es Nada* was brave enough to follow the Indian woman in the waters of tangled brown seaweed. Kanaka-born as the sailors were, they could not live in such a sea. They turned their eyes away as Juana María disappeared, a daring suicide. Some of the Indian mothers on board hugged their infants to their breasts—at least their own babies were safe, as safe as they could be huddled together on the deck of a schooner in churning waves.

The *Peor es Nada* ran before the wind to San Pedro and put the Indians ashore. Some were housed by the *padre* at the old Plaza Church Los Angeles; others were sent to San Gabriel. Captain Hubbard believed that the Indian woman was dead but he planned to return to the island for a final search.

Then he was ordered to sail for San Francisco. At the entrance to the Golden Gate his schooner capsized. The crew escaped. Few craft larger than Indian canoes remained on the coast, and no one dared attempt passage of the channel in a canoe. Juana María and her baby were forgotten....

For fifteen years! Then out of the past spoke one of the Indians, Jesus, to the Reverend Vicar General Gonzales Rúbio at Santa Barbara. He had been rescued by Captain Hubbard of the *Peor es Nada;* he had never forgotten the sight of the Indian woman swimming alone in that terrible sea back to her baby.

"Padre, I think she still lives on San Nicolas Island."

Padre Rúbio was shocked and grieved by the recital. He offered two thousand dollars reward to anyone who could give him information about the lost woman. Funds at Mission Santa Barbara were at their lowest, but *Padre* Rúbio paid Thomas Jeffries two hundred dollars to visit the island and rescue the woman if she still lived. Jeffries returned and reported, "There is no one living on San Nicolas."

Padre Rúbio would not give up. He sent George Nidever, a hardy pioneer of Santa Barbara, back with Jeffries and a crew of Indians. The *padre* admonished, "Do not return until you find the woman."

Nidever, Jeffries, and a crew of six Indians sailed over to San Nicolas and landed near the lower end of the island. They walked along the beach near a bluff for several miles; then—"Footprints! A human being!" The footprints were small like those of a woman and sunk deep in the hard dry ground. Probably they had been made during the previous rainy season.

Nidever led the company on. They found three small sagebrush enclosures a mile apart near the beach, on slightly rising ground. Human habitations! Suspended from stakes or driftwood stuck in the earth at a height of five or six feet were pieces of dried blubber well preserved. The windbreaks might have been built years before, but the blubber had been placed there within a few weeks. The men were greatly excited. The lost woman was alive! They would find her!

When a strong wind sprang up Nidever and his men hastened back to the schooner. The southeaster roared into a gale. Fearing for the safety of the schooner, they boarded it, and under the lee of the island the ship remained eight days. The anchor dragged. A second anchor was improvised by filling a bag with stones. San Nicolas had become a danger to Nidever and his men. They left for Santa Barbara and reported their discoveries to *Padre* Rúbio.

"Now I am certain the Indian woman lives," said the *Padre*. "You must go back."

Nidever had seen large numbers of otter on the island. Their pelts were valuable for fur, so he was eager to return to San Nicolas. He took with him Charles Brown and two sailors. The boat was anchored at the south end of the island with Indians in charge. Nidever and Brown walked along the beach northward.

"If the woman is alive," said Nidever, "she will be found here. It's a better place for both fish and seal." The huts of the preceding year were unaltered. There was seal blubber, but again it was fresh. *"Padre* Rúbio is right," said Nidever. "The woman is alive."

In the neighborhood of the huts were seven or eight wild, barking, black and white dogs, about the size of a coyote. Indians in the northwest had such dogs, and the impression was confirmed that the San Nicolas Indians might have been brought there by the Russians. At sight of Nidever and Brown the dogs fled.

The men reached the upper end of the island. No signs of the woman were found.

"The dogs must have eaten her," said Nidever. "Not even her bones are here."

A keen wind rose and Nidever was anxious about his boat. "No woman is living on the island," he finally declared.

Suddenly in the crotch of a *malva* bush he discovered a basket covered with sealskin. Within was a dress of shagskin cut in squares carefully pieced together, a sinew rope, abalone-shell fishhooks and bone needles.

"Her storeroom!" shouted Nidever. "She is alive!"

He scattered the various articles about on the ground. "If when we return we find them replaced in the basket, we will have definite proof of the woman's existence."

Nidever and Brown continued exploring the eastern end of the island. Another southeaster arose. It soon increased to a furious gale and Nidever was again driven back to Santa Barbara.

Padre Rúbio was impatient. "You must go back," he said. "Find that woman."

In July, 1853, Nidever returned with Charles Brown, an Irishman, and four Mission Indians in charge of the boat. Nidever and Brown camped on the island. At the end of San Nicolas Nidever found fresh tracks.

Excitedly he followed them on the beach and up over the bank where they were lost in the moss. Early next morning they all set out looking for the lost woman. Nidever continued along the shore to the head of the island. He found the storeroom—everything had been replaced in order.

"The woman is alive!" he cried.

Brown and four men crossed to the far side of the island. He sent the men to search among the bushes where the basket had been found. He saw the track he had noticed the night before and followed it up again, then lost it. He continued up the side of the ridge until he discovered a short piece of driftwood that had been washed ashore. The woman had been down to the beach for firewood, and had dropped this piece in returning! Farther up the ridge were three habitations. Breathlessly the men went forward.

They found some huts made of whale ribs covered with brush, open on all sides. Brown was in despair, for grass had grown tall in the huts. For some time they had been unoccupied. From the high part of the ridge he looked in all directions. A small, distant, moving black object caught his eye. Perhaps it was a crow. He went toward it. The object grew larger. On, on, he advanced cautiously.

There was an enclosure. Within was the Indian woman lost for eighteen years, her head and shoulders barely visible. Three black and white dogs seated near her began to growl.

Within a few yards of the woman Brown halted and silently signaled his men by placing a hat on the ramrod of his gun which he raised and lowered. They came toward him. Still the woman had not seen Brown.

He stood watching her. Cross-legged she was seated on the grass that covered the ground within the enclosure and which served as her bed. Her shoulders were bare, her dress was made of shagskin cut in squares and sewed together, the feathers pointing downward. Her bare head was covered with matted hair which seemed half rotted from exposure to sun and weather. Across her knee she held a piece of blubber she was stripping from a seal's skin with a makeshift iron knife. Near her was a smoldering fire. Outside the enclosure was a large pile of ashes and another of bones. Evidently she had lived here a long time.

Still the woman had not seen Brown, but he observed her astonishment when she saw his men approaching. She kept up a continuous talking to herself, occasionally shading her eyes with her hand and gazing steadily at the men drawing near. Brown wondered what she would do. Silently he signaled the men to spread out so as to prevent her escape. Just before they reached her camp Brown suddenly appeared before her. To his great surprise, she bowed, smiled and received him with much politeness and dignity, all the while speaking her unknown tongue.

When the men came up she greeted them in the same way and continued chattering. They seated themselves around her and she kept on talking. Although the Indians spoke several dialects, they did not understand a word she said.

Eighteen years had passed since the woman of San Nicolas had looked upon a human being, but she had graces of hospitality. Toothless, she smiled continually. From a sack made of grass she took some roots known among Spanish-Californians as *carcomites*. She roasted them on the fire and offered them as food. They proved nutritious and palatable.

Nidever wished to take her on board the boat and all the men made signs to her, "Come with us!" She did not understand. Finally they made her realize that she must gather up all her food and leave. With great alacrity she set about making ready. She placed her dried blubber of seal and sea elephant in a large Indian basket. She wished to take even a seal's head so decayed that the brains were oozing out. Nothing should be cast aside. For eighteen years she had felt pains of hunger and had subsisted on the wild provender of San Nicolas. Generous with her few possessions, she offered her rescuers native foods.

In order to please her, Nidever and Brown permitted her to take the seal's head with her. Her aesthetic triumph!

The woman had no conception of candles, coal oil, or lamps. She took her burning torch, a stick, in one hand and departed from her island home. Each of the men carried a portion of her possessions. Especially eager was she to keep the lines she had used for fishing and a large rope she had made for snaring sea otter when they came to sleep on the rocks. She led her rescuers to a spring that supplied her with water. In the clefts of a rock was her food arsenal—her store of bones that she sucked. Here also she kept dried blubber. In order to gain the woman's confidence Nidever and Brown preserved all her belongings.

In spite of her isolation for eighteen years she had her own special bathing spring. She stopped there and washed her hands and face. She showed the men her cave where she slept in stormy weather.

Then she went down to the landing to visit Nidever's schooner. She knelt in the bow of the boat and clung to the sides. So much had she suffered from cold on the island that she kept near the schooner stove. She ate with relish pork and hardtack given her by Nidever and Brown, preferring them to native food. Of sugar she could not get enough. Greedily she smacked her lips and asked for more. Remembering the eighteen years, she saved every scrap of food left after the first meal, even the bones.

That afternoon on the schooner Brown made her a skirt out of bedticking. Greatly pleased, she put it on and continually called their attention to it. Proudly she looked at her skirt, her man's shirt and necktie—her new costume of civilization of the mainland.

While Brown was sewing she made signs, "Let me sew"; and he gave her needle and thread. How to put the thread through the eye baffled her until he showed her the way. She thrust the needle into the cloth with her right hand, pulling it through and drawing the thread tight with her left. Nidever gave her a dilapidated but heavy cape serviceable in cold weather.

Returning to the island, Nidever and Brown made a hunting camp between the beach and rocks. Their shelter of poles against the rocks was covered with sailcloth. They erected a similar shelter for her at a distance, roofing it with brush. During the month they remained on the island she made no effort to leave. In eighteen years she had talked so much to herself and her dogs that she could not chatter enough, although her rescuers could only guess at her meaning. She talked, talked, and sang.

Gratefully she brought wood and water for her rescuers. She fashioned unique grass vessels for holding water, each like a demijohn. The wide mouth was lined with a coating of asphaltum found on the beach. Ingeniously she put several pieces of asphaltum in the bottom of the basket, and hot pebbles on top. When the asphaltum was melted, by a quick motion she covered the inside of the basket with an even coating and threw away the surplus. These containers were watertight and lasted a long time.

When Nidever and Brown killed otter, after skinning them, they cast the bodies into the sea. One day they killed a large female which was with young. When the hunters were throwing it away the woman protested. The young otter which was nearly grown and covered with fur was taken out and the skin stuffed. This delighted the woman—it seemed to take the place of her baby. She suspended it to a pole in her shelter and swung it back and forth for hours, crooning to it in singsong.

During their otter hunt on the island, Brown and Nidever made shift to piece out her story. Certainly she had reached the island after her leap from the *Peor es Nada* eighteen years before, but whether she found her baby alive, dead or missing no one could know—or, if alive, how long it had survived the hard island life. She had her dogs for companions at the end—that was all.

They could see how she had contrived to exist; making fire with flint, digging native roots and bulbs from the ground, gathering sea-gulls' eggs, and cooking them over driftwood coals. They saw she was expert at trapping sea otter and killing them with spears she had made with flints as tools; saw how she had dried their flesh and strung it high on poles to keep it from preying animals. She had fished too, with lines made from otters' sinews and fishhooks chipped from abalone shells. When roots, fish and otter failed, she had her storehouse in rock clefts filled with bones for her and her dogs to gnaw.

And she had fashioned clothing from other otter skins—the men saw the castoff iron hoop she used in skinning the animals, the bone needles and sinews with which she patched the squares of skin together. They saw a dress she had woven of feathers, white, blue, yellow, black and red, left by birds of passage—a long, vividly colored garment which was a masterpiece of workmanship.

As for her shelter, the rescuers had seen the small huts she had built, circular sagebrush enclosures six feet high on small elevations near the shore in different parts of the island. One was more elaborate than the others, with its framework of whale's ribs covered with brush.

Thus from the visible signs of her life on the island they could fill in a part of her story.

The woman of San Nicolas had a species of religion too. Her faith was revealed when the schooner sailed for Santa Barbara and she entered her new life. A furious gale arose and the little vessel was threatened. The woman made a sign as if to say, "Let me allay the wind." Kneeling down she turned her face toward the gale and commenced making incantations. The storm did not cease. Again she knelt. And again! When the wind abated she pointed to the clear sky. "See what I did!"

Santa Barbara with its Mission and its colorful gardens was her delight from the time they approached the shore early in the morning. Perhaps she had never before seen a settlement of civilization. She clapped her hands and danced when she saw an ox team with a Spanish cart. She touched the wheels, the yoke, the animals tied to each other—laughing, talking, gesticulating all at once.

Another new wonder was a horseman riding along the beach. She embraced the horse, caressed the saddle, touched the man. She straddled the first two fingers of her right hand over her left thumb imitating the gallop of the horse, and she shouted with delight.

Santa Barbara made *fiesta* for the lost woman of San Nicolas. George Nidever's dwelling became the court of the South with the lost woman as queen! Vicar General Gonzales Rúbio and *Padres* Sanchez and Jimeno gave her their blessing. They baptized her Juana María. Hundreds flocked to see her. Indians came from Santa Inés, San Gabriel, and Los Angeles. Not one of them understood her language. Somewhere she had acquired the words "pickaninny" and *"mañana."* She conversed by signs.

Everyone in Santa Barbara paid Juana María tribute—in money, clothing and trinkets. Usually she gave them to children. She loved the picture of the Infant and all children. She looked at them tenderly, crooned with tears in her eyes as she held them in her arms. Nearly two decades had passed, but her empty arms still ached with longing for her lost baby.

In these years—the 'fifties of the gold rush—the Panama steamer touched at Santa Barbara, and passengers asked to see the lost woman. For them she would put on her fine feather dress into which she had woven so much loveliness, and would dance the dances of her people.

Juana María was like a greedy child with no control over her appetite. Fruit she ate inordinately, and at all hazards. An intestinal disease developed. She had careful nursing and attendance. It was thought that her customary diet of seal meat would restore her health; so a meal was prepared and roasted. She shook her head and laughed, rubbing her finger along her gums. It was too late.

Alone on the Island of San Nicolas Juana María had survived eighteen years, but seven weeks of civilization killed her. George Nidever made her a rough board coffin, and she was buried by the Fathers in the cemetery near Mission Santa Barbara. Most of her trinkets, including the beautiful feather dress, were sent by Father Gonzales Rúbio to Rome.

For years Juana María's grave was neglected, but since 1928 it has been marked by a tablet on the Mission wall below the tower— placed there by the Santa Barbara Chapter of the Daughters of the American Revolution. Father Augustine Hobrecht accepted it on behalf of the *Padres*. One of the last points of interest stres; d to tourists leaving the Santa Barbara Mission cemetery is this tablet in memory of Juana María, devoted mother, the woman Robinson Crusoe of San Nicolas Island.

XXII

VASQUEZ AND ROSARIO

1873

FRANCISCANS brought to California tolerance for crimes of violence. In the beginning San Diego Mission was wiped out, Padre Jayme was killed and others lost their lives. Padre *Panto was poisoned by his Indian cook, but the murderers were not executed, nor were they punished by death at other Missions where they killed* padres. *The Indians were regarded as ignorant, willful children.*

Some of that spirit lingered in California when the Americans came by the thousand in 1849 after the discovery of gold. Law and order were not easily maintained in the world's greatest mining camp. In the early 'fifties one person in every six met violent death. Some men were lynched, not so often for murder as for the state's most heinous crime, horse-stealing.

Several great purges of criminals took place in San Francisco, one in 1851 when the Sidney Ducks and an organization called the Hounds burned San Francisco for the fifth time, sweeping away the last of the old Mexican buildings of Yerba Buena. Even easy-going San Francisco then lost patience and shipped the Sidney Ducks and the Hounds out of the country on a warship.

There were endless duels in California, and disorder was so great that Vigilantes were formed throughout the state with several thousand members. Governor J. Neeley Johnson hysterically ordered out the militia and summoned Federal troops, saying there was an insurrection in California. After several men were lynched, the situation clarified, but hatred continued to embitter the descendants of those Spanish pioneers who had come to California more than seventy years before the Stars and Stripes were raised. Joaquin Murietta, avenger of Rosita, was dead, but his spirit burned with dark splendor in the hearts of Spanish-Californians. They would not admit that he had been shot down on the Tulare plains. To this day old Californians will assure one that Murietta died years later in Mexico. One Spanish-Californian especially cherished Murietta's memory— Tiburcio Vasquez. He was born in a little adobe house just back of Colton Hall in Monterey. It stands today after more than a hundred years. It is one of the landmarks of Monterey, and is owned by Mr. Louis Hill.

Vasquez came of a family that had helped to found San Francisco. His grandfather, Tiburcio Vasquez, was alcalde of San José and well educated by the standards of his time. He himself had gone to good Monterey schools, learning to write poetry and play the guitar.

When he was seventeen Vasquez was falsely accused of having shot an American constable at Monterey and was exiled from the old Spanish capital. After he was outlawed he joined men older and more bold. For years he lived recklessly, robbing rich gringos and often giving his plunder to the poor, but he would weep on reading Paul and Virginia. Like Murietta he found at every Spanish-Californian ranch a refuge, friends and facile loves. Reasonable security was his until he met Rosario.

TIBURCIO—in the 'sixties and 'seventies to Spanish-Californians that word meant Tiburcio Vasquez, young, pale, with deep-set gray eyes, over his shoulders a black cape lined with red!

To Americans Vasquez was only a "greaser" bandit with a price on his head. To Old California he was the last valiant protest against *gringo* conquest. *Señoras* and *señoritas* loved him—how many, he alone knew. And Vasquez loved *señoras* and *señoritas*.

I will not tell of them. Not even of *Señora* Salazar who fled with him from Mission San Juan Bautista, died in his arms, and was brought back to be laid on the doorstep of Salazar her husband, an escapade nearly costing Vasquez his life. I write only of his last love—Rosario.

Both Vasquez and Rosario had the heritage of founders of San Francisco, the Spanish pioneers in the Anza expedition of 1776. Both families were grantees of leagues of land. Alviso, the town, still bears Rosario's family name. Like Vasquez, Rosario was part of the warm coppery soil of California.

But they did not meet until she was the wife of Abdon Leiva of Chualar and mother of his two children. Vasquez had no wife. He belonged to all women, especially to women of Spain—like Rosario, with passion-flower lips and scarlet dancing slippers. When Vasquez and Rosario met at the *fandango* at the New Idria Mine their wild hearts flamed together.

Already Rosario knew Vasquez's story. Outlawed at seventeen from Monterey for a crime he did not commit, he became the avenger of the conquest of California. No *gringo* property was safe from him. He outrode sheriffs. He ruled in the mountains and in the sunny valleys. Wherever Spanish-Californians were, there was his home. Saint Never-Say-a-Word was the patron of his kingdom.

"Tiburcio is back from Mexico!" passed from lip to lip as Vasquez flung like a *magnifico* into the dancing *sala* at the New Idria. *Caballeros* embraced him. *Señoras* and *señoritas* offered wine, tamales, *enchiladas, tortillas.*

"*Gracias,* no feasting!" he cried. "On the way from Monterey I outrode a posse in the valley below."

There was almost royal authority in his manner as he strode across the *fandango* house floor to Rosario. He gave an order to the musicians.

Vasquez and Rosario danced. "*Señorita—*"

Feebly trying to erect a barrier Rosario corrected, "*Señora*—Rosario Leiva—"

"Rose of the mountain," he gallantly interpreted.

Vasquez's lieutenant, burly young Cleodoveo Chavez, hastened into the room with the warning, "*Capitán!*"

Before Chavez spoke Vasquez's quick eye saw the slouch hat of the stocky sandy-haired sheriff. "Hands up, Vasquez!"

"Hands up, yourself!" gaily sang out the outlaw. Gun in each hand, he plunged across the room and out of an open window guarded by Chavez.

Vasquez's blood stained the windowsill, but once more he and Chavez were on the road, matching their wits with the law. The sheriff declared that he had driven the outlaws into Mexico. After twisting over trails, fresh bullets in their bodies, Vasquez and Chavez appeared at Abdon Leiva's small *rancho* in the vicinity of Chualar not far from Mission Soledad. Leiva was only one of many who sheltered Vasquez. His *ranchito* became the outlaw's refuge.

Vasquez's pockets were always overflowing. Often in the night Vasquez and Chavez rode swiftly down the mountain into the Salinas and Santa Clara Valleys, waylaid travelers, ventured into San José and Monterey, bought Manila shawls and slippers for Rosario, and toys for the shining-eyed, sturdy Leiva children. There were always fresh horses for Vasquez at the valley *ranchos*. Spanish-Californian *rancheros* thought it a small crime to rob *gringos*. Had not Americans taken California from them?

Vasquez and Leiva became as brothers. When drouth killed sheep and cattle, Vasquez lent Leiva money. To Rosario it seemed fairy gold. Abdon would not have believed it, unless Rosario herself had told him, that Vasquez had charmed her conscience away. One day as she was riding back from Mission San Juan Bautista she had fallen into Vasquez's arms on a field fragrant with spring flowers. Her children's faces flashed before her, even while she said:

"Tiburcio, let me go away with you."

"Some day. Now the danger is too great."

"I want to share your danger."

"You're too precious to be risked. One more great raid! Then Mexico—you and I!"

Her arms seemed to strangle him with love. Those soft clinging arms, how could they know that they were symbol of a noose?

Rosario felt more deeply united with Vasquez than with Leiva.

To the *Padre* at Mission San Juan Bautista she said, "Tiburcio Vasquez is to be the father of my next child."

"Unless you give up this man, you will never see your children in heaven."

Unashamed she replied, "I shall be with my new child and Tiburcio."

Drouth was prolonged. Even autumn flowers died. Leiva's crops failed. Cattle cried out piteously for food and water in the wide thirsty spaces. Their bones whitened on the hills. The Leivas became dependent upon Vasquez. Rosario suggested to her husband, "Why not join Tiburcio?"

Dull, well-meaning Leiva was horrified. "*Caramba!* Rosario! Me, a thief! Would you steal?"

"*Madre de Dios!*" she stormed. "We both are poor today because of those pie-eating Yankees. Tiburcio doesn't think it a crime to rob *gringos*. Neither do I. They beggared us. Tiburcio is man enough to fight back."

"I'm not strong enough to fight law."

"There is no law in California for Californians. Law is made by *gringos* for *gringos*. Tiburcio is no coward."

"*Caramba!*" cried Leiva. "Neither am I!"

"The children and I starve. Tiburcio risks his life in the valleys. You play safe, borrow his money. If that isn't being a coward—*Dios de mi vida!*"

Drouth aided Rosario. Leiva weakened before his wife's renewed taunts. But in his first holdup on the Monterey road he deserted Vasquez. Back at his *ranchito* he dreaded meeting neighbors. He winced even when his dog nuzzled his hand.

Again Rosario goaded him into joining the raid on Firebaugh's Ferry. Fear of the future made clammy sweat stand on his forehead. With a hand on Leiva's thick shoulder Vasquez rallied him laughingly.

"Abdon, be as good a man as Rosario."

"*Bien, Capitán,*" feebly answered Leiva.

Vasquez saluted Rosario, *"Señora Capitán!"*

A great new plan—a whirl into the valley, rob stores, hold up the New Idria stage—then Mexico! Happiness, sweet-to-do-nothing, liberty! Rosario made Leiva as enthusiastic as Vasquez.

On the day of the great robbery Rosario and the children rode southward. Vasquez, Leiva, Chavez, and their company ostentatiously escorted them down the mountain and over the sultry, hazy plain. They pretended they were all leaving together, but Rosario and the children were to meet them at San Emidio.

After *Adiós* to Rosario, Vasquez and his company galloped north to the wide, rocky Tres Pinos Creek. There they cleaned guns. A mile distant lay their first booty, the Tres Pinos supply store. All that hot August day in 1873 they lay under oak and sycamore trees waiting. Night came and Vasquez commanded, "Tie everybody. If anyone resists, shoot. Take everything you can carry!"

Pell-mell they rode over the dusty road to Tres Pinos and plunged toward the store. "Lay down, everybody! *Pronto!*"

Tres Pinos had seen many holdups. Loungers dropped as though shot. They were tied. A deaf man resisted. Vasquez's gun brought him down and the outlaw crossed himself. "Hurry through the safe! Then for the hotel!" The landlord tried to close the front door. Pistol in hand, Vasquez was on the porch and a bullet crashed through the door into the landlord's brain.

All horses at Tres Pinos were taken to prevent pursuit. The bandits packed the store supplies on horses' backs.

Vasquez led. Chavez guarded the rear. "Faster, *amigos!*" shouted Vasquez. "Hurry!"

When they met travelers they hid in the chaparral. Then on they went at high speed. Vasquez's horses gave out. Chavez's horses failed. They mounted the stolen animals. "Faster!" shouted Vasquez.

They thought they were galloping away from the noose. But no matter how fast they went they could not leave behind the picture of the accusing men on the bloody ground at Tres Pinos.

When Vasquez divided booty on the range between San Benito

and Fernandez Valleys he gave his followers money only. Jewelry and telltale objects he kept back. Chavez protested.

"*Amigo,* I am lost," replied Vasquez. "These murders will arouse California. You boys have a chance. Nothing can save me. I am finished!"

For safety they separated. When they met at the Higuera ranch at dinner Leiva accosted Vasquez, glowering savagely. "Tiburcio, they say I should put a bullet into you."

Vasquez tried to laugh down Leiva's white anger. "Let the sheriff do that." He offered Leiva a cigarette.

Abdon's hand was on his hip as he said, "They say Rosario—"

Vasquez had met many wrathful husbands. "No one can say a word against Rosario. She is like my sister." He flung his arm over Leiva's shoulder.

"People talk, Tiburcio."

"*Caramba!* Of course! They want to break up our company. We must stick together. Those three men at Tres Pinos—remember! May the saints rest their souls!"

Leiva was humbled. "*Perdón!*" Arm and arm with Vasquez he walked into the arbor of pine branches where the Higueras were entertaining a large company.

Soon Leiva's heavy face hardened. He sat thrusting the blade of his sharp knife through his hat crown. Vasquez observed him and smiled fraternally.

"*Vamos!*" ordered Vasquez. Some of the company he sent northward to establish an alibi. As he rode southward with Leiva and Chavez, Vasquez observed Abdon furtively scrutinizing him.

At San Emidio Rosario embraced Vasquez as if she were welcoming the entire world. She kissed Leiva also, even Chavez. But she kissed Vasquez first. Something different in that kiss! The blackness in Leiva's eyes deepened.

Vasquez detected suspicion under Leiva's friendliness. It was not concealed in his tenderness for Rosario, nor during his frolics with the children, nor when he said, "Isn't it great to be here with Rosario

ADOBE BIRTHPLACE OF TIBURCIO VASQUEZ AT MON-
TEREY.

LAST PHOTOGRAPH OF TIBURCIO VASQUEZ
BEFORE HIS EXECUTION IN 1873.

LYNCH LAW IN CALIFORNIA.—SURRENDER OF PRISONERS AT THE COUNTY JAIL, SAN FRAN-CISCO [From an old woodcut].

again?" His eyes followed every word and look passing between Vasquez and Rosario. When they went on to Elizabeth Lake, Leiva still watched.

Camp was struck in a canyon under cottonwoods and sycamores. No danger of posses! Safety from everyone—save themselves.

Leiva set his trap.

He left for Elizabeth Lake to buy supplies. Feebly Vasquez volunteered to go. Leiva would not listen. "I am not known in the vicinity. I'll return about midnight, possibly in the morning. *Adiós!*"

Rosario and Vasquez did not try to conceal their joy in the first words, "At last, alone!"

It was the first time that they had been freely together since the sacking of Tres Pinos. The children played in the dry gravelly arroyo. Chavez went hunting and brought back quail and jackrabbit which Rosario cooked over the open fire. They supped on boiled jackrabbit, wild onions and wine from the Leiva *ranchito*. The children went to sleep in the tent. Chavez rolled up in his blanket in the thicket. Rosario played the guitar and sang Spanish songs.

At last Rosario and Vasquez lay in each other's arms on the golden sycamore leaves. *"Madre de Dios!* How long it has been, Tiburcio."

"I feared I should be shot before seeing you again. Now let the posses come."

Posses! Danger—they forgot all. Then—

Leiva stood before them. "Traitors!"

Chavez was startled out of his sleep by Leiva's coyote cry when he found Vasquez and Rosario together, passion-pale. Like a black panther he sprang between Vasquez and Leiva.

"Vasquez, defend yourself," shouted Leiva.

Within the week Vasquez had committed murder, but he defined his code. "Abdon, I'll not kill you after taking your wife. Honor—"

Leiva went mad. *"Sangre de Cristo! Honor!"*

Chavez pressed his dragoon pistol against Leiva's heart. Abdon knew that Cleodoveo Chavez would give his life for Tiburcio Vasquez.

Leiva dropped his gun and roared, "Choose weapons, Vasquez!"

"No, Abdon, I should kill you. Your children need you. I'll not kill you unless you attack. Then I'll defend myself."

"You ruined my home, made me an outlaw, a sharer in your murders. You—worse than *gringo*."

Vasquez raised his gun. "Don't," pleaded Chavez. "Sheriffs may be near—"

Leiva turned away. "Rosario, get the children ready!"

"Where are we going?" asked Rosario.

"Get ready, I say."

Rosario looked at Vasquez. Would he let her go?

Vasquez's eyes were on the ground. What-can-I-offer? Sheriff's-bullets. Her-children. Our-child. Leiva-will-protect-her-better-than-I-can. Why-doesn't-he-shoot? Leiva-will-kill-me.

Rosario dressed the sleepy children. Leiva harnessed the horses. Chavez helped place their belongings in the wagon. Leiva shook Chavez's hand. "Cleodoveo, quit," he said. "If you stay with Vasquez the *gringos* will hang you."

Chavez grinned. "Not till I split a few of their tongues."

"No more of this life for me," said Leiva. As he prepared to leave with his wife and children he turned to Vasquez. "Wherever we meet, shoot me first. If you don't—"

Rosario's head bent over her children. Her body seemed crumpled with age as the wagon rattled out of the rocky arroyo. "Tiburcio failed me—he let me go!" she thought.

Chavez found Vasquez face downward on the gray leaf-covered gravel where he and Rosario had fallen like blind things into each other's arms. His hand held a pistol. He lay like a man already dead.

"*Capitán*," said Chavez gaily, "thank the saints that woman has gone. Now we can get away."

Vasquez was silent. Chavez tumbled into his blanket. Vasquez sat up and rolled a cigarette. When Chavez woke he found Vasquez smoking. He lighted a fire and made coffee, but Vasquez would neither eat nor drink. Chavez wolfed dried meat. As he went to the creek to fetch water he picked up a Los Angeles paper dropped the previous evening by Leiva. Staring he read.

"Four sheriffs looking for us! *Cristo!* The Governor's reward— $5,600! Dead or alive!"

"I'm going to find Rosario," said Vasquez.

Chavez protested. "I like women, but Tiburcio—"

"Rosario—"

"Rosario should not come with us."

"She must."

"*Gringo* sheriffs may be here any minute. What can we do for Rosario?"

"Risk nothing for me, Cleodoveo. Strike out for yourself. I'm going to Rosario."

Chavez's face twisted. The scar stood out on his brow and cheek. "I'm not trying to save my own neck. It's you, *Capitán.* I'll never leave you, whatever comes." They shook hands.

At sunset Vasquez and Chavez followed Leiva's trail out of the canyon to find Rosario.

Posses.... Vasquez heard them behind trees, in crackling brush, in the sound of fallen leaves! Posses were hot on their heels. From Tres Pinos. From Cantua Canyon. Through the furnace-like desert surrounding Fresno and Bakersfield. Over marshes, past Lake Tulare. And on to San Emidio. On a mesa a few miles from Jim Heffner's road house, in a thicket of vines, poison oak, sycamores and alders, Vasquez and Chavez met the sheriffs. At two hundred yards they fought. The sheriffs took refuge behind boulders. Vasquez and Chavez slid their horses down a precipice and were away.

"To Rosario!" said Vasquez.

"*Caramba!* Rosario is death."

"Those posses showed me death, Cleodoveo. I am going to Rosario."

Chavez argued no further with his mad leader. "*Bien!* May San Antonio save you!" In silence Vasquez and Chavez embraced. Each had a foreboding that it was for the last time.

A swift ride over the trail, and late that night Vasquez rapped at the door of Jim Heffner, friend of the lawless. "Is Leiva here?"

"He left two hours ago. His wife and children are upstairs."

Vasquez stalked through the house to Rosario asleep with her children, a rosary in her hand. "Come!" She did not understand. "*Querida,* come!"

"Tiburcio, you! I've been praying to save you from Leiva."

"Where is he?"

"Gone to betray you to the sheriff. You escaped! Thank the Mother of God!"

"Hurry, my heart! We shall never be separated again."

"My children—"

"Our child will soon be here, Rosario. We can get away to Mexico."

"If we can't—"

"I am doomed. We shall be homeless as mountain lions. Will you come?"

"It will be too hard for you—"

"If it is but an hour, Rosario, I want you."

Even her sleeping children did not stay her flight. Her unborn child and its father outweighed the years behind. Weeping, she kissed the children *Adiós.*

"Courage, Rosario." Together they went down the creaking stairs and plunged into midnight future of fugitives.

Vasquez lifted her to his waiting horse and swung into saddle behind Rosario. Up the steep trail from Heffner's house they rode. In ascending they saw sheriffs coming down the opposite side of the mountain. Soon Vasquez and Rosario were out of sight, miles away on the mountains where they met Chavez.

The lovers learned anew love's cost—hiding in thickets, saddle blankets for bedding, no sleep, cold food, two days without eating, raw deer meat eight days, battles with cougars, death always on the next curve of the trail! Alone in their great house with its quivering walls by day and its shimmering roof by night, their love was bounded by the stars.

One late October night they struck camp in the mountains not far from Mission San Fernando. New danger! As unattended as a mountain lion Rosario prematurely gave birth to a son. She tore off her own garments and wrapped them around the weak child. Blankets were her only clothing.

Vasquez rode down into the valley, robbed a peddler of garments and bedding and hurried back to Rosario.

The baby lay in a stupor. Rosario held the little wrinkled body. *"Madre de Dios!* You must not die!" He chafed the baby's hands, breathed into his mouth, tried to give him some of his own fierce strength.

"What if he should die, Tiburcio—without baptism? *Dios de mi vida!* He must not! For love of the Holy Mother, fetch a *padre!* Save the baby!"

Long since Vasquez had lost faith in all save his own destiny, but he rejoiced that Rosario still had faith. "I'll ride till I find a *padre, querida."*

Rosario touched a small silver crucifix suspended from her throat. Tiburcio would come back.

At Mission San Fernando among palm and olive trees Vasquez aroused the aged *padre* from his sleep. "My child is dying in the mountains, *Padre.* Will you come quickly to baptize him? I'll take you on my horse and bring you back."

Rosario was lying on her bed of straw and blankets when they arrived, attempting to shield her son from the sharp autumn wind. *"Pronto! Padre,* save my baby!"

The infant was baptized Tiburcio. Rosario promised to take the baby to the Mission to complete the ceremony.

"My son," said the *Padre* when he got down from the horse at the Mission, "why do you and your *señora* live in such poverty?"

Vasquez knew there was no danger of betrayal. *"Padre,* I am Tiburcio Vasquez."

"Unfortunate man."

"The mother of my son left husband and children to come with me."

The priest shook his head. "Unhappy—"

"We're happy, *Padre mio*. We have risked life together. We're going to Mexico."

"Poor erring children. Send the woman back to her family."

"Impossible."

Vasquez found Rosario peering into the baby's closed eyes. "He doesn't move. He is cold." She knew that her son was dead. Softly she rocked him in her arms and shivered. Vasquez placed more blankets over her shoulders. As they sat looking at their child their love was deepened by tears.

With sticks and pointed rocks Vasquez and Chavez hollowed out the shallow grave. They covered the body with wild vermilion fuchsias and white starry tarweed. On the scarred earth they planted poppies.

"Come away, Rosario," urged Vasquez. But when she tried to mount the horse she fainted.

Rosario's cough, sunken chest and hollowed eyes alarmed Vasquez. Autumn rains began. He took her to the cabin of a Spanish-Californian sheepherder, where for the first time in weeks she tasted bread and coffee. From the sheepherder Vasquez learned that already some of his company were in prison.

In court at San José Leiva testified, "My wife is with Vasquez. I don't know where. I would like to find him with a gun."

Rewards increased. Posses tore over California. Dead or alive Vasquez must be found. Rosario feared that her frail arms were holding him for death.

"Go," she begged. "If you don't, they'll find you. Hurry away."

At first Vasquez would not listen. "One more raid to the north. Then back to you, *querida,* and over the border to Sonora! Forever!" Love's eternal mirage!

Once more Vasquez was on the road, north, south. Five sheriffs raced after him and Chavez. The Governor's reward was $15,000 for

Vasquez dead or alive. At Greek George's ranch [now Hollywood], he was trapped and brought back to the old Pueblo San José de Guadalupe where his grandfather, the *Alcalde* Don Tiburcio Vasquez, once ruled.

Rosario followed Vasquez. "Forever" had been transformed into "never." She implored Leiva, "Do not testify against Tiburcio. It will only please the *gringos.*"

Wasted words. Vain tears! It was Leiva's day. There was more than one way to kill! He took the slow easy way—not a bloodstain on his own hands. Smiling he watched Vasquez's white face as he heard the sentence, "Hanged by the neck.... And may God have mercy on your soul."

Rosario wracked and broken choked out her grief, "I killed you, Tiburcio."

"Don't be sad, *querida*. Our love was worth it. This isn't the end. It will go on."

March 18, 1875, closed Vasquez's material existence. He had dared death too often to fear the black cap that shut out the light. With a crucifix in his hand he cried to the approaching darkness, *"Pronto! Pronto!"*

Through that night all Spanish-California—the mighty and the lowly—prayed with Rosario for the soul of their defender, the man with the sinister deep-set gray eyes and the black cloak lined with red.

Prolonged misery was Rosario's life. Where she rests is unknown. For more than half a century Tiburcio Vasquez's grave at Santa Clara was marked only by a weather-beaten board cross that was often battered to the ground by storms. But spring never failed to recarpet his earth-house with orange poppies. Often in the autumn the grass was charred black with flames that seemed hungry to obliterate Vasquez.

Then a man of God remembered—one of Tiburcio Vasquez's own faith. He erected a headstone and planted a palm of Saint Francis. So the Man of Assisi loved and forgave sinners.

XXIII

SHARON'S ROSE AND TERRY

1881

THOUSANDS *who had been lured to California by the siren summons of gold found none in the placers, but they were charmed by the climate and the new free life. They bought Spanish land grants, or established themselves in business. They sent for their families and friends, and the sleepy little settlement, Yerba Buena, became San Francisco, the metropolis of the Pacific Coast.*

In the 'sixties the mountains gave the Pacific Coast another surprise. The silver mines of Nevada opened, and adventurous Californians, mostly San Franciscans, rushed to the Comstock Lode. Nevada's silver made more millionaires. Fair, Flood, Mackay and Senator William A. Sharon brought their millions to San Francisco and became part of its life.

Even more exciting than the Nevada discovery of silver for all California and the Pacific Coast was the driving of the golden spike of the overland railroad on May 10, 1869. Now there was a railroad from the Atlantic to the Pacific! A new group of millionaires, Huntington, Hopkins, Stanford and Crocker, vied with each other in erecting handsome dwellings on San Francisco's high hill—Nob Hill it was called.

Of course, San Francisco had its great promoter, William C. Ralston, the magnificent. Under his wizard's touch, theaters, factories, and irrigation schemes developed; there arose also the Palace—not only the largest building in the West but the greatest hotel in the world— and San Francisco's pride. A day came, however, when Ralston's wand no longer performed magic and his body was found in San Francisco Bay. Ralston's Palace became the property of his partner,

Senator William A. Sharon, who was cool-headed in finance, but careless in his relations with women. One of them, Sarah Althea Hill, suddenly startled San Francisco by announcing that she was his wife.

And into the maelstrom of charges and counter-charges was drawn David S. Terry, former Justice of the Supreme Court of California. Terry who had a heightened sense of life in a storm; Terry who had held off Vigilantes single-handed in 1856, planting his dirk in the neck of Vigilante Hopkins; Terry who had laid low United States Senator David C. Broderick in a duel—now Terry had a new battle to fight, for a tantalizing slip of a Southern girl.

SAN FRANCISCO in the 'eighties argued fiercely over Sarah Althea Hill, the girl with hair of raw gold, moss-rose cheeks, and a rosebud mouth. She was Senator Sharon's Rose. But was she his secret wife?

The legal battle between Sharon and his cast-off Rose divided families, disrupted friendships and was as tragic as a Greek drama. Numerous law books have been written about Sharon *vs.* Sharon.

Sharon was the Pacific Coast Vanderbilt. When he passed up Market Street, San Francisco did not see a delicate little man with stone-gray eyes. San Francisco beheld the Palace Hotel, the Bank of California, millions in bonds, Nevada's fabulous Comstock Lode, with the United States Senate as decoration. Powerful, shrewd, precise, a poker player who coldly wagered $10,000 on a hand, with an ever-changing succession of mistresses to whom he admittedly paid $500 a month— could it be that at sixty he had married Sarah Althea Hill because he could possess her in no other way?

Sharon's North said "No." Sarah Althea's South said "Yes." Was she not one of their own kind, gently born, convent bred, a lady? The South knew ladies. Men died on the dueling field for the honor of ladies. When the divorce case Sharon *vs.* Sharon went to trial in Judge Sullivan's court in 1881, the South stood with its own daughter. Rudely Sharon denied he had ever married his Rose.

Three years before the battle began, Sarah Althea Hill—an orphan with a depleted inheritance from her father, a Missouri attorney—

sought out Senator Sharon, the great financier, for advice in stock investments. She was living modestly at the Baldwin Hotel. Sharon dwelt luxuriously at his own magnificent Palace Hotel, the largest in the world. Impoverished though she was, Sarah Althea considered Sharon her social inferior, an old Yankee moneybags who should be delighted to aid a Southern lady in distress.

Sharon was flattered, even charmed. He invited her to the sumptuous Palace. How lonely he was since his wife's death! His children had their own interests. And wasn't Sarah Althea a pretty girl? Weren't her eyes blue? Wasn't her hair golden? Weren't her cheeks like apples? Weren't her hands soft? Weren't her feet tiny? He had a poetic flight—Shakespeare. He sang *Auld Lang Syne*. He drove her down to his magnificent country home Belmont, erected by William Ralston, his partner who had committed suicide after building the Palace Hotel. Here in the music room where Ralston had entertained Adelaide Neilson, Sharon sang for his Rose.

Was all this effort and scenic effect that Sharon might make her one of his five-hundred-dollars-a-month mistresses? So he testified.

Under oath Sarah Althea contradicted him. She swore that because of family hostility to his remarriage the Senator gave her a secret contract. Sitting on his knee, she said, she wrote from his dictation:

In the City and County of San Francisco, State of California, on the 25th day of August, A. D. 1880, I, Senator William Sharon, of the State of Nevada, aged sixty years, do here, in the presence of Almighty God, take Sarah Althea Hill of the City of San Francisco, to be my lawful and wedded wife, and do here acknowledge myself to be the husband of Sarah Althea Hill.

> William Sharon of Nevada,
> August 25, 1880.

I hereby agree not to make known the contents of this paper or its existence for two years, unless Mr. Sharon himself sees fit to make it known.

> S. A. HILL.

Of this document Sarah Althea Hill said in court, "I have regarded it as my honor for three long years." Her golden hair seemed to send out sparks of fire. Her blue eyes were avenging as she leveled a gloved finger toward Senator Sharon, "He dictated it to me."

Never before had the Pacific Coast seen the stone-eyed Sharon lose his poker calm, his senatorial dignity. On his feet, he gripped the table shouting, "It is the damndest lie ever uttered on earth. The paper is a forgery....I'm a pretty old fish, not to be caught with that kind of bait."

Sarah Althea's lover was now her enemy; every line of expression disclosed it. Lovely and pallid, she appealed to the court. "I do not like to offend Your Honor, but he has his millions against me. I'm only a woman. I've been driven from my home. He has taken my money. I have no money to defend myself with."

Every minute of the trial was torment to the silvery-haired Senator and to his highly placed daughter in England, Lady Thomas Hesketh. Three years of his life were in the spotlight. Sharon had kept Sarah Althea at the Grand Hotel, which was connected by a bridge with the Palace where he lived. "My little wife," he had introduced her to his friends. Day and night she had nursed him during a desperate illness. In white satin, it was said, she had been one of the guests when his daughter Flora became Lady Hesketh at Belmont.

Finally Sarah Althea declared she had demanded recognition as his wife. Sharon replied, "You must give up your marriage rights or leave this hotel." She refused to go. He choked her.

Sharon's testimony was that he sent her away from the Grand Hotel because she tried to enter his rooms through the transom. "I wish you would break your damn neck," he said.

Ah Ki, Sharon's dramatic little Chinese servant and bodyguard, described the last dinner served for the Senator and Sarah Althea. Roses in her hair, face glowing with happiness, beautifully gowned she came. With frosty eyes Sharon showed her the dinner table. "You will never sit there again. You know what you have done. Go!"

While Ah Ki spoke Sarah Althea put her lace handkerchief to her eyes, her satin-covered shoulders shook and her golden plumes quivered. When Sharon's Rose did not leave the Grand Hotel, Manager Thorn testified that he ripped carpets from the floor and tore bells from walls. He removed doors so that she slept exposed to passersby. Only then did she depart for a house near fashionable Rincon Hill.

Sharon swore that later he gave her $7,500 to sign a quitclaim to all claims upon him. After the document was signed he gave her more money. When payments ceased, he asserted that she desperately fabricated the marriage contract by writing it above his signature surreptitiously obtained, and that she had then treated the paper to make it look old and worn.

Even voodooism was summoned by Sharon's Rose to gain control of the Senator's affections. Mammy Pleasance, Voodoo Queen, the colored woman with mysterious eyes, one black and the other blue, always sat at Sarah Althea's side in the courtroom. From Mammy Sarah Althea learned strange sorceries. In her room at the Grand Hotel, over a spirit lamp she had compounded a love potion of sugar, molasses and black tea. She paid a maid $20 to place the potion in the Senator's wine, to sprinkle cloves under his pillow, to scatter black mesmeric powder on his chair. All the while she herself uttered wild incantations. Sharon's Rose even cut open a wild pigeon, stuck nine pins into it and wore it in a silk bag around her neck.

Strangest of all was Sarah Althea's fatal death charm. She bribed a grave digger to let her bury the Senator's socks at night under a cadaver in the cemetery; at the same time she gave away silver to make the charm work. After the garments rotted, if the Senator did not love her, Sarah Althea believed death would come to him.

Sharon had the grave opened and the socks brought into court and exhibited. He was promptly sued for violating the grave.

Mammy Pleasance, the black spell-worker at Sarah Althea's side, stared at Sharon in malicious triumph. As the case wore on, in spite of his subtle smile of confidence, every time the Senator looked at Mammy Pleasance he seemed to pale and shake.

Handwriting experts contradicted one another in the usual way, but Sharon's "My dear wife" letters presented by Sarah Althea were unshaken. Her witnesses vanished mysteriously or were arrested. Sharon's Rose interrupted proceedings with impertinent remarks to suave General W. H. L. Barnes, Sharon's chief counsel, leader of the San Francisco Bar.

And then entered David S. Terry, the giant, former Justice of California's Supreme Court—Terry, the comet, trailing behind him fire and fury and the ghost of United States Senator David C. Broderick, killed by Terry in a duel near Lake Merced.

"Terry is a man!" said the sorceress Mammy Pleasance to Sarah Althea. "Set your cap for him!" Mammy ignored Terry's devoted wife Cornelia at Stockton.

Red-bearded, shaggy-haired Terry took his seat at Sarah Althea's side, her shining deliverer. From the time Terry entered the courtroom Sharon's face wrinkled; his well-groomed hands seemed to wither.

To his friends Terry was a god adored, to his enemies he was a slayer of heroes. In legal practice Terry was above reproach. From the age of thirteen he had fought for what he called truth, right and honor. He had been in the fray at the battle of San Jacinto in the war with Mexico. In 1856 he stabbed Vigilante Hopkins of San Francisco and barely escaped hanging at Fort Gunnybags. Most spectacular of all was his resignation in 1860 from the California Supreme Court to fight a duel with the practiced marksman, United States Senator David C. Broderick. After killing that lone strange man, Terry had been swept out of California on a wave of hatred and horror into Nevada. The Civil War, in which he was a Confederate brigadier-general, had not helped to erase his fire-eating past. He was living at Stockton with his wife and children when chivalry called him to aid Sarah Althea.

Sharon, the Palace Hotel, the Bank of California, the Comstock Lode, millions in bonds and gold glared at Terry; but that giant with massive shoulders and fierce impulses glared harder at Sharon. Terry insulted General Barnes. General Barnes insulted him. Witnesses threatened each other. No one on Sharon's side stirred abroad without a bodyguard. Two burly gunmen protected General Barnes. An army of police was on duty at the City Hall. Terry alone carried no weapon, but his very presence seemed dynamite. The air quivered with violence.

Finally Judge Sullivan said, "I'm tired of conducting a trial in an arsenal."

Every morning all the attorneys and witnesses were searched, even Mammy Pleasance. She accepted it with a smiling roll of her wise aged eyes.

Chivalrous Terry believed in Sarah Althea, and his bushy brows worked in a passion of pity as she was smeared by the cynical General Barnes and by Sharon's witnesses. In his manner toward her he guarded the girl against the world.

At first Terry and Sarah Althea seemed like father and daughter. They ate candy and fruits together, chatted and laughed. Sadness left her blue eyes. Once more she had an anchor in life. She was the pert, quick-witted little convent girl. Daily she appeared in new clothes, gay dresses of velvet brocade, fur-lined coats, and plumed hats or bright bonnets.

As the months passed spectators at the trial noticed that Terry's shaggy gray hair and Sarah Althea's golden shimmering locks were ever closer together. His manner toward her altered. It was no longer paternal. He seemed to be living in a spell of enchantment.

Terry took a large photograph of Sarah Althea to his wife, gentle Cornelia of Stockton. In those perilous days she seldom saw her husband. Looking at the photograph she sighed, "I suppose we shall have to adopt the girl." Patient Cornelia dusted the photograph daily. She noticed that when David came home he looked at the picture long and intently.

The case was costing Sharon huge sums. This was not a $10,000 poker game; but millions were wagered. He rode to the City Hall attended by guards. When he finally testified, he was infirm and his false teeth had been left at home. Nervously he paced the platform as he spoke, "It tires me to sit still." All he would concede was, "I offered her $500 a month to live with me, and she accepted." He seemed to be slowly dying from within.

But the Senator's eyes burned with black hatred when General Barnes flayed the Rose as if he would strip the flesh from her body. "Sarah Althea is not a deserted wife, but a miserable sinner who has been publicly stoned."

The black plumes on Sarah Althea's hat trembled from the anger which distorted the lovely lines of her face. Tears of shame filled her eyes.

Terry pulled his massive shoulders erect and rose like an avenging giant. From the depths of his chivalrous soul he spoke as he had never spoken, draining his very life with words to vindicate the honor of the golden-haired woman at his side. As he went on, to Sarah Althea he seemed the embodiment of all the knights who had tilted a lance in medieval tournaments. His words were those of an adorer of Sharon's Rose. When he sat down Judge and audience sighed.

As soon as the case closed Terry was summoned to the side of his sick wife, Cornelia, at Stockton.

For fifteen months the case had been on trial, occupying eight courts. How would it all end? After a month's consideration, on the day before Christmas, 1884, Judge Sullivan rendered a decision recognizing the marriage contract and granting Sarah Althea Hill Sharon a divorce from William A. Sharon.

Sarah Althea, in black with pink ruching at wrists and throat and wearing a spangled bonnet, was pale with nervousness. When the Judge declared that she was Mrs. William A. Sharon she seemed about to faint. Someone helped her into the witness room, where she began weeping.

"Once I wished I had died before the shame and disgrace of the trial began," she said. "Now all that shame has been wiped away by the Judge's decision. I am Mrs. Sharon!"

Sharon was not in the courtroom. Terry was with his sick wife.

The Judge ordered a division of community property. General Barnes sat like a stone image.

Madness held the courtroom for fifteen minutes. People ran forward to kiss Sarah Althea Hill, now Mrs. Sharon with millions, the heroine of San Francisco that day.

It was a Christmas-present decision, and in Christmas fashion Sarah Althea celebrated, hastening into big shops to buy gifts for all who had befriended her. Seventeen dollars she paid for a lace collar for her cook. Charming Mrs. Sharon herself received hundreds of bouquets.

Her divorced husband, Senator Sharon, announced, "I will sink every penny in the bay before I give that woman a dollar."

On the very day that Terry won his great legal victory, he lost his wife Cornelia at Stockton, his unfailing friend. Her pleadings had saved his life when he was held prisoner by the Vigilantes. Like a protecting mother she had stood at his side after he killed Broderick and during his stormy Nevada days. She had gone with him into exile in Mexico. Loyally she had awaited his return from the Civil War. In the last lonely days at Stockton she had patiently dusted Sarah Althea's photograph.

Terry was now a solitary giant and Sarah Althea was his only joy. On New Year's Day he appeared among her champagne-drinking guests at a party she gave, towering among pygmies. He brought her diamond earrings and a brooch. They made the wild roses reappear in her cheeks. She was witty, merry. Champagne was for everyone. She was rich; her greatest wealth was Terry. Now that death had made him free he told her that he adored her.

Only for a few days, sweet triumph! Sharon was so feeble that many thought Mammy Pleasance's sorcery had accomplished its work. But his attorneys filed suit to void the marriage contract. Sarah Althea demanded a division of the property, $10,000 alimony, and $150,000 for attorneys' fees. Terry took the "my dear wife" letters and Sarah Althea's contract to Stockton and hid them in his own safe.

Again the courts began to grind. The king of the Comstock was fighting with his last strength. "I will not pay that woman a penny until the Supreme Court has passed on the case," he declared.

The Supreme Being decided the case. In the midst of the bitter struggle death took William A. Sharon on November 13, 1885. Flags on the Palace and Grand Hotels were slowly lowered to half mast. He lay on ice under white roses and japonicas in the greatest hostelry in the world, his own Palace Hotel—Bonanza Inn.

Sarah Althea now tried to prove herself Sharon's widow. There was one who never doubted her—Terry. Two months after Sharon died she sailed up the Sacramento River on the *T. C. Walker* with sixteen large trunks and two truckloads of furniture. All Stockton assembled to see her disembark; Sarah Althea Hill Sharon was to take the place of Cornelia Terry.

Terry wearing his great slouch hat met her and they drove to the house of Father W. B. Connor. It was like most weddings. Terry had forgotten a ring. The best man forgot his purse when he went to the jeweler's to buy the ring. But at last the pair were married. Terry was sixty-two, Sarah Althea in her early thirties. He left his young bride with the guests at the breakfast table and hastened back to court.

Terry's friends were horrified. One week after Sarah Althea's marriage to Terry the United States Circuit Court in San Francisco declared her marriage contract to Sharon a forgery. She was forbidden to use it again, or to speak of it as genuine.

Sarah Althea was a fighter. Her courage matched Terry's, and he loved her valiance. The court she defied. "I will not surrender my marriage contract."

Terry carried the case to the California Supreme Court. There he thundered, "Before the decision was rendered by Judge Sullivan, an agent of Sharon's took the Judge a check made out to him to be filled out at his own price. The defense has said, 'Sharon is dead, there is nothing of importance left in this case.'" From the depths of his being Terry spoke, "There is the honor of a woman involved—past, present, future."

On January 31, 1888, the Supreme Court confirmed the judgment of the lower court. Sarah Althea said to the reporters, "Right has won against millions."

Terry's shaggy brows were in a frown. "The fight is not over."

In 1888 the personnel of the California Supreme Court changed and another appeal was taken by the Sharon forces.

With all the violence of their natures Sarah Althea and David S. Terry united in hatred of Judge Sawyer of the Circuit Court who had called the contract a forgery. They met the Judge on a train. Sarah walked down the aisle and gaily pulled his beard, then she began laughing. Terry scolded her, but he too laughed. The Judge was not amused.

The Circuit Court assembled to render the last decision. On the bench with the Judges was Justice Stephen J. Field, an old friend of Terry's, with whom he had sat on the bench. Field read the decision, pages of manuscript—Sarah Althea had never been married to Sharon; the contract should be canceled.

Everyone in the courtroom stood up. Sarah Althea addressed the Judge.

"Madam, sit down," commanded Justice Field.

With dramatic despair she said, "Justice Field, we hear you have been bought. How much have you been paid for this decision?"

Calmly Justice Field said, "Marshal, put that woman out."

Terry was a living shield before his wife. "Don't put your hands on her!" he ordered the marshal. "I'll take my wife from the courtroom."

The marshal caught Terry's collar. Terry struck him in the mouth. A dozen men brought the giant to the floor. Through all the commotion Sarah Althea was crying out to Justice Field, "You have been bribed."

She was dragged out by officers. Terry shook off his assailants and rushed after her. They surrounded him again. Sarah Althea was locked in a room. "Don't enter the door!" the officers commanded.

Terry drew a small dirk. Texans carried knives, not guns. "Stand aside," savagely ordered Terry the Texan. "I don't want to hurt anyone, but I'm going to her."

In her room Sarah Althea wailed against Field, "Bought, you have been bought!"

A dozen guns were turned on Terry. In agony he yielded up his knife, pleading, "Let me be with my wife."

When Field finished his decision ordering the contract to be given up, Sarah Althea's anguished screams had been turned into soft sobs. The Terrys sat in their room consoling one another. Crowds gathered in the streets retelling the story of the slaying of Broderick in 1859.

Field found his friend Terry guilty with Sarah Althea of contempt of court. Both were sentenced to the Alameda County jail—Sarah Althea for thirty days, and the former Supreme Justice David S. Terry for six months.

Armed deputies hurried the pair into a carriage. Through the window Sarah Althea appealed to the public, "Help us!"

Sarah Althea was released on bail, but she would not leave her husband. She served every minute of his sentence. The great generous Terry loved more deeply each day his volatile but determined wife. During the six months in jail he directed the fight. Sarah Althea Hill, daughter of an attorney, conducted her own case in court.

Terry appealed to the United States Supreme Court for freedom on a writ of *habeas corpus*. He applied to President Cleveland for pardon. Both were refused. Once his name had carried great weight but it had been sadly tarnished by the golden-haired Sarah Althea. Field wrote to Washington urging that Terry serve every hour of his sentence. This he did.

"You are a martyr to our cause," Sarah Althea assured Terry proudly. Robbed of millions by a corrupt decision, as they felt, and shamed by imprisonment, they thought they had reason to hate Justice Field, who had besmirched them with unwarranted stain.

Like a trapped tiger Terry roared to reporters and friends, "Field will never dare come back to California. I'll horsewhip him."

"If you do that," suggested a nervous friend, "he will surely avenge the insult."

"If he resents it, I'll kill him."

Once again free, Terry went back to practice law at Fresno. His open, fearless face was now dark with brooding. Chattering, golden Sarah Althea alone was his happiness. She talked more and more, always of her wrongs, with a strange new gleam. She asked for a receiver for the Sharon fortune. Her beauty grew pale and wild.

Sharon had been dead for four years, but still the case went on. Field was back in California from Washington. Always with him was a small silent lightning-rapid bodyguard, David Nagle. Terry thought himself menaced. To add to his despair the new Supreme Court reversed Judge Sullivan's decision, and ordered a re-trial of the Sharon case.

Terry's Southern chivalry suffered. "They made out my wife a strumpet. What can one person do against Sharon's millions?"

The Terrys always brooded over the burning of the marriage contract. How could they fight the ghost of a dead man? The trustees of the Sharon estate could not be made parties to a suit for divorce. Terry was sixty-six when by chance he boarded the Southern train at Fresno as Justice Stephen A. Field was returning from holding court at Los Angeles. Next morning the train stopped at Lathrop. Passengers swarmed into the large dining room for breakfast. Field with his bodyguard Nagle was among the first served. Terry was seated at a table in the dining room when he saw the Justice.

The great Colossus rose staring hard at Field, struck him on both cheeks, left and right.

Without leaving his seat Nagle shot Terry, who had neither knife nor gun. Terry sank to the floor.

Slowly he arose, gazing into the bewildered eyes of the man who had once been his friend.

With an anguished wail Sarah Althea broke through the crowd and sank upon her knees, pressing her husband, her champion, to her breast. Dying he kissed her farewell.

"Who did this? Who?" she demanded.

"Nagle guarding Field."

"Kill his murderers!"

She would not leave the dead man. When he lay outside the station, a sheet over his stark body; when he was carried on special train and engine to Stockton; when a wagon conveyed him to the morgue—through the days and nights she would not quit his side. "She is like a mad woman," they said.

A grave was dug in the family plot between the graves of Terry's first wife and his son. Sarah Althea lifted her still golden head in understanding. "Then there will be no room for me beside him?"

In spite of her protesting friends she was at the grave when all that was left of courageous, chivalrous David S. Terry was given over to dust. For days she remained in a darkened room behind locked doors sobbing, refusing food, speaking to no one.

Both Field and Nagle escaped punishment, but when Nagle shot Terry the bullet deadened the essence of Sarah Althea Terry. Her large eyes grew larger and stranger, but her head was always held high like a gallant soldier's. She visited mediums, "talked" with Terry. In death he was her comfort, as he had been in life. She wandered about among her friends, and was especially loyal to the Voodoo Queen, Mammy Pleasance.

When the beautiful doomed figure of a woman walked San Francisco's streets at noonday dressed in an evening gown asking plaintively, "Where is Mammy Pleasance? Where—" the world knew that Sarah Althea Hill Terry was mad. Protesting, kicking officers, she was placed in the hospital for the insane at Stockton not far from Terry's tomb. There she long survived Mammy Pleasance and even Justice Stephen J. Field. People forgot that she lived until she was found by Evelyn Wells, her first guest in a quarter of a century.

During her fifty years at the Stockton Asylum sometimes Sarah Althea was Mrs. Sharon, sometimes Mrs. Terry, sometimes the wife of General Grant, often the Queen of Hawaii, always a leader of society! To the last she was smiling, gracious, with fine rosy features, blue eyes, snow-white hair and a sharp humorous tongue. She owned the Bank of California, the Palace Hotel. The President had given her the Stockton slough! "Won't you let me present you with a check for $25,000?" A rare light of tenderness came into her face when she spoke of Terry. "Such a big fellow, a Brigadier-General! They couldn't get him inside of a house without taking down the walls. They hanged the man that shot him. He deserved it."

In February, 1937, at last Sarah Althea Hill Sharon Terry had her way. She was placed beside David S. Terry and his wife Cornelia in the cemetery at Stockton, California.

XXIV

STEVENSON AND FANNY OSBOURNE

1880

CARMEL is the literary capital of the western United States. Here from 1773 to 1776 lived California's first historian and biographer, Padre Francisco Palóu. *At Mission San Carlos (Carmelo) he began the first books written west of the Alleghenies,* La Vida de Padre Junípero Serra *and* Las Noticias de las Californias. *Palóu was the morning star of California literature and fine living.*

Even in this primitive life, threatened with Indian attacks, the gray-robed padre *bordered his vegetable garden at Carmel with azaleas, himself planting and watering them. He also made two trips to San Francisco Bay before he founded Mission Dolores on June 29, 1776, beginning a great unique city.*

For nine years Palóu lived at Mission Dolores, during that period completing Serra's biography. After his friend's death at Carmel, Palóu returned to Mexico, became guardian of San Fernando College and was buried in the church of San Fernando.

Mission San Juan Bautista had its cultured Padre *Arroyo de la Cuesta, who two decades later wrote an Indian grammar and a dictionary of the Mutsun language. In the 1820's at Mission San Juan Capistrano a book on the natives and their god,* Chinigchinich, *was written by* Padre *Gerónimo Boscana. Aside from these books old California produced no literature, but Governor José Figueroa brought the first printing press in 1833.*

With the coming of the Americans appeared newspapers, the first being Walter Colton's The Californian, *in 1846 at Monterey. Soon came the great gold discovery, with adventure rushing in from every path and fortune just around the corner. During the twenty-five years following 1849 nearly two hundred volumes were written in California, more than in all the other states and territories west of the Mississippi.*

There was also a magazine, the Overland Monthly, *founded in 1868 in San Francisco, edited by F. B. Harte [Bret Harte]. The delighted public read not only its editor's stories, but articles by Mark Twain and Henry George. To the* Overland *came that Byron of Oregon, Cincinnatus Heine Miller with red shirt and cowboy boots, living a daily life of poetry. Because of his sympathy for the wronged Joaquin Murietta, he changed his own name to Joaquin. All these writers were reborn in California and they gained fame, but they did not come to Carmel or Monterey.*

At this same time, however, life stirred at Mission Carmelo. The roofless ruin touched the pity of Father Angelo Casanova, rector of the Monterey parish. Determined to bring back its glory he began by trying to find Serra's grave. After obtaining funds he removed three feet of debris from the abandoned Mission, had the grave opened and invited friends of California to witness the solemn event. By the hundreds they gathered and beheld Serra's dust.

From that day once more the great founder of the Missions seemed abroad in the state. Mrs. Leland Stanford reroofed the church and others aided in its restoration. Activity at Carmelo stimulated other Mission friends. Once more the bells rejoiced, and today only four of California's twenty-one Missions are unrestored.

Artists in that early day appreciated the beauty of Carmelo and Monterey. Jules Tavernier, Julian Rix and Joe Strong came to paint the buildings, the whalers and the fantastic cypress. Fanny Osbourne, an artist from San Francisco, also came. It was she who drew Robert Louis Stevenson from across the sea to Monterey with its guitar-playing and heart-breaking old Spanish songs of love.

IN the very garden at Monterey made historic by the Sherman Rose, culminated one of the memorable romances of English literature, that of Robert Louis Stevenson of Scotland and Fanny Van de Grift Osbourne of California. Three years previously they had met at Grezsur-Loing, a village in the Fontainebleau forest. There Fanny was stopping at a little green inn frequented by artists and writers, formerly a ruined castle in a lovely garden. With her were her two children, Isobel and Lloyd.

Seeking to escape unhappy marriage with philandering Captain Samuel Osbourne of San Francisco, she had gone to Antwerp and later to Julien's *atelier*, Paris. Her small son Hervey died in Paris and she sought solace in change of scene. She went to the inn at Grez to paint the River Loing. Because of delicate health Stevenson had been ordered from chill foggy Scotland south to France. He came to Grez seeking strength.

One soft summer evening Fanny was seated at a long table in the inn dining room, which had panels painted by many artists who had lodged there. Suddenly at the wide-open window appeared a slim youth of twenty-six with blazing dark eyes, long hair, and a hectic flush in his cheeks. He wore a picturesque velvet jacket. Later Isobel described him as "nice looking, but ugly."

For a moment he gazed vividly at Fanny. At the height of her exotic dark beauty, she resembled, so her Indiana mother said, a native tiger lily. Several years older than Stevenson she turned the intent regard of her grave, deep, experienced face to his. In that first glance Stevenson afterwards said he loved her. Lightly he vaulted through the window and was soon seated at her side. So vitally alive was he that he made other writers and artists in the room seem colorless. His own entrancing personality brought out the best in Fanny and everyone. She was from America, the country of Walt Whitman, one of Stevenson's literary heroes.

After dinner the group sat in the arbor till late drinking coffee and talking. Fanny glowed and melted. To Stevenson her very blood seemed made of flowers. He became her constant companion, and was never far from her easel. He amused Isobel and Lloyd. They canoed in his *Rob Roy*, he leading the races. Laughing they overturned each other's canoes. Dressed as gods and goddesses, Fanny and Stevenson, costumed in sheets, wreaths on their heads, danced. Fanny enthralled Stevenson's reason and his senses. With joy he gave his life into her power.

Fanny's firm, manly, well-stocked mind commanded the group made up of Stevenson and his friends. She was more like a woman of the *quattrocento* than of the nineteenth century. She might have been one of the Medicis, or a leader of a great cause. She became a serious friend to Stevenson, such as he later created in the Countess von Rosen of *Prince Otto*. Sometimes he addressed her as "my dear fellow." She sat in the hammock at Grez while the others lounged on the grass at her feet and discoursed on the problems bedeviling life. She had a musical, well-modulated voice, but she talked little and listened much. "Fascinating silence" enveloped her, although her friends were really stimulated to speak for her approval. Soon it was evident that Stevenson was indissolubly bound to this rich-hearted woman who enchanted him like a wine-red jewel. This life continued more than two years.

Fanny Osbourne found it impossible to maintain herself in Paris, although she and her children sometimes lived on smoked herring and bread. They returned to California and left Stevenson to a stark existence.

Fanny determined not to renew the unhappy life with Sam Osbourne. At Monterey where the customs of Spain and Mexico still lingered, she found cool, high whitewashed rooms in one wing of the Sherman Rose adobe of Doña María Ignacia Bonifacio. With her lived Isobel and Lloyd and her youngest sister, Nellie Van de Grift. When Osbourne occasionally came from San Francisco to call, the children realized that grave matters were being considered. It was at a time when divorce was considered a tragedy and the Van de Grift relatives were appalled when the news was broken to them— Fanny was to divorce Sam Osbourne.

Under the strain of objections Fanny fell ill. Stevenson heard. To his Scotch parents from whom he was receiving an allowance until he could establish himself as a writer, divorce was even more distasteful than to the Van de Grifts. Their son was in love with a married woman, an American, a foreigner.

Stevenson determined to stand on his own feet. No longer would he accept an allowance from his parents. He booked third-class passage for New York. *The Amateur Emigrant* had begun. He was going to the country of Fanny Osbourne and Walt Whitman—the West seemed luminous.

"What shall I find in America?" he wrote, two days at sea from New York. "I dare not wonder."

On Sunday he arrived. Monday saw him on an emigrant train for California, a journey of from ten to fourteen days. Unaccustomed to hardship, he traveled almost in beggary. He washed in a tin bowl with three others. His head went round. Robert Louis Stevenson seemed to have died. He thought it would be easy to commit suicide. He wore only an unbuttoned shirt and a pair of trousers, but it was impossible to rest on the train. In order to sleep he took laudanum.

"Man," he wrote to an English friend, "I can't sleep, but I can eat." The food was heavenly.

He saw a yellow butterfly or two, a patch of wild flowers, some frame houses, a wooden church, a windmill, miles of waste, herds of cattle, ghostly deserts, alkali and rocks without form or color. In one tug all the past had been uprooted. On through the strange country the train bore him. California, what would it bring him?

In Doña María Ignacia Bonifacio's secluded Monterey garden with its roses and fuchsias tree-high, again Stevenson found Fanny. He had made no mistake in coming. After three years their love was still reality. Fanny lived with the same great intensity, scorning all that was not simple and true.

She had Stevenson's own gypsy passion for freedom. She would marry him. For Fanny with her direct honesty of speech and conduct there was no other way. She went to San Francisco to arrange a divorce.

The excitement of Stevenson's transplanted existence, the unaccustomed hardships, the fog in Monterey without summer or winter, brought on chills and fever. Night sweats and a cough developed. He took his camp blankets and rode twenty miles to Captain Smith's angora goat ranch in the Santa Lucia Mountains. He was seeking the sun cure in the open air that once had re-established his health at Mentone in the south of France.

For four days Stevenson lay under a tree in a stupor. He scarcely thought, ate, or slept. Fever consumed him. He did little but fetch water for himself and horse, light a fire and make coffee. At night he heard goat bells ringing and tree frogs singing. A crowing cock made him homesick. Each new noise drove him mad. He would have died, he wrote, but his spirit rose in a "divine frenzy"...kicked and spurred his vile body forward.

After three weeks in the sunshine and sleeping on camp blankets on the ground in the dry mountain air he revived. He taught the ranch children reading. Wife and children he envied any man. He envisioned his own future. Not alluring! He was earning less than $500 a year. He was determined, however, to support Fanny and himself and the children that he hoped would be theirs.

September, warm and summery, found him back at Monterey with Fanny. In the Indian summer the air was like drinking elixir of the lotus. Stevenson cared little about flowers, but clouds, thundering surf and Monterey's resinous pine forests enchanted him. Pillowed on fragrant roseleaf cushions as he lounged in Doña María Ignacia's garden listening to Fanny, life seemed exciting and worth while.

At times he was frightened about his work. He earned two dollars a week writing for a Monterey paper, but he had so many anxieties that he thought of returning to his profession—the law. Three books haunted him, however; one of them, *Prince Otto*, must be his masterpiece. If only he could earn a thousand dollars a year, Fanny and he would be rich.

What if all three books should fail! What if he could not support Fanny, his adored sweet-hearted woman! *"The Amateur Emigrant* must sell in spite of the deil and the publishers." If it didn't, the next book would. Stevenson was not yet thirty, and he wrote, "Vividness and not style is my line. If a thing is meant to be read, try to make it readable." He maintained that Rawdon Crawley's blow made *Vanity Fair*.

At this time Stevenson was at his lowest in health. His career never seemed to promise so little, but Fanny had profound faith in his genius. This faith helped him have faith in himself.

A few doors from Doña María Ignacia's adobe house Stevenson found a great airy room with five windows opening out on the balcony in the dwelling of Dr. Heintz, a son-in-law of Jules Simoneau who had a French restaurant. Stevenson's letters pictured his life. He breakfasted on a dirty tablecloth in the little whitewashed back room at Simoneau's. To Sanchez's saloon near the post office he strolled for a drink. The walls of the bar had been decorated by the painters Jules Tavernier, Julian Rix, and Joe Strong who later married Isobel. He played chess with Simoneau and discussed the universe with him. To François the baker, Augustin Dutra, and an Italian fisherman, Robert Louis became "Don Roberto Luis." He wrote that he grew "to love this lovely place." The Pacific "licked all other oceans" with its eternal roaring surf.

Mornings Stevenson was at his desk. Then he hastened to Fanny to read aloud what he had written, with her sister Nellie and the Osbourne children also his audience. When he brought forth his morning's creation his face was flushed and his manner shy, but for a body so frail his voice was full and sonorous. Afterwards he wrote of Fanny as chary of praise but prodigal of counsel. He profited by her reach of imagination, sense of humor, wealth of experience, and fairmindedness. She burnished his soul, blew on the drowsy coals, ever held the target higher. "If any fire burns in the imperfect pages, the praise is hers."

Again in the evening he was with Fanny. Doña María Ignacia, straight as an arrow, springy as a girl, like an alert bright-eyed young bird, brought them *tamales, enchiladas, frijoles* and coffee.

Stevenson and Fanny studied Spanish by reading aloud. Frequently they strolled on wooden sidewalks through Monterey's crooked streets, or wandered on the white sandy beach around the sweeping curves of the bay. At times the blood-red harvest moon sprang up suddenly, making the water phosphorescent. Serenaders still strummed guitars under Doña María Ignacia's windows, and Nellie and Isobel lighted candles as Doña María Ignacia had in her youth. Stevenson and Fanny gathered shells at Point Cypress. She rode her mustang Clavel. They went to a rodeo. Pastoral Spanish-California still had cascarone balls when dancers broke egg shells filled with tinsel paper upon each other's heads. The entire population irrespective of age, arrayed in silks or flannel shirts, danced all night.

On San Carlos Day Stevenson and Fanny attended Mass at Carmel Mission. He was touched by the abandoned church and much moved when he heard Indian singers at an altar in the sacristy chanting hymns taught them by Serra when they came from the mountains to worship. Stevenson liked it all, including the *merienda* after Mass under the trees.

But his immediate goal was to acquire a thousand dollars a year. He went on writing *Prince Otto* and *A Vendetta in the West*.

Christmas found Stevenson living at a workingman's lodging house in Bush Street, San Francisco, existing on forty-five cents a day, sometimes less. Frequently he dined for ten cents on a roll and a cup of coffee. He sat up nights for a week trying to help his landlady save the life of her dying child. In this period he abandoned his old longing to be a father. Ever he grew weaker. It took him six hours to do a page. "God only knows," he wrote, "how much courage and suffering is buried in that manuscript."

He was seized with cold sweats, fever, prostrating attacks of coughing, sinking fits in which he lost power of speech, many symptoms of galloping consumption. For six weeks Fanny was a great fighting woman standing between Stevenson and death. She never left his side. When he recovered he felt that he owed her his life. As he put it, "Hell went off once more discomfited."

Stevenson longed to go to the mountains as soon as the weather cleared. When he was stronger he went to live in Oakland with

Nellie and her husband, Adolfo Sanchez, in an old cottage covered with Banksia roses. Stevenson was still too weak to write and Nellie became his amanuensis. To her he dictated part of *Prince Otto*, in his enthusiasm pacing up and down the room. Adroitly Fanny devised ways to keep him quiet by placing tables and chairs to obstruct his path. Finally he worked calmly, enjoying his dictation. "*Prince Otto* isn't exactly funny, but some of it is smiling."

Daily Stevenson helped wash and polish dishes, reciting Spanish conjugations. "There is no doubt about it, I was born to be a butler."

Evenings Lloyd Osbourne pleaded with Stevenson for a sea tale, and to amuse the boy, the group invented long continued stories. So began *Treasure Island,* which Stevenson afterwards wrote for little Lloyd Osbourne.

On May 19, 1880, Fanny Osbourne became Stevenson's wife. They were married at Oakland by the Reverend Mr. Scott. Mrs. Virgil Williams, one of Fanny's art teachers, and Mrs. Scott were the only witnesses.

"It was a sort of marriage *in extremis,*" wrote Stevenson. "If I am where I am, it is thanks to the care of that lady who married me when I was a mere complication of cough and bone, much fitter for an emblem of mortality than a bridegroom."

At the time of their marriage Fanny believed that her husband could live only a few months, but her daughter Isobel Field writes that after her mother was married to Stevenson she entered Fanny's room in San Francisco and stopped with a sudden shock, hearing her laugh happily for the first time in her life.

On their honeymoon trip the Stevensons set out for Silverado, a deserted mine near Calistoga Hot Springs in Napa County, three thousand feet up cindery Mount St. Helena. With them went Lloyd Osbourne, a setter dog Chuchu, four cats and two horses. Another book had begun, *The Silverado Squatters.*

The Stevensons' first family altar was eight miles up a mountain on the Coast Range in a deserted miner's bunkhouse. There were three rooms with sashless windows. Each room was virtually atop the other. Both Stevenson and Fanny wore miner's boots found in the shack. She called herself ugly in her rough clothing, but he told her she was his Forty-Niner and the most beautiful creature in the world.

Stevenson admired Fanny's housewifely ability, her ingenuity in putting in doors and windows of light frames covered with cotton. From her Dutch ancestors she inherited skill in sewing and cooking. Red and white wine and dried fruit were found by her. She filled the house with wild tiger lilies from the thicket, always her own symbol.

In the "blessed sun" Stevenson could sit out in the haven on Mount St. Helena and look forth into a great realm of the air, down upon tree tops and hilltops, and far and near on a wild varied country. In this deep wooded glen filled with a thousand fragrances Fanny bloomed. She belonged in the country and her very presence made Stevenson more alive.

In far Scotland Stevenson's parents heard of his illness, and they were moved by Fanny's care. They recognized that their son had found in her a character as strong, as unusual as his own. Hearts and purses were unlocked. Funds came across the sea. Stevenson's health improved. With his wife he returned to San Francisco. His pockets were full of twenty-dollar gold pieces. To touch them made him feel rich. "Just look!" he laughed to Fanny. "I'm simply lousy with money!"

In Scotland Fanny made immediate conquest of Stevenson's parents and charmed his friends. But his illness drove Stevenson from Scotland to the Swiss Alps, to London, to the English countryside, to France and across the water to the Adirondacks. Fortune came to him. *Prince Otto, Treasure Island,* and *Kidnapped* were published. The unexpected success arrived from a book he dreamed—*The Strange Case of Dr. Jekyll and Mr. Hyde.* He thought it the best thing he had done, but Fanny considered it the worst. With his entrancing personality and his distinguished mastery of style he became the most attractive man of letters in his generation, but he was compelled to leave his own setting and seek the will-o'-the-wisp health in the South Seas.

On a three-hundred-acre plantation in a mountain cleft near Apia, Samoa, the Stevensons made their first permanent home. Here Fanny supervised the building of Vailima with cannibal workmen. "My marriage has been the most successful in the world," wrote Stevenson. "She is everything to me; wife, mother, sister, daughter, and dear companion, and I would not change to get a goddess or a saint."

Vailima prolonged Stevenson's life by five years. The natives regarded him as their chief. He was planning to return to America to lecture, and was at his happiest and gayest, chatting on the veranda of his house Monday, December 3, 1894, when suddenly he placed his hands to his head and said, "What is the matter? Do I look strange?" After fourteen years of happy life with Fanny he sank at her feet. Robert Louis Stevenson had escaped from his body which he called his "dungeon."

Sixty sturdy natives carried his remains to the summit of Vaea. Gelett Burgess designed Stevenson's tomb, which was built by native workmen. On one side is a brass tablet engraved,

> *Under the wide and starry sky,*
> *Dig the grave and let me lie.*
> *Glad did I live and gladly die,*
> *And I laid me down with a will.*
> *This be the verse you grave for me:*
> Here he lies where he longed to be;
> Home is the sailor, home from the sea,
> And the hunter home from the hill.

After the light went out of Samoa and the South Seas for Fanny, her sable hair turned rapidly white. Twenty lonely years she spent wandering. No dwelling long made her happy. Finally her own ashes were taken by Isobel Field and her husband Salisbury Field from San Francisco to the summit of Vaea and there deposited with those of Stevenson. A bronze tablet was placed on the side of his tomb and inscribed:

> *Teacher, tender comrade, wife,*
> *A fellow-farer true through life,*
> *Heart whole and soul free,*
> *The August Father gave to me.*

On Stevenson's tablet is the thistle of Scotland with the hibiscus of Samoa. On Fanny's tablet is Samoa's hibiscus with the tiger lily, the name given to Fanny Van de Grift by her mother in Indiana.